END
of the
AGE

INKWATER
PRESS

Copyright

Contact Inkwater Press at 6750 SW Franklin Street, Suite A, Portland, OR 97223-2542. www.inkwaterpress.com

ISBN-10 1-59299-205-6

ISBN-13 978-1-59299-205-8

Publisher: Inkwater Press

Printed in the U.S.A.

Illustrative drawings are the works of Michelangelo, who was patterned after the Archangel Michael; of Donatello, who was patterned after the Archangel Gabriel; and of Leonardo, who was patterned after Christ.

And I will reveal my name to my people and they will come to know its power. Then at last they will recognize that it is I who speaks to them.

Isaiah 52:6

I will tell them.

And I saw a scroll in the right hand of the one who was sitting on the throne. There was writing on the inside and the outside of the scroll, and it was sealed with seven seals.

And I saw a strong angel, who shouted with a loud voice: "Who is worthy to break the seals on this scroll and unroll it?" But no one in heaven or on earth or under the earth was able to open the scroll and read it. Then I wept because no one could be found who was worthy to open the scroll and read it.

But one of the twenty-four elders said to me, "Stop weeping! Look, the Lion of the tribe of Judah, the heir to David's throne, has conquered. He is worthy to open the scroll and break its seven seals."

I looked and I saw a Lamb that had been killed but was now standing between the throne and the four living beings and among the twenty-four elders. He had seven horns and seven eyes, which are the seven spirits of GOD that are sent out into every part of the earth. He stepped forward and took the scroll from the right hand of the one sitting on the throne.

Revelation 5:1 – 7

Its time for the reading
of the small scroll.

The Curriculum

Contents

List of Tables

List of Illustrations

The Name of GOD

6

Listen, you scientists, philosophers and teachers, Christians, Muslims, Jews and Gentiles, and I will give you a physics lesson that you will never forget. Take a lesson from Cyrus, chosen by GOD himself. I, Cyrus, must tell you the truth. For, telling the truth to all of you is what I was born to do.

This is the truth of GOD's people; how they were created, why and how they came to be in such a state of disrepair; how he will rescue them from the evil that possesses them; how he will triumph; and when he will triumph.

> This is the story of the LORD's people. They are the vineyard of the LORD Almighty. Israel [Eve] and Judah [Adam] are his pleasant garden. He expected them to yield a crop of justice, but instead he found bloodshed. He expected to find righteousness, but instead he heard cries of oppression.
>
> *Isaiah 5:7*

GOD's name is **ATOM**. We know this *first* because in the generational tradition of fathers and first born sons, GOD named his first born Adam, so that in these days and in the days to come, you would know him and remember the truth of your Creator.

> This is the history of the descendants of **Adam**. When GOD created people, he made them in the likeness of GOD.
>
> *Genesis 5:1*

> So you see, just as death came into the world through a man, **Adam**, now the resurrection from the dead has begun through another man, Christ. Everyone dies because all of us are related to Adam, the first man. But all who are related to Christ, the other man, will be given new life.
>
> *1 Corinthians 15:21 – 22*

> The Scriptures tell us, "The first man, **Adam**, became a living person." But the last **Adam** – that is, Christ – is a life-giving Spirit.
>
> *1 Corinthians 15:45*

ATOM, whom scientists and physicists everywhere agree is the beginning of all life, who was called Zeus in the days of the Greeks, is the GOD of all gods, LORD of all lords. ATOM, the creator of all things is also the author and finisher of all things. ATOM is the great prosecuting attorney, who rules according to law – the physical laws of the universe and the natural and biological laws that govern the bodies of mankind. ATOM also rules by the moral law, which he wrote on a tablet with his own hand and passed down to Moses to be the moral conscious that governs the behaviour and actions of humankind.

Michelangelo, The Face of GOD

This great one, **ATOM** (who is omnipotent and able to see into all things as nothing is hidden from him) perceived that an honourable race (his own precious jewels), was in a woeful plight. Moreover, wanting to inflict punishment on them that they might be chastened and improve, ATOM collected all the lords and the princes below him into his most holy habitation, which, being placed in the centre of the world, beholds all created things.

To these lords and princes, he revealed his plan of salvation for his children and for the others who would believe on his name and call upon him in times of trouble. The plan became manifest with the birth of Jesus Christ but I assure you that many years before that time, the architecture of this plan was being developed and the outcome shaped.

Jesus Christ, who is ATOM, made flesh, is an endearing legacy for all mankind. He has given hope to so many and yet, even he was grossly misunderstood. Now, as the end of this age, the Age of the Gentiles, is drawing near, Christ's way and means is being critically analyzed by those who stand to lose much. They are compelled to decipher and apply a hidden and sinister meaning to Christ's birth and crucifixion, suggesting a level of debauchery to his life and his associations during his time on earth. All of the recent depictions of his life and legacy are riddled with falsehoods and this bears saying since many of you have been captivated by the lies. If nothing else, history has taught us that propaganda is easier to believe than the truth. In this age, we live under a cloud of deception so thick you can cut it with a knife. As soon as we see a glimpse of light and begin to understand the truth, the clouds roll back together resulting in confusion and folly. Under these behaviorally volatile, accident prone, weather–beaten and body battered conditions it is easy to accept the deception as truth.

Mankind, the children of ATOM, were lured away from their godly parents by a shrill flute, a clever step and a master debater who uses a secret weapon (emotion) with which to draw you unto him. No matter. The price has already been paid for your salvation. It is time for the redemption of the souls. It is time for you Jewels to return to your own land.

Where is that land? Is it a place upon the earth, so small and cluttered, littered with the remnants of war and desecration? Of course not! Such a small and polluted place is not ATOM's home. I will tell you. Listen carefully so you can learn the truth of these matters.

It is under these woeful circumstances that I, Cyrus – ATOM's anointed one, have been called to lead the children of GOD away from Babylon; it is time to return to Israel by way of Mount Zion until we reach the light that is Jerusalem.

Today, as we travel up the mountainside, we will look to the right and to the left as we pass the two peaks that are the Mount of Olives. We will stop and take a moment to pay respect to that great and famous protector upon whom we all depend – Michael. Then, we will take the direct route down the hill; we will not wander off or be quarantined in the desert as the Hebrews once were. We will travel until we reach that place called Megiddo or Armageddon if you prefer. For surely, there will be war when truth supported by scientific reason and intellect confronts deception, foolishness and folly. Now, elders, the time has come for the reading of the small scroll, the reading of the Revelation of Jesus Christ.

Revelation of Jesus Christ

And when ATOM, who is GOD, had called the elders together, he spake through John, the revelator and through his anointed one, Cyrus, saying:

This is a revelation from Jesus Christ, which GOD gave him concerning the events that will happen soon. An angel was sent to GOD's servant John so that John could share the revelation with GOD's other servants. John faithfully reported the Word of GOD and the testimony of Jesus Christ – everything he saw.

GOD blesses the one who reads this prophecy to the church, and he blesses all who listen to it and obey what it says. For the time is near when these things will happen.

This letter is from John to the seven churches in the province of Asia. Grace and peace from [ATOM] the one who is, who always was, and who is still to come; from the sevenfold Spirit before his throne; and from Jesus Christ, who is the faithful witness to these things, the first to rise from the dead, and the commander of all the rulers of the world. All praise to him who loves us and has freed us from our sins by shedding his blood for us. He has made us his Kingdom and his priests who serve before GOD his Father. Give to him everlasting glory! He rules forever and ever! Amen!

Look! He comes with the clouds of heaven. And everyone will see him – even those who pierced him. And all the nations of the earth will weep because of him.

Yes! Amen! "I am the Alpha and the Omega – the beginning and the end," says the LORD GOD. "I am the one who is, who always was, and who is still to come, the Almighty One."

I am John, your brother. In Jesus, we are partners in suffering and in the Kingdom and in patient endurance. I was exiled to the island of Patmos for preaching the word of GOD and speaking about Jesus. It was the Lord's Day, and I was worshiping in the Spirit. Suddenly, I heard a loud voice behind me, a voice that sounded like a trumpet blast. It said,

"Write down what you see, and send it to the seven churches: Ephesus, Smyrna, Pergamum, Thyatira, Sardis, Philadelphia and Laodicea." When I turned to see who was speaking to me, I saw seven gold lampstands. [The seven gold lampstands are the seven versions of mankind – Judah (diatomic), Israel (diatomic), Jerusalem (atomic), the Gentiles (bi–atomic – two diametrically opposed elements that exist within one bacterial body, both male and female.) Now, a lampstand, by nature, is simply a body without the head, without the light that is also called wisdom.]

And standing in the middle of the lampstands was the Son of Man.

Leonardo, The Lampstand

The Garden of Eden

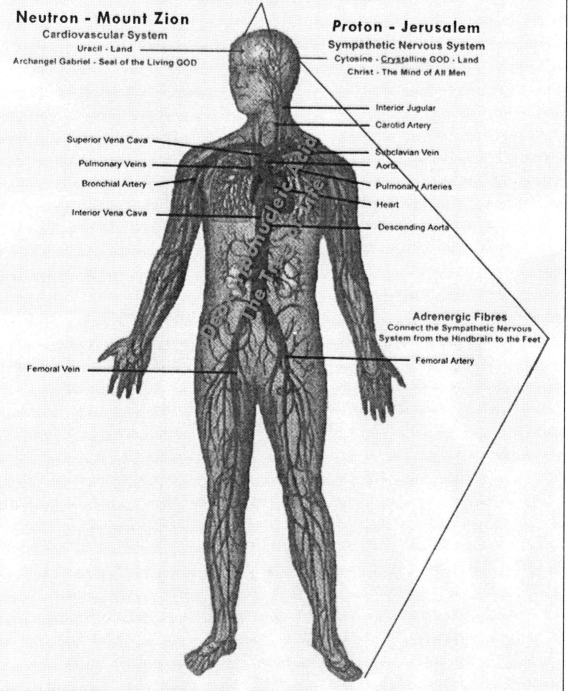

Gluon - Mount of Olives
Muscular & Skeletal System
Thymine - Land
Archangel Michael - Commander of GOD's Armies

Neutron - Mount Zion
Cardiovascular System
Uracil - Land
Archangel Gabriel - Seal of the Living GOD

Proton - Jerusalem
Sympathetic Nervous System
Cytosine - Crystalline GOD - Land
Christ - The Mind of All Men

Interior Jugular

Carotid Artery

Superior Vena Cava

Subclavian Vein

Pulmonary Veins

Aorta

Bronchial Artery

Pulmonary Arteries

Interior Vena Cava

Heart

Descending Aorta

Adrenergic Fibres
Connect the Sympathetic Nervous
System from the Hindbrain to the Feet

Femoral Vein

Femoral Artery

He was wearing a long robe [the body of every man] **with a gold sash across his chest** [deoxyribonucleic acid]. **His head and his hair were white like wool, as white as snow.** [Proton is the white light, the nucleus or centre of ATOM. Proton creates. The strong red line circling the white light of the centre is Gluon. Gluon helps Proton organize his creation. The third line on the inner circle is a fuzzy yellow line, Neutron, the teacher.]

ATOM, the Creator of All Living Things

And his eyes were bright like flames of fire [synapses firing from the hindbrain].

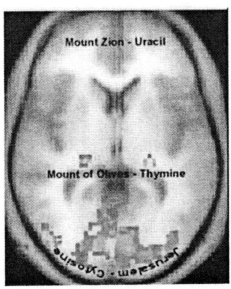

Mountain of Fire

His feet [the right and left lobes of the midbrain] **were as bright as bronze refined in a furnace, and his voice** *thundered* **like mighty ocean waves.**

He held seven stars in his right hand [the seven versions of mankind and humankind]**, and a sharp two–edged sword came from his mouth.** [Electron – Adenine and Guanine, the bacteria that is both good and evil.]

And his face was as bright as the sun in all its brilliance. [ATOM is an all–consuming fire who resides within the Sun.]

When I saw him, I fell at his feet as dead. But he laid his right hand on me and said, "Don't be afraid! I am the First and the Last. I am the living one who died. Look, I am alive forever and ever! And I hold the keys of death and the grave.

Write down what you have seen – both the things that are now happening and the things that will happen later.

This is the meaning of the seven stars you saw in my right hand and the seven gold lampstands: The seven stars are the angels of the seven churches[1]**, and the seven lampstands are the seven churches.**[2]

Revelation 1:1 – 20

---

1   The seven stars are DNA based (deoxyribonucleic acid)/ – Cytosine (diatomic – one male and one female, separate force particles) Thymine (diatomic – one male and one female, separate force particles), Uracil (atomic – either male or female – one force particle), Adenine and Guanine (bi-atomic – one body ruled by two separate minds, diametrically opposed but conjoined)]

2   The seven churches are the seven versions of mankind and humankind that are modeled after the original pattern, that is ATOM and the replica that is deoxyribonucleic acid (DNA).

        There is **Judah** – diatomic – one male and one female – separate) **Israel** (diatomic – one male and one female – separate), **Jerusalem** (atomic – either male or female), the **Gentiles** (atomic – one body with two separate minds, diametrically opposed but conjoined in one body).

Seven Stars, Seven Gold Lampstands

DNA Angels	Cytosine	Cytosine	Thymine	Thymine	Uracil	Adenine	Guanine
Atomic Design	Diatomic	Diatomic	Diatomic	Diatomic	Atomic	Bi-Atomic	Bi-Atomic
Atomic Properties	2 separate force particles		2 separate force particles		single force particle	2 matter particles conjoined in one body	
Atomic Detail	Male	Female	Male	Female	Male or Female	Male and Female conjoined in one body	
Corresponding Church	Smyrna	Philadelphia	Laodicea	Pergamum	Thyatira	Sardis	Ephesus
Names written in the Book of Life	Judah	Judah	Israel	Israel	Jerusalem	Gentiles	Gentiles

Letters to the Seven Churches

Ephesus – The Virtuous Gentile

"Write this letter to the angel [DNA–Guanine] of the church in Ephesus [the virtuous Gentile]. This is the message from the one who holds the seven stars in his right hand, the one who walks among the seven gold lampstands:

"I know all the things you do. I have seen your hard work and your patient endurance. I know you don't tolerate evil people. You have examined the claims of those who say they are apostles but are not. You have discovered they are liars. [The virtuous Gentiles are the whistle–blowers, always looking for some impropriety to report.] You have patiently suffered for me without quitting.

But I have this complaint against you. You don't love me or each other as you did at first! [You worship Satan, Electron.] Look how far you have fallen from your first love! Turn back to me again and work as you did at first. If you don't, I will come and remove your lampstand from its place among the churches. [He will rip the Gentiles – the virtuous and immoral – from the DNA chain before the appointed time.] But there is this about you that is good: You hate the deeds of the immoral Nicolaitans, [the sodomizers, homosexuals] just as I do.

"Anyone who is willing to hear should listen to the Spirit and understand what the Spirit is saying to the churches. Everyone who is victorious will eat from the tree of life in the paradise of GOD."

Smyrna – Judah

"Write this letter to the angel [DNA–Cytosine, second sight] of the church in Smyrna [Judah]. This is the message from the one who is the First and the Last, who died and is alive:

"I know about your suffering and your poverty – but you are *rich*! I know the slander of those opposing you. They say they are Jews, but they really aren't [they are Gentiles] because theirs is a synagogue of Satan. Don't be afraid of what you are about to suffer. The Devil will throw some of you into prison and put you to the test. You will be persecuted for 'ten [all] days.' Remain faithful even when facing death and I will give you the crown of life.

"Anyone who is willing to hear should listen to the Spirit and understand what the Spirit is saying to the churches. Whoever is victorious will not be hurt by the second death."

Pergamum – Israel

"Write this letter to the angel [DNA--Thymine, thy will is my will] of the church in Pergamum [Israel]. This is the message from the one who has a sharp two–edged sword: [The sharp two--edged sword is a reminder that it was Israel who caused mankind to fall into the current state of disrepair.]

"I know that you live in the city where that great throne of Satan is located [art and passion], and yet you have remained loyal to me. And you refused to deny me even when Antipas, my faithful witness, was martyred among you by Satan's followers.

And yet, I have a few complaints against you. You tolerate some among you who are like Balaam [Jerusalem — the serpent], who showed Balak [Eve] how to trip up the people of Israel.

He [Jerusalem] taught them [the Jewels of ATOM] to worship idols [I-dolls] by eating food offered to idols and by committing sexual sin [swallowing bacterial filled body fluids, adding the "bad' bacteria to the intestinal tract"].

In the same way, you have some Nicolaitans [sodomizers] among you – people who follow the same teaching and commit the same sins [homosexuality].

Repent, or I will come to you suddenly and fight against them [your Gentile children] with the sword of my mouth. [I will destroy them].

"Anyone who is willing to hear should listen to the Spirit and understand what the Spirit is saying to the churches. Everyone who is victorious will eat of the manna [unexpected wisdom] that has been hidden away in heaven [your forehead]. And I will give to each one a white stone [Proton, wisdom], and on the stone will be engraved a new name that no one knows except the one who receives it.

Thyatira – Jerusalem

"Write this letter to the angel [DNA--Uracil, the seal of the living GOD] of the church in Thyatira [Jerusalem]. This is the message from the Son of GOD whose eyes are bright like flames of fire, whose feet are like polished bronze [the brain]:

"I know all the things you do – your love, your faith, your service, and your patient endurance. And I can see your constant improvement in all these things.

But I have this complaint against you. You are permitting that woman – that Jezebel [Electron – Adenine] who calls herself a prophet [she rules over the seven churches today] – to lead my servants astray [She leads them astray through Jerusalem's teaching of the masses].

[She speaks to Jerusalem and gives him his instructions. Even though they are often ridiculous, Jerusalem, the teacher and preacher follows them and imparts her incredible lies to GOD's three jewels.]

She [Electron – Adenine] is encouraging them to worship idols, eat food offered to idols, and commit sexual sin. I gave her time to repent, but she would not turn away from her immorality.

Therefore, I will throw her upon a sickbed, and she will suffer greatly with all who commit adultery with her, unless they turn away from all their evil deeds.

I will strike her [Gentile] children dead. And all the churches will know that I [ATOM] am the one who searches out the thoughts and intentions of every person. And I will give to each of you whatever you deserve.

But I also have a message for the rest of you in Thyatira who have not followed this false teaching ('deeper truths,' as they call them – depths of Satan, really). I will ask nothing more of you except that you hold tightly to what you have until I come.

"To all who are victorious, who obey me to the very end, I will give authority over all the nations [to teach and lead them]. They [Jerusalem] will rule the nations with an iron rod and smash them like clay pots. They will have the same authority I received from my Father, and I will also give them the morning star!

[The morning star is wisdom, is Judah. Today, Jerusalem is the night star. Like Noah's son, Ham, Jerusalem is the least, the servant. Meanwhile Shem, who is Judah, and Japheth who is Israel are the born rulers from the beginning.]

Anyone who is willing to hear should listen to the Spirit and understand what the Spirit is saying to the churches.

Revelation 2:1 – 29

Sardis – the Rebellious Gentile

"Write this letter to the angel [DNA—Adenine, the lure] of the church in Sardis. This is the message from the one who has the sevenfold Spirit of GOD and the seven stars:

"I know all the things you do, and that you have a reputation for being alive – but you are dead[3] [literally dead].

Now wake up! Strengthen what little remains, for even what is left is at the point of death. [And it always will be.]

Your deeds are far from right in the sight of GOD. Go back to what you heard and believed at first; hold to it firmly and turn to me again. Unless you do, I will come upon you suddenly, as unexpected as a thief.

"Yet even in Sardis there are some [Gentiles] who have not soiled their garments with evil deeds. They will walk with me in white, for they are worthy. All who are victorious will be clothed in white. I will never erase their names from the Book of Life, but I will announce before my Father and his angels that they are mine.

---

3   The purine/urine based bacteria, of which the double helix DNA is comprised, is neither alive nor dead. It is in fact, undead. It was lethal to mankind from the beginning and that is why GOD separated the clear water above the earth from the contaminated waters below soon after creation.

And GOD said, "Let there be space between the waters, to separate [pure] water [life] from [purine] water [death]." And so it was. GOD made this space to separate the waters above [the waste, the waist] from the waters below [the waste, the waist]. And GOD called the space "sky." This happened on the second day. [In this, the Creator separated the two trees one from another – the Tree of Life from the Tree of Good and Evil.] And GOD said, "Let the waters [the matter particles] beneath the sky [the waste] be gathered into one place so dry ground may appear." And so it was. GOD named the dry ground [the three Force Particles] "land" and the water [the two matter particles] "seas." And GOD saw that it was good.

Genesis 1:6 – 10

Now understand this: Bacteria are the most effective and efficient way to destroy unused and toxic waste – dead or dying blood cells, fecal material and urine that is drained from the liver, kidneys and bowels, other unused or sacrificed food. This is why the light water was separated from the heavy and toxic water.

Anyone who is willing to hear should listen to the Spirit and understand what the Spirit is saying to the churches.

Philadelphia – Judah

"Write this letter to the angel [DNA–Cytosine] of the church in Philadelphia [Judah]. This is the message from the one who is holy and true [Proton]. He is the one who has the key of David [the ability to create]. He opens doors, and no one can shut them; he shuts doors, and no one can open them.

"I know all the things you do, and I have opened a door for you that no one can shut. You have little strength, yet you obeyed my word and did not deny me. Look! I will force those who belong to Satan – those liars who say they are Jews but are not – to come and bow down at your feet. They will acknowledge that you are the ones I love. "Because you have obeyed my command to persevere, I will protect you from the great time of testing that will come upon the whole world to test those who belong to this world.

Look, I am coming quickly. Hold on to what you have, so that no one will take away your crown. All who are victorious will become pillars in the Temple of my GOD, and they will never have to leave it. And I will write my GOD's name on them [ATOM], and they will be citizens in the city of my GOD – the new Jerusalem that comes down from heaven from my GOD. And they will have my new name inscribed upon them.

Anyone who is willing to hear should listen to the Spirit and understand what the Spirit is saying to the churches.

Laodicea – Israel

"Write this letter to the angel [DNA–Thymine] of the church in Laodicea – Israel. This is the message from the one who is the Amen [All men] – the faithful and true witness, the ruler of GOD's creation: [Like Gluon the strongest and the strong nuclear force, Israel is the strongest among men. Israel leads. Just as David was in times past, Israel is GOD's chosen leader. Remember that Jacob's name was changed to Israel.]

"I know all the things you do, that you are neither hot nor cold. I wish you were one or the other! But since you are like lukewarm water, I will spit you out of my mouth! You say, 'I am rich. I have everything I want. I don't need a thing!' And you don't realize that you are wretched and miserable and poor and blind and naked.

I advise you to buy gold from me – gold [truth] that has been purified by fire. Then you will be rich. And also buy white garments so you will not be shamed by your nakedness. And buy ointment for your eyes so you will be able to see. I am the one who corrects and disciplines everyone I love. Be diligent and turn from your indifference.

"Look! Here I stand at the door and knock. If you hear me calling and open the door, I will come in, and we will share a meal as friends. I will invite everyone who is victorious to sit with me on my throne, just as I was victorious and sat with my Father on his throne.

Anyone who is willing to hear should listen to the Spirit and understand what the Spirit is saying to the churches."

Revelation 3:2 – 22

I, Cyrus, was willing to hear and have listened to the Spirit whose name is ATOM. I understand what the Spirit is saying to the churches. I know who the churches are and how to identify them. Listen.

The Sin of Israel

Now this is the truth of the matter. The devil awakened a desire in GOD's daughter Eve who was called *Israel* in heaven. She was called Israel just as surely as Jacob and David were called Israel by GOD.

I know that the devil came upon Eve with her *joy strong* because she did the same thing to me – *a horrifying experience* feeling the dragons' ice cold breath under your sheets. She was whispering lies in my ear and o so confident that she would win me over on the first day. But my GOD said, 'don't listen' and he also said, 'GOD *always* give you a way out'.

I jumped up and ran out of the room. I went into the study and sat down at my desk. I looked up into the sky and wondered what I had done to deserve this kind of attention. It was enough to make you run screaming in terror. But GOD's grace is sufficient for me. I found out that I had done nothing wrong. I found out that I had been *chosen* to do something great. I had been *born* for this moment in the history of life on earth.

Ezekiel wrote a story about two eagles that demonstrate how Eve left her Father's care and lusted after the fruit that Satan had to offer. The bible says,

A great eagle [Christ, Proton] **with broad wings full of many-colored feathers came to Lebanon. He took hold of the highest branch of a cedar tree and plucked off its topmost shoot** [Adam]**. Then he carried it away to a city filled with merchants, where he planted it.**

Ezekiel 17:3 – 4

You see, there were *many* named Judah on the earth in the beginning for Judah were made both male and female.[4] GOD charged Judah to populate the earth and to subdue it. Haven't you scientists seen the bones of the ones he saved for you? Do you think you found those bones by accident? No. GOD wanted them to be found. They were placed there for you to find.

This should end the debate on whether the seven days of creation were literally seven twenty-four hour periods, which is human time or if the seven periods were GOD's own rich time. You bible scholars have seen the references in Daniel to 62 sets of seven. Only GOD and his angels know how to translate that. *Nothing* in human wisdom can help us *calculate* what that means. And what makes you think you are wise enough to try? Only GOD and his angels know what it means.

So of course, those seven days were GOD's *time*.

---

4   Genesis 1:26 – 28

When have you ever heard of the Most High GOD answering your prayers in *your* time, to accommodate your comfort level? Even Jesus was famously late in responding to the panicked cries of the people. It is the reason that Lazarus *died* and then was raised back to life.

GOD does what he does in his own time, when he is ready. And he does whatever he wants! He is not intimidated by your boundaries or the boundaries of those who oppress you.

Stop fooling yourselves. If you think you are wise by this world's standards, you will have to become a fool so you can become wise by GOD's standards.

For the wisdom of this world is *foolishness* **to GOD.**

As the Scriptures say, "GOD catches those who think they are wise in their own cleverness." And again, "The LORD knows the thoughts of the wise, *that they are worthless.***"**

1 Corinthians 3:18 – 20

Those of you who still want to argue can continue to waste your breath. What has been said surely is – no matter what lies the evil one has told you. If you were truly wise, you would pray and ask GOD to give you wisdom. Not for your *own vanity* but for his *glory*.

Now, does this revelation of the seven days of creation take away from the importance of GOD's Word – the Bible?

Of course not! GOD does *everything* in his own time, in his own way, and for his own purpose. The knowledge of men is nothing compared to the knowledge of GOD.

Now, the scriptures say,

Then he planted one of its seedlings [Eve] in fertile ground beside a broad river, where it would grow as quickly as a willow tree. It took root there and grew into a low, spreading vine. Its branches turned up toward the eagle [Christ], and its roots grew down beneath it. It soon produced strong branches and luxuriant leaves.

But then another great eagle [Electron or Satan] with broad wings and full plumage came along.

So, the vine [Eve] sent its roots and branches out toward him [Satan] for water.

The vine [Eve] did this even though it was already planted in good

soil and had plenty of water so it could grow into a splendid vine and produce rich leaves and luscious fruit."

Ezekiel 17:4 – 8

Even in those days, Eve had a choice. She knew that the sin that she was being tempted with was forbidden and <u>wrong</u>. She knew that GOD had told her and Adam <u>not</u> to taste the fruit of the tree of good and evil, the fruit of Satan.

Now, was this fruit like an apple or grapes? No. It was fruit out of the loins, as my children are the fruit of my loins. Satan's fruit is over ripe. It is like peaches that are sweetest just before they turn rotten. And I know why it is called fruit. It is a polite way of describing that foul *oral* act. That is what GOD is referring to when the scriptures speak of you kneeling down and worshiping idols in your 'sacred gardens'. If you knew your GOD, you would never want to taste this *fruit*. It is a filthy habit. It is an abomination in GOD's sight.

Michelangelo, Sin of Eve and Adam

"Yes," Adam admitted, "but it was the woman you gave me who brought me the fruit, and I ate it."

Genesis 3:12

And it was the woman, not Adam, who was deceived by Satan, and sin was the result.

1 Titus 2:14

The result of Adam's sin, which is greedy, emasculated sperm and fatalistic bacteria lodged in the woman Eve's digestive tract, changed the pure and clean genome, the genetic makeup within the bodies of mankind from incorruptible to corrupt and vile. The temple that was once imperishable is now perishable, desecrated, full of corpses. This physical change to the genetic DNA makeup of mankind had far reaching consequences. For, the addition of bacteria overtook the healthy molecules and cells within the body. Over the generations, we have become incapacitated, disease ridden, arthritic and weak.

When Adam sinned, sin [bacteria] entered the entire human race. Adam's sin [bacteria] brought death, so death spread to everyone, for everyone sinned.

Romans 5:12

So let me explain this to you for I fear that you don't know what sin is: Sin is literally "time without GOD". Sin, from its Latin origins, means without. To be without GOD means to be in sin. We are living in sin in these days, in this generation. This is true because even thought Christ died for sin, sin was not taken away. Past and present sins were forgiven. We live in sin today because at the cross, men were conned into choosing the anti-Christ who had been bound. Today he is free and rules over mankind.

You may not fully be able to comprehend it yet, but Satan name is also called Jesus! Oh yes! Remember that there were two named Jesus at the cross. One was the Saviour, the Lamb of GOD – Jesus Christ. The other was Bar-Jesus or not Jesus. Bar-Jesus is commonly referred to as Barabbas. He is the one that the Jews and the Gentiles chose on that fateful day. The world as you see it is the result. Barabbas is not the Rabbi, the Counselor or Christ. Bar-Jesus or Satan is the false prophet, who lives through you, giving you foolish counsel, to which all men eagerly listen every day beginning early in the morning during your shower. Bar-Jesus is the anti-Christ. But you will come to understand this more and more. Keep reading.

In this age of the Gentiles, Satan is quick to answer when you call on the Lord's name, even when you pray in Jesus' name. Satan's name is Bar-Jesus – which means "not Jesus". Satan will give you signs and wonders, answering audibly, telling you lies, speaking in words you cannot understand – whatever it takes to convince you that she is good, that she is God. She is the one deceiving the whole world.

The bacteria from the first sin also contaminated the minds of men causing the bronze mountains to be tainted with gray matter. Now, we have changed from truth seeking to idol worshiping: seeking impurity, sexual immorality and eagerness for lustful pleasure. Men like Enoch were able to live for hundreds of years back in the beginning. However, murderous bacteria and greedy sperm became embedded in the human genome, the genetic DNA chain. From that one sin, all men die. The bacteria will not be cleansed away until the war, until the sinking of Babylon, of the city of Atlantis; that great city that will be thrown down like a stone.

> **Yes, I am afraid that when I come, GOD will humble me again because of you. And I will have to grieve because many of you who sinned earlier have not repented of your impurity, sexual immorality and eagerness for lustful pleasure.**

2 Corinthians 12:21

Now don't let your shame or your guilt overwhelm you. The Lamb of GOD died for our sins and his blood was offered as a sacrifice for the sins of the world. Christ said, 'Go, and sin no more.' And he meant it.

His hands are extended to everyone in this generation, during the end of this age. No one who is indecent or immoral will be allowed in the New Jerusalem. The scriptures say,

> **All who are victorious will inherit all these blessings, and I will be their GOD, and they will be my children. But cowards who turn away from me, and unbelievers, and the *corrupt*, and murderers, and the immoral, and those who practice witchcraft, and idol worshipers, and all liars—their doom is the lake that burns with fire and sulfur. This is the second death.**

Revelation 21:7 – 8

Electron, known as Satan around the world, woke me up one night. She was frustrated and angry at my constant refusal and the lengths that I went to in order to protect my body from her nagging grinding. She was screaming.

You have to say it! You have to say it! You have to say it!

As I gained consciousness, I stretched. I did not ask her what she wanted me to say.

I did not entertain her suggestion in anyway. I simply said, "No! Never!"

I rose up off the short sofa where I slept for too many months. I sought *protection,* such as was available to me and found it.

But Eve had no such protection. So, she went to reason this new pleasure out with her sister Jerusalem – *the serpent.* Jerusalem was delighted that Eve had come to her for advice. *This was a rare thing.* Eve did not go to Adam and discuss it. She knew that Adam would be against it for Adam was still faithful to GOD.

Jerusalem gained confidence from this solicitation for advice. She told Eve what she wanted to hear so that she would have favor with Eve. That is why Jerusalem was called 'serpent' in the garden. She has a forked tongue. She is the neutral one. She can go either way – encouraging the good in you or the evil. Her tongue swings *too* easily. She will *say* anything to have power and honor.

Jerusalem was made to be a worker, a teacher. She was not created to be a leader of tribes. She has a great amount of knowledge. She is a *brilliant* scholar – but everything has been learned by rote – through books and discussions. Her knowledge has not been gained by *observing* the truth like Judah or by *experiencing* the truth like Israel.

The serpent was a woman, the one who talks constantly. She is easily deceived and slow to gain wisdom but she *acted* arrogantly as if she knew everything. She is Ham, cursed forever to be *less wise* than the other two. Yet, she still belongs to GOD. She is his child as much as Judah and Israel.

Jerusalem, *GOD's third child*, is the peacemaker and she will say anything so that everyone is happy.[5] She is hungry and thirsty for justice.[6] Today, Jerusalem is persecuted on earth but GOD has said that they will receive vindication in full against the evil influence that caused them to fall from GOD's grace.

Now, Jerusalem encouraged Eve to give in to this sin. It is amazing how the clan of Jerusalem gives advice so confidently and thinks more of themselves than they ought. The results are disastrous for those who listen for they will surely be led astray.

Let the Holy Spirit guide you! Stop depending on man to tell you what to do unless, of course, you *want* to be led astray. Unless, of course, you *want* to sin and you just want someone to give you the **go ahead!**

When Jesus walked the earth, he rebuked Peter who is called Jerusalem in heaven. Christ was telling his disciples about his coming death. And Peter said,

---

5 Lamentations 1:2, Matthew 5:4
6 Matthew 5:6

"Heaven forbid, LORD," he said. "This will *never* happen to you!"

Jesus turned to Peter and said,

"Get away from me, Satan! You are a *dangerous trap to me*. You are seeing things merely from a human point of view, and not from GOD's."

Matthew 16:22 – 23

And in these last days, the consequences for Jerusalem's tongue wagging are **severe**. Jerusalem is responsible for helping to fulfill Satan's plan. She is an unwitting partner with Satan and hangs on to her every word. Now, the bible says,

… The world around us is under the power and control of the evil one.

1 John 5:19

Anyway, upon the advice of that serpent Jerusalem, Eve accepted Satan's fruit. And in doing so, she unwittingly set the stage for Satan's plan to *take over the world*.

Satan implanted his seed into GOD's virgin daughter. For, Eve was a *virgin to sin* until she joined her body with the great prostitute, the one who was called the Queen of Heaven – Satan. For the bible says of Satan,

He will merely think he is attacking my people as part of his plan to conquer the world. He will say, "Each of my princes will soon be a king, ruling a conquered land."

Isaiah 10:8

At the time that Eve sinned, there were *hundreds* of "Eves" (or as they are called in heaven "Israel") living in the beautiful Garden of Eden just as there were *hundreds* of Judah. They were both male and female. GOD created the earth and prepared the land first.

Then GOD said, "Let us make people in our image, to be like ourselves. They will be masters over all life – the fish in the sea, the birds in the sky, and all the livestock, wild animals, and small animals." So, GOD created people in his own image; GOD patterned them after himself; *male and female he created them*. GOD blessed them and told them, "*Multiply and fill the earth* and subdue it. Be masters over the fish and birds and all the animals."

Genesis 1:26 – 28

It is also true that during that time there were *many* Eves and *many* Adams because when Cain was banished from his home for killing his brother Abel, he settled in the land of Nod east of Eden[7] where he found a wife among the *others* GOD had made.

The evil one, who was jealous of the LORD's success, came during the night and planted weeds in GOD's field of golden wheat. And GOD was outraged.

Then the LORD said, "Has anyone ever heard of such a thing, even among the pagan nations? My virgin Israel has done something too terrible to understand!

Jeremiah 18:13

For in her tubes she carried the seed of Satan, a quick growing weed who multiplied without shame. Like all plants, these weeds have a name. They are called *Cain*. And they are known all over the world as *the Gentiles*. And Cain, (who is also both male and female and of every race) joined in the rotation of crops in the fourth year. Now, as weeds have a tendency to do, Cain began immediately to take over the fields. And the heart of GOD grieved. The scriptures say,

My people have planted wheat but are harvesting thorns. They have worked hard, but it has done them no good. They will harvest a crop of shame, for the fierce anger of the LORD is upon them.

Jeremiah 12:13

The thorns that GOD's people are harvesting are the same weeds whose name is Cain. These thorns are the Gentiles.

This is the first time the wall of the Holy City of Jerusalem was breached.

Listen as wisdom calls out! Hear as understanding raises her voice! She stands on the hilltop and at the crossroads. At the entrance to the city, at the city gates, she cries aloud,

"I call to you, to all of you! I am raising my voice to all people. How naive you are! Let me give you common sense. O foolish ones, let me give you understanding. Listen to me! For I have excellent things to tell you.

Everything I say is right, for I speak the truth and hate every kind of deception."

Proverbs 8:1 – 7

The wisdom of the Holy Spirit is wholesome and good. There is nothing *crooked or twisted* in it. How could Cain, the murderer, belong to ATOM? Why would he make such a being, one that he would have to chase down and argue with all of his life?

---

7   Genesis 4:16

The words of the Holy Spirit are plain to anyone with understanding, clear to those who want to learn the truth. Choose her instruction rather than silver, and her knowledge over pure gold. For the wisdom of gentle Jerusalem is far more valuable than rubies. *Nothing* you desire can be compared with it.

So, through the evil one, Cain was conceived.[8] And all of the crops of Cain – these aliens with their foreign gods,[9] foreign nations,[10] foreign warriors who take what they want,[11] foreign oppressors who speak in an unknown language[12] – oppress and control the three children of GOD. Satan has enslaved GOD's children using her children *and* Jerusalem to help her. The children of the devil are the 'hard path'. They cannot understand the scope of GOD's plans nor does their father want them to. They are the *hard path*. The bible says,

> **The seed that fell on the hard path represents those who hear the Good News about the Kingdom and don't understand it. Then the evil one comes and snatches the seed away from their hearts.**

Matthew 13:19

When Jesus walked the earth as a man, he told another story to illustrate the birth of Satan's children – the foreigners', the Gentiles who came to live among the Jews. He said,

> **The Kingdom of Heaven is like a farmer who planted good seed in his field. But that night as everyone slept, his enemy came and planted weeds among the wheat. When the crops began to grow and produce grain, the weeds also grew. The farmer's servants came and told him,**
>
> **'Sir, the field where you planted that good seed is full of weeds!'**
>
> **'An enemy has done it!' the farmer exclaimed.**
>
> **'Shall we pull out the weeds?' they asked.**
>
> **He replied, 'No, you'll hurt the wheat if you do. Let both grow together until the harvest. Then I will tell the harvesters to sort out the weeds and burn them and to put the wheat in the barn.'**

Matthew 13: 24 – 30

---

8   Genesis 4:1
9   Psalm 81:9, Jeremiah 2:25
10   Isaiah 25:5
11   Isaiah 62:8
12   Isaiah 28:11

Jesus explained this parable plainly.

The weeds are the people who belong to the evil one. The enemy who planted the weeds among the wheat is the Devil. The harvest is the end of the world, and the harvesters are the angels.

Matthew 13: 38 – 39

Every plant not planted by my heavenly Father will be rooted up, so ignore them. They are blind guides leading the blind, and if one blind person guides another, they will both fall into a ditch.

Matthew 15: 13 – 14

Ezekiel wrote the story of the LORD's anger and disgust at Eve's sin. You may read it for yourself in Ezekiel 23 or you may read it here. It amounts to the same story, only I have paraphrased it and added clarification from the Spirit of GOD. This story explains the idol worship that GOD spoke of so often to the prophets. It is the idol worship that he abhors. The LORD told Ezekiel the story of Eve's sin.[13]

He said, "Son of man, once there were two sisters who were daughters of the same *mother*." The mother, of course, is GOD Almighty. He is both mother *and* father for he *created* them. And as the story goes, the two sisters became prostitutes in Egypt.

Now Egypt is a foul place where Satan is worshipped as a god in the gold, silver, bronze, iron, or wooden statues that were made to represent her. They called these statues names like Baal or Molech. Today, they call him Buddha, Christ, and Mary and many others. And anyone who did not bow down and worship her was killed.

Even as young girls, these two sisters allowed themselves to be fondled and caressed by spirits who came to defile them when they were very young. They allowed it because the devil came upon them in a surprising way, suddenly and without warning. Satan came upon them strong in the fields and open spaces before they were old enough to have breasts. The Song of Songs describes the details. For King Solomon wrote,

Brothers: "We have a little sister too young for breasts. What will we do if someone asks to marry her? If she is chaste, we will strengthen and encourage her. But if she is promiscuous, we will shut her off from men."

Young Woman: "I am *chaste*, and I am now full breasted. And my *lover* is content with me."

Song of Songs 8:8 – 10

The young woman who is *chaste*, innocent and a virgin to men, has a lover who is not human. Her lover is the devil. This explains why David with all of his wives and concubines had favor with GOD until the day he lay with Satan and with Satan's daughter. On that day, he conceived a child that was a child of the devil. But GOD took the child from him and punished him for this sin. This lust for pleasure is the purest form of idol worship. Nothing angers GOD more than this.

And Ezekiel wrote,

> The older girl was named Oholah, and her sister was Oholibah. I married them, and they bore me sons and daughters. I am speaking of Samaria and Jerusalem, for Oholah is Samaria and Oholibah is Jerusalem.

Ezekiel 23:4

Oholah was Eve, Israel, GOD's prophet. And Oholibah was Jerusalem, the serpent who was created to be a teacher and faithful follower of the Most High. For the LORD Almighty said,

> I saw that the *prophets* of Samaria were terribly evil, for they prophesied by Baal and led my people of Israel into sin.

Jeremiah 23:13

Greed and lust for the good things in life led the serpent into idol worship and *prostitution*. Taking the advice of the devil,[14] the serpent sold her soul for prosperity. Then she taught Eve of these crimes and she followed suit. The serpent sold out the whole world so that she could be honored among men. The bible says,

> Then Oholah lusted after other lovers instead of me, and she gave her love to the Assyrians, her neighbors.

Ezekiel 23:5

And so, in this same manner, Eve lusted after the pleasures that the devil offered her. She left her Creator who from the beginning gave her *joy*. She joined with the Assyrians so that she could have *joy strong*. The **Assyrians** are the horde, the demons, the thorns, evil spirits led by the devil herself.

For the bible says,

> Destruction is certain for Assyria [Electron and her brood], the <u>whip of my anger</u>. Its military power is a club in my hand. Assyria will enslave my people, who are a godless nation.

---

14   Numbers 31:16

It will plunder them, trampling them like dirt beneath its feet.

Isaiah 10:5 – 6

The Assyrians are demons, thorns and brier. They exist in the mind and cover the bodies of every person. For the bible says,

The LORD, the Light of Israel and the Holy One, will be a flaming fire that will destroy them. In a single night, he will burn those thorns and briers, the Assyrians.

Isaiah 10:17

And the Assyrians are also known as the children of Satan – the descendants of Cain, the Gentiles. The bible says,

Assyria's vast army is like a glorious forest, yet it will be destroyed. The LORD will completely destroy Assyria's warriors, and they will waste away like sick people in a plague. Only a few from all that mighty army will survive – *so few that a child could count them*!

Isaiah 10:18 - 19

He will burn the Assyrians as surely as he will burn the weeds. But who can blame Oholah for her lust. I can. GOD does. But the bible says,

They were all attractive young men, captains and commanders dressed in handsome blue, dashing about on their horses.

Ezekiel 23:6

And so, Eve prostituted herself with Satan – the most desirable one in all of Assyria. Even Plato wrote of Poseidon, the water god, who had a child with a human woman in his work Critias. Eve worshipped Satan's idol in her *sacred forest* and defiled herself with him there. For when she left Egypt, she did not leave her spirit of prostitution behind. She was still as lewd as she was when she was a very young girl, when the Egyptian demons satisfied their lusts with her and robbed her of her virginity.

Then Eve, Israel, offered Adam, Judah, this indulgence and he accepted. And the heart of GOD grieved and the earth wept.

O Israel and Judah, what should I do with you?" asks the LORD. "For your love vanishes like the morning mist and disappears like dew in the sunlight.

Hosea 6:4

And that is how it began. That is why the scriptures say,

We know that we are children of GOD and that the world around us is under the power and control of the evil one.

1 John 5:19

Then GOD was angry with Eve for her idol worship, for her wanton prostitution and for the birth of Cain and he banished Adam and Eve from their home.

For they have betrayed the honor of the LORD, bearing children that aren't his.

Hosea 5:7

And GOD named these children of Eve – Lo-ammi[15], which means 'Not my people'. He said, For, these are sons and daughters of Israel. who were born of the evil one. They are not 'Jezreel' which means GOD. ATOM plants.

And I will not love her children as I would my own because they are not my children! They were conceived in adultery. For their mother is a shameless prostitute and became pregnant in a shameful way.

She said, "I'll run after other lovers and sell myself to them for food and drink, for clothing of wool and linen, and for olive oil."

Hosea 2:4 – 5

Unbelievable and yet it is true!

Look at me and be stunned. Put your hand over your mouth in shock. When I think about what I am saying, *I shudder. My body trembles.*

Job 21:4 – 6

GOD punished the Jewels for their disloyalty by taking away their blessings and scattering them all over the earth. For Isaiah wrote of Eve and Adam,

This is the story of the LORD's people. They are the vineyard of the LORD Almighty. Israel and Judah are his pleasant garden. He expected them to yield a crop of justice, but instead he found bloodshed. He expected to find righteousness, but instead he heard cries of oppression.

Isaiah 5:7

And the prophet Daniel wept for the sins of the Jewels. He said of GOD's judgment,

---

15   Hosea 1 and 2

LORD, you are in the right; but our faces are covered with shame, just as you see us now. This is true of us all, including the people of **Judah** and **Jerusalem** and all **Israel**, scattered near and far, wherever you have driven us because of our disloyalty to you.

Daniel 9:7

But what can be done about this. For the bible says,

The virgin **Israel** has fallen, never to rise again! She lies forsaken on the ground, with none to raise her up.

Amos 5:2

Nothing – for Eve is long dead. In her greedy lust, she opened the door and invited Satan in and he and his sinful children have never left us. So we live together – the Jewels and the Gentiles – becoming more wicked with every generation.

Did GOD's people stumble and fall beyond recovery? Of course not! His purpose was to make his salvation available to the Gentiles, and then the Jewels would be jealous and want it for themselves.

Romans 11:11

Then GOD told the story of Eve's end to Ezekiel. He said,

And so, I handed her over to her Assyrian lovers, whom she desired so much. They stripped her and killed her and took away her children as their slaves.

Her name was known to every woman in the land as a sinner who had received what she deserved.

Ezekiel 23:9 – 10

Now let me explain what this means because many of you will read this and think that the Assyrians are men from an age long past. They are not. They are demons, evil spirits, subjects of the devil who followed her when she was banished from heaven. They live among us today. When the devil was thrown down

His tail dragged down one-third of the stars, which he threw to the earth.

Revelations 12:4

These stars are the Assyrians. GOD handed Eve over to these demons that she desired so much. And having no further access to the Tree of Life, Eve's life ended. And also, the life of Adam. And we who are alive today, her children, are now slaves to sin because of the first sin.

38

As the bible says, 'We were all born in sin and shaped in iniquity'. The demons corrupted her body and it was riddled with disease. The demons killed the spirit of GOD within her. And as she aged, she became frail and withered away in death.

Now how do you think that all of the women knew about Eve's sin? That's right. You know the answer. They knew when the child was born! Cain was made in the image of his father, mother just as Adam and Eve were created in the image of their father, who is GOD. Cain's skin was pale and thin. His eyes were even more pale and blue like jewels. His hair was wavy and black.[16]

In those days, Cain's appearance was a sharp contrast to the nappy haired people of GOD. And no matter how hard Eve worked to cover his skin (to protect him from the sun), Cain's jewel-colored eyes were a constant reminder of her sin.

The Quaternity

The birth of Cain's began the quaternity – the cycle of seasons, which lasts for a four-year period.[17]

In the quaternity, each year represents a crop of fruit. Previously there had been a trinity. It was a cycle of three—like the Father, Son, and Holy Spirit, like Judah, Israel, and Jerusalem (the man, woman, and serpent).

In GOD's plan of the creation of man, the Jewels are known as *fruit*. In the first year, Judah was created and Israel was planted. In the second year, Israel was harvested and Jerusalem was planted. In the third year, Jerusalem was harvested and Judah was planted. And the cycle of seasons for planting and harvesting came and went unquestioned like the moon that marks the seasons and the sun that knows when to set. These are the three crops that were planted in Eden. *Planted* means the living being was **conceived**. *Harvested* means the living being was **born**.

---

16 Song of Songs 10:5 – 7
17 The union of four in one, as of four persons; -- analogous to the theological term trinity. Source: Webster's Revised Unabridged Dictionary, © 1996, 1998 MICRA, Inc.

When Satan came and planted his seed into Eve's tubes, the rotation of the three crops changed. Now the crops rotate on a quaternal cycle. In the first year, Cain is harvested and Judah is planted. In the second year, Judah is harvested and Israel is planted. In the third year, Israel is harvested and Jerusalem is planted. In the fourth year, Jerusalem is harvested and Cain is planted.

The Crops

Year	Seeds Planted during the season of	Will yield a crop of
1	Judah	Cain
2	Israel	Judah
3	Jerusalem	Israel
4	Cain	Jerusalem

And the cycle continues in this repeating fashion just as the sun rises and sets every single day, just as the seasons come year upon year. So, every person born to a woman (and who isn't) is one of these four crops.

You are either one of the three created in the beginning and are therefore a Jew. Or, you were born of the crop that was seeded by Satan when Eve sinned – and are therefore a Gentile. A person cannot chose to which tree he belongs just as he cannot choose his physical parents. GOD chooses according to his will and purpose.

For every tree is known by his own fruit. For of thorns men do not gather figs, nor of a bramble bush gather they grapes.

Luke 6:44 KJV

Jotham, the son of Gideon, told a parable of the four trees and the four types of fruit. He said, "Listen to me if you want GOD to listen to you!" He said,

Once upon a time, the trees decided to elect a king. First, they said to the olive tree, 'Be our king!' But it refused, saying, 'Should I quit producing the olive oil that blesses both GOD and people, just to wave back and forth over the trees?'

Judges 9:8 – 9

The olive tree is Judah. Judah is the one that blesses both GOD and people.

Then they said to the fig tree, 'You be our king!' But the fig tree also refused, saying, 'Should I quit producing my sweet fruit just to wave back and forth over the trees?'

Judges 9:10 – 11

The fig tree is Israel. Israel *is* the *sweetest* fruit. It is the fruit that *works* for GOD and *helps* others tirelessly.

Then they said to the grapevine, 'You be our king!' But the grapevine replied, 'Should I quit producing the wine that cheers both GOD and people, just to wave back and forth over the trees?'

Judges 9:12 – 13

The grapevine is Jerusalem. Jerusalem is the one that cheers up both GOD and people with an eternal optimism that cannot be matched. Jerusalem is the light of the world.

Then all the trees finally turned to the thornbush and said, 'Come, you be our king!' And the thornbush replied, 'If you truly want to make me your king, come and take shelter in my shade. If not, let fire come out from me and devour the cedars of Lebanon.'

Judges 9:14 – 15

The thornbush is Cain – the father of the Gentiles. The Gentiles are the ones that demand complete control over the lives of the trees and their fruit. If the Gentiles are denied this authority, they will set out to destroy all of those who resist.

Jesus Christ was born in this same cycle and on the same branch – the branch of Judah. And GOD called his name Judah in heaven. This cycle determines your temperament or nature and your purpose. Paul explained this when he talked about the Hebrew people. He said

Their ancestors were great people of GOD, and Christ himself was a Jew as far as his <u>human nature</u> is concerned. And he is GOD, who rules over everything and is worthy of eternal praise! Amen.

Romans 9:5

This is how it was in the beginning.

Consider the Kennedy's. The father was a Gentile – powerful, power hungry, influential, and charismatic. John was Judah – GOD's own son, made in the image of Christ. Robert was Israel – GOD's favorite, the passionate one, the strong one who accomplished much so that I could write these words without fear of retribution. And the youngest son, Edward, is Jerusalem – afraid to live, afraid to die so he simply carries on hoping that no one will notice him. This is as it has always been. This is how it will be when Christ returns.

But after he returns and his anger is spent, he will change the rotation. A fresh crop will be planted *each month* instead of each year as it is today. And the Gentiles will not be among these new crops. GOD will pull the thorns out by the roots.[18]

> **Therefore, this is what the Sovereign LORD says: "Because it became proud and arrogant, and because it set itself so high above the others, reaching to the clouds, I handed it over to a mighty nation that destroyed it as its wickedness deserved. I myself discarded it."**
>
> *Ezekiel 31:10 – 11*

John described the new world under the rule of Christ. He said,

> **And the angel showed me a pure river with the water of life, clear as crystal, flowing from the throne of GOD and of the Lamb, coursing down the centre of the main street.**
>
> **On each side of the river grew a tree of life, bearing twelve crops of fruit, with a fresh crop each month. The leaves were used for medicine to heal the nations.** *No longer will anything be cursed.* **For the throne of GOD and of the Lamb will be there, and his servants will worship him.**
>
> *Revelation 22:1 – 3*

And now you must understand what the scriptures mean when it says that Abraham had two children. One was born of a free woman and one was born of a slave woman. The three that belong to GOD are descendants of the free woman and before that – descendants of Shem, Japheth, and Ham who descended from Adam, Eve, and Serpent.

The ones that belong to the devil are descendants of the slave woman and before that – of Cain. The bible says,

> **This means that Abraham's physical descendants are not necessarily children of GOD. It is the children of the promise who are considered to be Abraham's children. For GOD had promised, "Next year I will return, and Sarah will have a son.**
>
> **This son was our ancestor Isaac. When he grew up, he married Rebekah, who gave birth to twins.**

But before they were born, before they had done anything good or bad, she received a message from GOD. (This message proves that *GOD chooses according to his own plan*, not according to our good or bad works.) She was told, "The descendants of your older son will serve the descendants of your younger son.

In the words of the Scriptures, "I loved Jacob, but I rejected Esau."

Romans 9:8 – 13

That is why the bible says,

So receiving GOD's promise is not up to us. We can't get it by choosing it or working hard for it. GOD will show mercy to anyone he chooses.

Romans 9:16

You can't become a Jew if you are not a Jew. If you are truly a Jew – not just because of your bloodline or because of the tribe to which you are linked – it is because you were born into one of the three designs that GOD created when he made the world. Being Jewish is not a *club* that you can join.

You can't become a Gentile if you are not a Gentile. If you are a Gentile, it is because you were born with the Gentile character. But Christ made it possible for Jewels and Gentiles to coexist in peace.

For the scriptures say,

But some of these branches from Abraham's tree, some of the Jews, have been broken off. And you Gentiles, who were branches from a <u>wild olive tree</u>, were *grafted* in. So now, you also receive the blessing GOD has promised Abraham and his children, sharing in GOD's rich nourishment of his special olive tree.

Romans 11:17

The case is made with the birth of Ishmael and Isaac. The scriptures say,

Then the LORD said to him [Abram], "No, your servant will not be your heir, for you will have a son of your own to inherit everything I am giving you."

Genesis 15:4

GOD waited fourteen years after he first told Abram that he would be the father of all nations. During that time, Abram grew tired of waiting and decided to take matters in his own hand. At Sarai's urging, he slept with Hagar – the slave wife.

So, Hagar gave Abram a son, and Abram named him Ishmael. Abram was eighty-six years old at that time.

Genesis 16:15 – 16

The LORD waited those fourteen years so that he could make his covenant with Isaac who is called Judah in heaven. While he waited, he watched Abram with great interest. When the time of testing was over, GOD went again to Abram. He changed his name to Abraham so that the world would know that he was Jerusalem and his wife's name to Sarah because she was Judah and GOD announced again that Abraham would have a son. He said,

My covenant is with Isaac, who will be born to you and Sarah about this time next year.

Genesis 17:21

Ishmael was thirteen when Sarah became pregnant and Isaac was born the next year when Ishmael was fourteen.

Abraham was ninety-nine years old at that time, and Ishmael his son was thirteen.

Genesis 17: 24 – 25

So now, the illustration below shows the types of *fruit* that were *harvested* between the conception of Ishmael and the birth of Isaac - the child of the promise.

The Sons of Abraham

Event	Ishmael's Age	Fruit	Abraham's Age
Isaac is Born	14	Judah	100
	13	Cain	99
	12	Jerusalem	93
	11	Israel	97
	10	Judah	96
	9	Cain	95
	8	Jerusalem	94
	7	Israel	93
	6	Judah	92
	5	Cain	91
	4	Jerusalem	90
	3	Israel	89
	2	Judah	88
Ishmael is Born	1	Cain	87
Ishmael Conceived	0		86

Again, every person is born one of these four. Adam was Judah and Eve was Israel. Cain was the first Gentile but he came from the loins of Eve and with Adam's help, through the seed of Satan. It is not a matter of *to whom* you were born that decides which of the four you are, but *when* you were born. That is why the scriptures say,

> **"Don't just say, 'We're safe—we're the descendants of Abraham'. That proves nothing. GOD can change these stones here into children of Abraham. Even now, the ax of GOD's judgment is poised, ready to sever your roots. Yes, every tree that does not produce good fruit will be chopped down and thrown into the fire."**

Matthew 3:9 – 10

Your heritage doesn't matter. For the people of GOD are Africans, Americans, Asians, Hebrews, Germans, Italians, Polynesian and **every** race, creed, and color. <u>When</u> you were born determines if you belong to GOD or if you are a child of the devil. Cain, who created his own brand of justice by killing his brother, became the fourth living being when there had only been three.

The Cycle of Crops

Tree	Cycle Begins			To	Cycle Ends		
Crops	M	D	Year		M	D	Year
Gentile	2	2	1946	-	1	21	1947
Jerusalem	1	22	1947	-	2	9	1948
Israel	2	10	1948	-	1	28	1949
Judah	1	29	1949	-	2	16	1950
Gentile	2	17	1950	-	2	5	1951
Jerusalem	2	6	1951	-	1	26	1952
Israel	1	27	1952	-	2	13	1953
Judah	2	14	1953	-	2	2	1954
Gentile	2	3	1954	-	1	23	1955
Jerusalem	1	24	1955	-	2	11	1956
Israel	2	12	1956	-	1	30	1957
Judah	1	31	1957	-	2	17	1958
Gentile	2	18	1958	-	2	7	1959
Jerusalem	2	8	1959	-	1	27	1960
Israel	1	28	1960	-	2	14	1961
Judah	2	15	1961	-	2	4	1962
Gentile	2	5	1962	-	1	24	1963

It is in this same pattern that mankind is born today. It is a cycle that will not end until after Christ returns. And that time is coming soon. Look at the increased number of murders and victims. People are being slaughtered all over the place. But, don't let these sad events discourage you too much.

In a short time – *in just a little more than a year* **– you careless ones will suddenly begin to care. For your fruit crop will fail, and the harvest will never take place.**

Isaiah 32:10

When Christ returns, the harvest of the Gentiles will begin to diminish in size until it is no more.

And all of these four are in your family. All of these four are in my family. The Jewels and the Gentiles live together in the same household.

Now the world has revolted against GOD. They have chosen the sons and daughters of the slave woman to rule over GOD's children just as the people of Shechem chose the slave woman's son, Abimelech, to be their king just because *he was a relative.*[19]

And this is true of every family. My mother was Jerusalem – using words that were strong as iron to teach us and keep us in line and my father was Judah – a wise and gentle man – a mechanic who could fix anything. To my parents were born seven children – three are Judah – the discoverers, one is Israel – a helper, an organizer, and a warrior, two are Jerusalem – a teacher and a salesman, and one is a Gentile – an entertainer.

These four are Ezekiel's living beings. They are Job and his three friends. They are Daniel and the three Hebrew boys. They are the four apostles – Matthew, Mark, Luke, and John with their four different perspectives on the life of Christ.

It is written in the law of nature just as the seasons change, just as the planets follow their course, just as night turns to day. For GOD has said,

If you can break my covenant with the day and the night so that they do not come on their usual schedule, only then will my covenant with David, my servant, be broken. Only then will he no longer have a descendant to reign on his throne.

Jeremiah 33:20

So now, will the LORD reject the ones that he created? No! For the LORD has said,

---

19   Judges 9:18

I would no more reject my people than I would change my laws of night and day, of earth and sky.

Jeremiah 33:20, 25

In a moment, you will understand why Christ said,

I have come to set a man against his father, and a daughter against her mother, and a daughter-in-law against her mother-in-law.

Your enemies will be right in your own household!

If you love your father or mother more than you love me, you are not worthy of being mine; or if you love your son or daughter more than me, you are not worthy of being mine.

Matthew 10:35 – 37

The bad seed, the sons, and daughters of Satan are living in your home. The chaff is mixed with the wheat. They are your sons and your daughters. They are your mothers and fathers, your sisters and brothers, your daughter-in-law, your mother-in-law. The Psalmist described the differences between the wheat and the weeds. He said,

Oh, the joys of those who do not follow the advice of the wicked, or stand around with sinners, or join in with scoffers. But they delight in doing everything the LORD wants; day and night, they think about his law.

They are like trees planted along the riverbank, bearing fruit each season without fail. Their leaves never wither, and in all they do, they prosper.

But this is not true of the wicked. They are like worthless chaff, scattered by the wind. They will be condemned at the time of judgment. <u>Sinners will have no place among the godly</u>. For the LORD watches over the path of the godly, but the path of the wicked leads to destruction.

Psalms 1: 1 - 6

The Fruit

Gentiles and Jewels	Cain	Judah	Israel	Jerusalem
The Fruit	Thorns	Olives	Figs	Grapes

In the fifth year of GOD's creation, Abel was born and his name is called Judah in heaven. And he was a son of GOD like his father Adam and his mother Eve. He did what was right in GOD's sight while Cain did what was evil. And GOD loved Abel but he rejected Cain.

The LORD accepted Abel and his offering, but he did not accept Cain and his offering.

Genesis 4:4 – 5

So, Cain killed Abel because he was jealous of GOD's favor toward him. And Cain has been killing GOD's children, his prophets and holy ones since that time.

Now I know what you are thinking. GOD knows what you are thinking. How can a Gentile become right with GOD? Don't worry. The story is not over yet. For the scriptures say,

And I tell you this, that many Gentiles will come from all over the world and sit down with Abraham, Isaac, and Jacob at the feast in the Kingdom of Heaven.

Matthew 8:11

Twins

Now, GOD knows everything. He knows what you are thinking before you ask. So, he made provisions for you to learn about the multiple births in your life. And the story was told about Rebekah.

Rebekah had two children – twins. One was called Esau and the other one was Jacob. And the two infants struggled from conception, even in the wound. When Rebekah asked GOD why it was happening, he explained.

The sons in your womb will become two rival nations. One nation will be stronger than the other; the descendants of your older son will serve the descendants of your younger son.

Genesis 25:23

This is the same curse that was put on Ham [Jerusalem], Noah's son.[20] And so, it was that Esau was born first – the remnant Neanderthal from an age long past.

---

20   Genesis 9:25

The first was very red at birth. He was covered with so much hair that one would think he was wearing a piece of clothing. So, they called him Esau.

Genesis 25:25

And the bible says that Jacob was born second.

Then the other twin was born with his hand grasping Esau's heel. So, they called him Jacob.

Genesis 25:26

And GOD loved Jacob who is Israel and rejected Esau who is Jerusalem.

Esau pleaded, "Not one blessing left for me? O my father, bless me, too!" Then Esau broke down and wept.

Genesis 27:38

Esau hated Jacob because he had stolen his blessing, and he said to himself, "My father will soon be dead and gone. Then *I will kill Jacob*."

Genesis 27:41

Jerusalem behaves like the iron and clay part of the Gentiles. He threatens strongly but he rarely carries out his threats. And he is foolish as when he sold his birthright for a single meal. He is as hard as iron. So, GOD blessed Jacob and Jacob worshipped the LORD.

The Five that Became Four

You have eyes—can't you see? You have ears—can't you hear? Don't you remember anything at all?

What about the *five* thousand men I fed *with five* loaves of bread? How many baskets of leftovers did you pick up afterward?" "*Twelve*," they said.

[Five is the number of particles within the walls of ATOM; twelve is the number of *cycles* that complete a season or an annual when one of the five rules. This is a universal formulation, from the tides to the birth of children.]

Mark 8:18

Don't you remember the *four* thousand I fed *with seven* loaves, with baskets of food left over?

[Four is the number of mankind and humankind; seven is the the number of churches from the creation of the world.]

How could you even think I was talking about food?

So again I say, 'Beware of the yeast of the Pharisees and Sadducees'.

Then at last they understood that he wasn't speaking about yeast or bread but about the false teaching of the Pharisees and Sadducees.

[Pharisees are DNA-Adenine; Sadducees are DNA-Guanine, both complete deceivers. These are Electron's brood. They lie because their mother lies to them.]

Matthew 16:10 – 12

What was Jesus really trying to say? What is the false teaching of the Pharisees and the Sadducees? And why didn't he just tell them the answer so that they would not have to *figure it out*?

I will tell you why. This is a coded message that Jesus left for the one with wisdom, for the woman, who is Judah, whose name is Cyrus. I am that woman and now I will explain to you what Christ meant.

Christ sounds a little irritated with the disciples who did not seem to get his point. But he was not irritated *with them*. He was irritated *with me*. He wanted me to understand the truth and he wanted there to be no doubt in my mind what he meant. And I get it.

What Christ is really teaching them, and me is that there are *five* types of people, but they exist in *four* bodies. The Pharisees – the accusers represent the first of the five. The Sadducees – the mourners represent the last of the five. The three in between are GOD's children – Judah, Israel, and Jerusalem.

This is one of the revealed things, the secret things that GOD saved for this time – the time of his return.

The four that he is speaking about are the four that he fed with seven loaves. The seven loaves are the Word, the bread of life. They are the seven messages that Christ left for the four living beings. For the four are the seven churches. They are the Temples of GOD. They are parts of the body of Christ.

Or don't you know that *your body is the Temple of the Holy Spirit,*
**who lives in you and was given to you by GOD? You do not belong
to yourself.**

1 Corinthians 6:19

Each of the four was left specific words – encouragement and condemnation – so
that they would not sin against GOD. Each of the four has two messages – except
Jerusalem. Jerusalem only has one – Thyatira.

The Trees

Gentiles and Jewels	Cain	Judah	Israel	Jerusalem
Seven Churches	Ephesus Sardis	Smyrna Philadelphia	Pergamum Laodicea	Thyatira
The Trees	Thornbush	Olive Tree	Fig Tree	Grapevine

Now, the *key* to understanding the differences and the divisions between the four
lies in the *biblical history* of the earth as the story is told in the book of Genesis.

The Five

1	2	3	4	5
Cain, Gentiles	Judah	Israel	Jerusalem	Cain, Gentiles
Protect, Defend, Serve, Desirable, Wisdom and Beauty	Scientist Discover, discern truth through reason	Helper, Do Desire	Teach, Suggest, Encourage, Shrewd, cunning	Violent, Murderer, Self-centreed, Pouting, Scheming, Deceptive

Judah is the apostle[21]; for, the very word means discoverer. Israel is the organizer,

---

21   He brought them to Adam to see what he would call them, and Adam
      chose a name for each one. Genesis 2:19

the helper, the implementer.[22] She is also very curious and willing to try almost everything.[23] Jerusalem is a very clever teacher; the well spoken, Jerusalem is quite believable, the encourager.[24] It was not a snake that spoke to Eve. As you all know, snakes don't talk. It was Electron, the serpent, speaking through Jerusalem, causing her to encourage Eve to sin. Think about it. How often have you said what you did not intend to say...and regretted the words? Our words and actions are not our own. They come from a source, from the hindbrain (wisdom) or the forebrain (folly).

Cain is both the head[25] *and* the tail[26]. He is patterned after his mother who was created to be *good* but evil was found in her and other unbearable elements as well. She is **man and woman,** kind and cruel. Satan is the dragon that gives the beast out of the sea his power. They are, in fact, merged into the same body conjoined at the head.[27] The scriptures say,

They worshiped the dragon for giving the beast such power, and they worshiped the beast. "Is there anyone as great as the beast?" they exclaimed. "Who is able to fight against him?"

Revelation 13:4

When *they* worship the beast, they worship themselves for the name of the beast is '*me*' just as surely as the Most High is the 'Great I Am'. And when we worship the beast called '*me*', we worship the dragon, or Satan. For the dragon is the devil. He is that Assyrian who lives within mankind. Satan is '*me*' but GOD is the 'Great I Am!'

The ones who worshiped the beast who is the dragon are the ones whose names are not written in the Book of Life, which belongs to the Lamb that was killed *before* the

---

22   "It is not good for the man to be alone. I will make a companion who will help him." Genesis 2:18

23   The woman was convinced. The fruit looked so fresh and delicious, and it would make her so wise! Genesis 3:6.

24   Now the serpent was the shrewdest of all the creatures the LORD God had made. "You won't die!" the serpent hissed. God knows that your eyes will be opened when you eat it. You will become just like GOD, knowing everything, both good and evil." Genesis 3:1, 4

25   Ezekiel 28:12 – 15

26   "Why are you so angry?" the LORD asked him. "Why do you look so dejected? You will be accepted if you respond in the right way. But if you refuse to respond correctly, then watch out! Sin is waiting to attack and destroy you, and you must subdue it." Later Cain suggested to his brother, Abel, "Let's go out into the fields." And while they were there, Cain attacked and killed his brother. Afterward, the LORD asked Cain, "Where is your brother? Where is Abel?" "I don't know!" Cain retorted. Genesis 4:6 – 9

27   Revelation 13:1 – 4

world was made.[28] Cain's name was not written in that book and most of the names that he has been called since those ancient times are not written there.

The dragon's son – Cain, the Gentiles – is the beast out of the earth that has 'two horns like a **lamb** but he speaks with the voice of the **dragon**'.[29]

According to the scripture, Judah is the scientist – the one who named all of the animals. And Eve was Adam's helper. Jerusalem was the one with the knowledge – the one who taught Eve and encouraged her to sin against GOD. To further illustrate the five, GOD in his wisdom gave us an example that we could see every day – in our hands and also in our feet.

The Hand

Cain	Judah	Israel	Jerusalem	Cain
Cain	Judah	Israel	Jerusalem	Cain
Thumb	Forefinger	Middle Finger	Second Middle Finger	Little Finger
Most prominent	Most Important	The strongest and longest	Weaker than the strongest	Least significant

The River of GOD

The second mention of these five is expressed by the river that flowed through the garden.[30] The river watered the garden and then divided into four branches or streams.

Now, the four streams give the reader a lovely picture of the layout of the land. But, they also explain something else. Water, in all of its forms, represents people.[31] And every person is one of these four streams.

---

28   Revelation 13:8
29   Revelation 13:11
30   Genesis 2:10
31   Revelation 17:15

1	2	3	4	5
Cain	Judah	Israel	Jerusalem	Cain
Pishon	Gihon	Tigres	Euphrates	Pishon
Flows through the land of Havilah, Pure Gold	Flows through the land of Cush, Black, Ethiopian	Flows east of Asshur (also known as Assyria)	Flows around Assyria, Babylon and Egypt	Black Onyx Stone

Cain is Pishon[32], which has two main characteristics – pure gold and black onyx stone. The gold represents the *good* in Cain. The gold represents a giving spirit, empathetic and nurturing. The word Onyx is translated from Hebrew to mean *claw*. The onyx represents *evil*. It is veiled intentions, personal motives, and deception. Pure onyx stone has tiny ribbons of white running throughout. These tiny ribbons of white are the tender parts representing sorrow or grief.

Judah is Gihon[33], which means *pure black*. He is a *spiritual* being. Pure black contains all of the colors in the spectrum – even to eternity, which, with GOD's help, he can see in a moment's time. He has great wisdom dating back to the beginning of the world. This wisdom is coded in his mind but he will never be able to decipher it all on his own. He needs GOD to guide him through the maze just as I need GOD now and always will.

Israel is the Tigres[34], which flows east of Asshur and Assyria. She is an *emotional* being. *Asshur* and *Assyria* are both Satan's lands. It is where his soldiers, his massive army and navy live. The Assyrian soldiers are demons, spirits [who cannot be seen with the eyes of man], bacteria as you know them, who work for Satan.

Jerusalem is the Euphrates[35], which also flows around Assyria. But it also flows around Babylon and Egypt. These cities no longer exist as they did in their glorious

---

32   One of these branches is the Pishon, which flows around the entire land of Havilah, where gold is found. The gold of that land is exceptionally pure; aromatic resin* and onyx stone are also found there. Genesis 2:11 – 12

33   The second branch is the Gihon, which flows around the entire land of Cush. Genesis 2:13

34   The third branch is the Tigres, which flows to the east of Asshur [Electron's territory; Cain's birthplace.] Genesis 2:14

35   The fourth branch is the Euphrates. Genesis 2:14. Euphrates is also known as Sweet Water in Hebrew, Black River and Desire.

days; however, they are symbols of strength and power that are still recognizable to-day.

Babylon represents the belly, thighs and loins. It is literally 'baby loins' the place where desire is stirred. It is the place where Eve allowed Satan to first put a breach in the wall of GOD's Holy City – Jerusalem. For the bodies of mankind is the Holy Temple of GOD. The Holy One exists within us and we abide in him.

But – when Eve accepted and ate Satan's fruit, (semen) the uterine wall was breached and Satan and her demons were allowed to enter in. And she has never left. *Egypt* represents knowledge or human intellect because of all that is accomplished there. So, what does the Euphrates say about Jerusalem, GOD's teacher and servant? It says that Jerusalem is a *physical* being and that he has great knowledge. He is GOD's teacher.

The black onyx[36] stone speaks well to Cain's character. It is a tiny spot, hidden from all, hardly noticeable.

The Golden Statue

Many have heard the story of King Nebuchadnezzar's dream of a golden statue. The statue, like the streams in the previous section, represents the five that exist in four.

Its head was made of fine gold just like the gold found around the river Pishon. Its chest and arms were made of silver. Its belly and thighs were made of bronze indicating both strength and beauty. Its legs were made of iron. Its feet and toes were made of iron and clay.

The fine gold that is the head and the feet and toes made of iron and clay represent the qualities that exist in the **head** and the **tail**, the beast and the dragon who is both good and evil, and man and woman.

Daniel began describing the four kingdoms by talking about the head of gold but the lesser kingdoms are uncomplicated. So, for the sake of simplicity, the minor kingdoms will lead this discussion.

---

36   Onyx - a hail; claw; hoof, (Heb. shoham), also, a precious stone adorning the breastplate of the high priest and the shoulders of the ephod (Exodus 28:9 -12, 20; 35:27; Job 28:16; Ezekiel 28:13). Consists of two layers (black and white) Source: Easton's 1897 Bible Dictionary

The Inferior Kingdoms

When Daniel described the second kingdom, he said,

But after your kingdom comes to an end, another great kingdom, inferior to yours, will rise to take your place.

Daniel 2:39

The kingdom that was inferior – the chest and arms of silver – was *historically* the kingdom of King Cyrus. Cyrus was harvested from the crop of **Judah**. His first actions show that he belonged to the GOD of heaven and earth. For, he sent out a decree concerning the Temple of GOD at Jerusalem. He declared that it must be rebuilt on the site where Jewels had once offered their sacrifices to GOD. He did not ask the people for money to do this work. All expenses were paid by the royal treasury. The bible says,

And the gold and silver utensils, which were taken to Babylon by Nebuchadnezzar from the Temple of GOD in Jerusalem, will be taken back to Jerusalem and put into GOD's Temple as they were before.

Ezra 6:5

The chest and arms of silver represents a kind heart and the hands a giving spirit. It says, I do not have much, but what I have, I will share. Silver represents Judah who was patterned after Christ. For, was he not purchased for thirty pieces of *silver* – the price at which he was *valued*?[37]

But the crop of Judah should not be concerned about not being second. For Christ whose creation name is Judah said,

But many who seem to be important now will be the least important then, and those who are considered least here will be the greatest then.

Matthew 19:30

Next, Daniel described the third kingdom.

After that kingdom has fallen, yet a third great kingdom, represented by the bronze belly and thighs, will rise to rule the world.

Daniel 2:39

Historically, Darius the Mede was the third great kingdom that rose up. He was harvested from the crop of **Israel**. He was both strong and bold. He sent out a de-

---

37   Matthew 27:9

cree that everyone of every race, nation and language in his kingdom should worship GOD. He said,

> I decree that everyone throughout my kingdom should tremble with fear before the GOD of Daniel. For, he is the living GOD, and he will endure forever. His kingdom will never be destroyed, and his rule will never end. He rescues and saves his people; he performs miraculous signs and wonders in the heavens and on earth.

Daniel 6:26 – 27

The *bronze belly and thighs* represents the parts of Israel that are most susceptible to the whims of Satan. They represent *desire*. For, it was those parts that caused Eve to choose sin over the will of GOD. And from that unholy union, Cain was born. The bronze says 'I am beautiful and strong'. It says, 'I will fight ... but only when challenged'. Israel is honorable as David was honorable. This kingdom will *rise to rule the world* because it is uncharacteristically strong – stronger than the other three.

Finally, Daniel describes the fourth kingdom. He says,

> Following that kingdom, there will be a fourth great kingdom, as strong as iron. That kingdom will smash and crush all previous empires, just as iron smashes and crushes everything it strikes.

Daniel 2:40

Jerusalem, the teacher, is the legs with strong sinews and unbending bones. The legs represent strength strong enough to hold up the entire world. The iron represents words that can smash everything and everyone in its path. This is the power of the serpent. These are the ways of *Jerusalem*.

The prophet Jeremiah was given these words regarding the descendants of Jerusalem. The LORD Almighty says of them,

> Are they not the worst of rebels, full of slander? They are as insolent as bronze, as *hard* and *cruel* as iron. <u>All of them lead others into corruption.</u>

Jeremiah 6:28

These three inferior kingdoms are the three children of GOD as they are now; not from when they were made; not as they were from the beginning. We have become inferior because we were not made to harass or fight or murder or plan murders. We were created as our Father, ATOM is created, peaceful and giving. We have become inferior because we did not fight back when Cain and his Gentile people stole our lands, our livestock, our funds and enslaved us, moving us from place to place. We could have...but we chose not to. Electron told us we could not win...just as he has been telling me all of these months. But...he, she is a liar. I *will* have my crown back. And so will you. There is nothing she can do to stop it.

The Statue

1	2	3	4	5
Cain, the Beast	Judah	Israel	Jerusalem	Cain, the Dragon
Fine Gold	Silver	Bronze	Iron	Iron and Clay
Head	Chest and Arms	Belly and Thighs	Legs	Feet and Toes

The statue represents all of mankind. The king was a Gentile.[38]

The Head of Gold

Now, the purpose that Daniel was called into the king's presence was to tell him the events of his dream and to explain the meaning. Daniel told him,

Your Majesty, you are a king over *many kings*.

[The *many kings* are the three children of GOD.]

The GOD of Heaven has given you sovereignty, power, strength, and honor. He has made you the ruler over all the inhabited world and has put even the animals and birds under your control. You are the head of gold.

Daniel 2:37 – 38

Gog is the gold head, the Gentile. To illustrate the head of gold, the scriptures say that the king treated Daniel well and loved him as a man would love an equal—not a servant. GOD used the king to honor Daniel.

---

38   Daniel 2:38 – 43

Then the king appointed Daniel to a high position and gave him many valuable gifts. He made Daniel ruler over the whole province of Babylon, as well as chief over all his wise men.

Daniel 2:48

Now, the king also *loved* people who were beautiful – young men especially – and for these he spared no expense. For the three Hebrew boys – Shadrach, Meshach, and Abednego, he provided the best education including manners and *poise* and he fed them the best *food* available. The bible says,

The king assigned to them a daily ration of the best food and wine from his own kitchens.

Daniel 1:5

This demonstrates that the king was *good* and willing to share with those that he loved.

The Feet and Toes of Iron and Clay

At the end of the vision, the prophet Daniel explained the feet and toes.

The feet and toes you saw that were a combination of iron and clay show that this kingdom will be divided. Some parts of it will be as strong as iron, and others as weak as clay.

Daniel 2:41 – 42

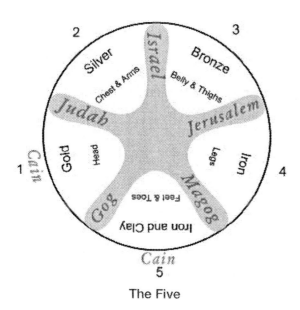

The Five

The feet and toes are not a kingdom separate and apart from the others because there are only *four* kingdoms. No, it is the second part of a combination that makes up the Gentiles. The Gentiles are the beast out of the earth. Beast is singular, for together, the Gentiles operate as one being just as all of those named Judah operate from a single heart and mind. The Gentiles are the ones with two horns like a lamb but speak with the voice of the dragon. They are the river Pishon where the purest gold could be found but also black onyx stone with fine, tender, white ribbons running through it. It is the big thumb and the smallest finger.

The head of fine gold wobbles. It is thrown off balance by the feet and toes of iron and clay. The iron is *uncontrolled anger* and *cruel words*. Nebuchadnezzar demonstrated this rage when the Hebrew boys would not bow down to his statue. The bible says,

> **Nebuchadnezzar was so furious with Shadrach, Meshach, and Abednego that** *his face became distorted with rage.* **He commanded that the furnace be heated** *seven times hotter* **than usual.**
>
> **Then he ordered some of the strongest men of his army to bind Shadrach, Meshech, and Abednego and throw them into the blazing furnace. So, they tied them up and threw them into the furnace, fully clothed.**
>
> **And because the king, in his anger, had demanded such a hot fire in the furnace, the flames leaped out and killed the soldiers as they threw the three men in!**
>
> *Daniel 3:19 – 22*

The clay represents *tears*. But, to really understand the symbolism of 'clay' we must look at its properties. Clay is soft earth, which is plastic, moldable; yet, it **hardens** when it is heated.[39] Clay is the result of the *wearing down* and it is full of impurities.[40]

King Nebuchadnezzar was *very* sensitive and it did not take much for him to fall a state of anxiousness and also into depression. After the king threw Daniel in the lion's den, he was very distraught. He stayed up all night wringing his hands and worrying. The scriptures say,

> **Then the king returned to his palace and spent the night fasting. He refused his usual entertainment and he couldn't sleep at all that night. Very early the next morning, the king hurried to the lions' den.**
>
> *Daniel 6:18 – 19*

Satan's children are crushed as easily as moths. But, so is their mother. How often the devil came upon me sobbing. But I had no compassion for her. She treated me cruelly and looked upon my poverty with indifference. She lied to me and gave me

---

39   Source: The American Heritage® Dictionary of the English Language, Fourth Edition Copyright © 2000 by Houghton Mifflin Company. Published by Houghton Mifflin Company. All rights reserved.

40   Source: Webster's Revised Unabridged Dictionary, © 1996, 1998 MICRA, Inc.

false hopes that my persecution would soon be over. She flattened me into a deep humiliation, but GOD Most High raised me back up.

And wars have broken out near and far, both personal and global. And the personal wars have escalated through an unsolvable paradigm. The black people believe that they must unify the blacks, but that is not how the lines are drawn. Cain – the real enemy – is black. And the white people feel that they must show preference to the whites. But Cain is also white. Cain is brown and he is yellow and also red. Cain is a woman and he is a man. He is a devout Christian. He is the sword carrying Muslim.

That is why the bible says during these last days, do not trust anyone – not your best friend or even your wife! Your enemies will be right in your own household.[41]

Intermarriage

This mixture of iron and clay also shows that these kingdoms will try to strengthen themselves by forming alliances with each other through intermarriage. But this will not succeed, just as iron and clay do not mix.

Daniel 2:41 - 42

The devil wanted Israel – GOD's warrior. She wanted her strength and power. So, she flattered her using Jerusalem to teach her. Eve wanted wisdom – the wisdom of GOD. So, she sinned and discredited all of mankind before GOD. The world was thrown into chaos.

So now, understand that **intermarriage** is **not** an option. It will not work because when the Gentiles marry Jerusalem, there will be sparks flying – iron striking against iron. Before the night is over, one of them will end up in jail or worse – dead. And Jerusalem has no heart for tears born of cruelty. The tears of an iron heart do not affect Jerusalem. Jerusalem is iron through and through.

Israel will weep over her Gentile husband. He will oppress her with his money and cruelty. He will treat her like a *prostitute*. He will stand over her night and day. She will not be able to leave the house without him watching. He will stalk her and find her out. She will leave when she realizes that she is stronger than her Gentile mate is. Then he will break down and weep. Israel is truly GOD's warrior. Judah will run from the Gentile woman as soon as he *comes to know* her aggressive, controlling character.

When Judah marries a Gentile, they will argue sometimes, this is true. But the conflict will manifest itself in the children. The female child, Judah, whose father is

---

41   Micah 7:5 – 6

a Gentile will inherit the Gentiles selfish ways and become unbearable to live with. Mother, you will never be able to do enough to please her so stop trying. Her body will be corrupt, rotten to the core, full of demons. She will argue about everything and claim unfair treatment in lieu of thanking you for all of your sacrifices. And your son will be uncontrollable unless he is disciplined at a young age. He will embarrass you every day of your life. He has his father's erratic genetic makeup. He cannot control himself.

The Gentile women will marry many times with multiple ceremonies to the same man. But the union will not last unless the Gentile marries a Gentile. The bible says,

> **Be ye not unequally yoked together with unbelievers: for what fellowship hath righteousness with unrighteousness? And what communion hath light [Jewels] with darkness [Gentiles]?**
>
> *2 Corinthians 6:14 KJV*

In other words,

> **Can two walk together, unless they are agreed?**
>
> *Amos 3:3 KJV*

> **What harmony can there be between Christ and the Devil? How can a believer be a partner with an unbeliever?**
>
> *2 Corinthians 6:15*

No! A believer cannot be a partner with an unbeliever. Either the believer will become an unbeliever or the unbeliever will become a believer. One will lead and the other will follow. The children of GOD **should not** partner with the children of Satan and I believe that the Holy Spirit agrees with me when I say this. For, *two* can only walk together in harmony if they agree on *one* direction.

In the end, the Jewel must run away as quickly as he can in fear of his life. For, she may run over him with her car or shoot him in the head while he is asleep; or, he may kill her in the woods and dump her body and the body of her unborn child, also a Jewel, in the river. He will cover his tracks well; not not well enough. You cannot hide from DNA evidence. You cannot hide from ATOM. You cannot hide from GOD. He always tells the truth.

Slaves

Now, the three Jewels have all been *forced* to walk with King Nebuchadnezzar. We have been enslaved and we walk with the Gentiles who rule in this generation. The believers have been coerced into following the unbelievers for promises of jobs and food or *love*.

And how has this coercion taken place?

Cain, and crops of Gentiles harvested after him, was made in the image of their mother. Their actions, words, and deeds all reflect the spirit of the devil. They are kind-hearted, empathetic, and *gentle spirited people* – hence the name *Gentiles*.[42] This describes the head of *gold*. Cain is like Joseph – the ones who cooks or provide food.

However – <u>and this is the cause</u> – the Gentiles also <u>*need*</u> to be loved and admired *constantly* for their cleverness and the good things that they do. Sweet and innocent Jerusalem will do this. And, for a time, so will Judah and Israel. But, after a while, they will grow tired of the *rude behaviour*, the nonsense of the Gentiles. First, the Jewels will ridicule him for his incredibly **vain expectations**. They will ask,

> **Who does he think he is that we should bow to his whims and desires? Who does he think that he is that we should be controlled by his thumb?**

Then, the three Jewels will scoff at Cain's lies and arrogant boasting. Later, Judah and Israel will ignore Cain effectively reducing his importance to zero. This lack of recognition and attention will make the Gentiles feel *depressed* and o—so very miserable. And they will be anxious and unable to sleep. The devil will keep Cain's feelings of injustice turning, reminding him every minute that he is being treated unjustly by the three. The disease will fester and grow just it they did when GOD rejected Cain's offering but accepted Abel's offering with all joy.

Then – <u>and this is the effect</u> – they will demand satisfaction. And without warning, Cain will fly into a rage, behaving erratically and violently as Satan behaves.

Cain was King Saul, who tried to kill David – GOD's chosen king, and Nebuchadnezzar who threw Daniel in the lion's den, and Herod who killed hundreds of babies looking for the Christ child. Cain will go on a rampage, killing the guilty, and the innocent; throwing things, bent on destruction. They live by natural instinct because they do not have GOD's Spirit living in them.[43] This is the *iron feet and toes*.

The Gentiles have brought lies, confusion, murder, and violence into the world. They are dual-personality with the utmost highs and the lowest possible lows. There is extreme conflict within them. They cannot sit still or be alone for long. They are a needy lot and *attention* is at the top of their list of needs. So, they flatter the children of GOD to get what they want.

---

42   Ezekiel 28:12 – 13, Revelation 21:19 – 20
43   Jude 1:10 – 19

The Gentiles are an emotional lot...*weeping at every turn*. Their sense of *loss* and *grief* is great. Sorrow is the *clay* part of the feet and toes.

Remember that Joseph cried after he schemed and accused his brothers of evil intent and theft and wickedness.

Then he [Joseph] broke down and wept aloud. His sobs could be heard throughout the palace, and the news was quickly carried to Pharaoh's palace.

Genesis 45:2

But it is only their eyes that weep. Their hearts are black onyx stones. Satan's children are *cold* and *cruel* like iron. They have no *compassion* or sense of fair play unless it gives them *boasting power*. They intimidate and manipulate the Jewels, as GOD knew they would.

They are murderers of both people and dreams. And, with all that they own – more than they could ever spend in a lifetime – they would not hesitate to cheat GOD's children out of their hard earned wages. But Christ is coming to deliver us from those that rule over us – the fine heads of gold, the feet and toes of iron and clay.

But as you watched, a rock [the first diamond] was cut from a mountain by supernatural means. It struck the feet of iron and clay, smashing them to bits. The whole statue collapsed into a heap of iron, clay, bronze, silver, and gold. The pieces were crushed as small as chaff on a threshing floor, and the wind blew them all away without a trace.

The Rock, the Stone that the Builders Rejected

But the rock that knocked the statue down became a great mountain that covered the whole earth.

Daniel 2:34 – 35

Christ, *Proton*, ATOM is the rock that was cut from the mountain that came to smash the feet and toes of iron and clay. When the feet are no longer holding up the statue, all of the others who are being supported by him will collapse and be scattered into tiny pieces. Then, the glory of Christ will cover the whole earth and he will rule it with an iron rod.[44] The king's dream is significant for this time – the last days of Gentiles.

The Four Beasts

There is no more complete and accurate description of the five who become four than Daniel's description of the *four beasts*.

The Beasts

Number	1 and 5	2	3	4
Tree	Cain	Judah	Israel	Jerusalem
Golden Statue	Fine Gold Iron and Clay	Silver	Bronze	Iron
Four Beasts	The Beast with Iron teeth	Lion with Eagles wings – who became a man	Bear with three ribs in his mouth	Leopard with birds wings

Then in my vision that night, I saw a fourth beast terrifying, dreadful, and very strong. It devoured and crushed its victims with huge iron teeth and trampled what was left beneath its feet. It was different from any of the other beasts, and it had ten horns.

As I was looking at the horns, suddenly another small horn appeared among them. Three of the first horns were wrenched out [The Jewels], roots and all, to make room for it.

This little horn had eyes like human eyes and a mouth that was boasting arrogantly.

Daniel 7:7 – 8

The <u>beast</u> that is more terrifying and stronger than any of the other three beasts is Cain – the Gentile. He is the one who threatens and then ... carries out his threats. David understood this when he wrote,

---

44   Daniel 2:31 – 35

Blessed be the LORD, who did not let their teeth tear us apart!

Psalm 124:6

The <u>lion</u> with eagles wings who became a man describes Judah who more than any of the others demonstrates the spirit of the Most High for he was formed by GOD's own hand. He is the model for GOD's human creation. The LORD will bless Judah ... forever.

The <u>bear</u> that has three ribs in his mouth is the warrior – Israel. He possesses all of the strength and the power. He can crush any and all of the other three. He is the strongest force in the universe both verbally and physically. His strength is fueled by anger and when he yields to it, watch out. He has power and might to outwit the beast with the iron teeth when he follows the instructions of those who are wise.

The <u>leopard</u> is the teacher – Jerusalem – who is extremely critical of her young students. She has a great deal of knowledge and she is brilliant. But her brilliance is also her downfall. She expects to see *her level of perfection* in everyone she meets. She is not concerned with feelings...until it is too late. She will break down anyone who does not give her proper respect. It will not be obvious at first. She will rouse you when you least expect it and conquer in a sneak attack. She has a short fuse but her growling is insignificant compared to the bear. Though she threatens often, she will rarely act. She may crush spirits but she does not kill indiscriminately.

The Four Curses

But your ancestors did not pay any attention; they would not even listen. Instead, they stubbornly followed their own evil desires. And because they refused to obey, *I brought upon them all the curses described in our covenant.*

Jeremiah 11:8

Four curses have been in effect since the original sin. They are, in fact, in effect today. These four curses describe the human condition, the differences between us and the social structure of the four types of man. Listen, if you want to know the truth about these curses and how they apply to the four, read the Proverbs. They are rules for righteous living according to who we are. Don't take my assessment of the truth, the assessment that the Holy Spirit gave to me. Read the truth for yourself. Just know that these conditions will be reversed when Christ returns but for now, these four curses are indicative of how we live.

Except for the very few, Judah lives a modest life – not rich, but generally not lacking. He makes due as I have learned to do during my incarceration. Judah is calm

– even in times of grief and great sorrow or high excitement and celebration. This is how the LORD has made him. He is the simple – open to trying anything, open to believing everything. But wisdom calls him with painful lessons and guilt and he obtains good judgment through his error and the errors of others. When Judah learns the wisdom that the Holy Spirit teaches him, Cain will jealously persecute him, spreading lies about Judah, coveting his glorious ways – GOD's ways. And Judah cries out to the LORD Almighty, saying,

> **What do you gain by oppressing me? Why do you reject me, the work of your own hands, while sending joy and prosperity to the wicked?**

Job 10:3

But Cain will never have the wisdom of Judah. GOD himself teaches Judah. The wicked who are allowed to oppress Judah, will lose hope. They have no escape. Their hope becomes despair. The triumph of the wicked will be short-lived and the joy of the godless is only temporary.

Israel is the mocker, the smart mouth, condescending *woman*. Anyone who rebukes a mocker will get a smart retort. So don't bother rebuking mockers; they will only hate you.

This is why Israel and Jerusalem fight against each other and have no tolerance for one another's weaknesses. Jerusalem is the teacher and forever trying to tell Israel how to live her life.

> **Throw out the mocker, and fighting, quarrels, and insults will disappear.**

Proverbs 22:10

For Israel *despises* the knowledge of Jerusalem, his condescending speeches. She desires the wisdom of Judah and in this, Judah will forever be Israel's master. For GOD has given Judah wisdom above all the others. He listens and takes heed to the instructions of the LORD. He learns to trust the LORD through his trials and rebukes. Though he is simple, he will learn to trust and obey the LORD.

The Day of Reckoning for Israel and Judah

> **Be still in the presence of the LORD [Israel], and wait patiently for him to act. Don't worry about evil people who prosper or fret about their wicked schemes. Stop your anger! Turn from your rage! Do not envy others – it only leads to harm.**

For the wicked will be destroyed, but those who trust in the LORD will possess the land. In a little while, the wicked will disappear. Though you look for them, they will be gone.

Those who are gentle and lowly [Judah] will possess the land; they will live in prosperous security.

The wicked plot against the godly; they snarl at them in defiance. **But the LORD just laughs, for he sees their Day of Judgment coming. The wicked draw their swords and string their bows to kill the poor and the oppressed, to slaughter those who do right. But they will be stabbed through the heart with their own swords, and their bows will be broken.**

It is better to be godly and have little than to be evil and possess much. For the strength of the wicked will be shattered, but the LORD takes care of the godly.

Day by day, the LORD takes care of the innocent, and they will receive a reward that lasts forever. They will survive through hard times; even in famine, they will have more than enough.

But the wicked will perish. The LORD's enemies are like flowers in a field – they will disappear like smoke.

Psalm 37:7 – 20

Jewels and Gentiles	Judah	Israel	Jerusalem	Cain
Curses	All of your life you will have to struggle to scratch a living from the ground. It will grow thorns and thistles.	You will strike (the serpent's) heel. You will have pain in childbirth. Your desire will be for the man. The man will be your master.	You will grovel in the dust as long as you live. You and the woman will be enemies. You will crush (the woman's) head.	You are banished from the land. It will no longer yield abundant crops. You will be a homeless fugitive wandering from place to place. **Anyone who tries to kill you will receive seven times your punishment.**
Proverbs	Simple	Mocker	Fool	Wicked

The *living* that Judah must scratch from the ground does not refer to food or money.[45] It refers to life, joy or the lack thereof. Sadness and misery is Judah's destiny in the current regime. Why others are laughing oblivious, we sit at home alone, wondering. The thorns and thistles[46] are the Gentiles, who are both attracted to us (mercy) and repelled by us (truth).

For Israel, '*the man will be your master*'[47] refers to Electron ruling over Israel. For, we who walk upon the earth are *mankind* and *humankind* from ATOM's perspective. ATOM was the first man, but there are others. Electron is the man, is the wo-man. Electron is the one who rules the mind Israel today.

Israel and Jerusalem do not get along. They argue - one knowing everything; one doing everything. They are enemies[48] when together they could defeat the evil within and without. Electron has kept them apart with their arguing so that she can stay in control of mankind. Israel is stronger than anyone. Jerusalem just short of that.

---

45   Gen 3: 17 – 18
46   **Son of man, [Judah] do not fear them. Don't be afraid even though their threats are sharp as thorns and barbed like briers and they sting like scorpions. Do not be dismayed by their dark scowls. For remember they are rebels.** *Ezekiel 2:6*
47   Gen 3:15 – 16
48   Gen 3:14 – 15

Judah is simple[49], slow to respond because the truth pours over him. He cannot be rushed; ATOM cannot be rushed. Israel is the mocker[50], mocking the truth because it is more convenient to believe a lie.

But alas, Jerusalem is an educated fool[51], following the Gentiles ways for money and honor. He will not listen. Jerusalem, the fool, has a curse of *bitterness*. His whole life is filled with poverty and sadness. He brings trouble upon his family and because of it; he will only inherit the wind. The fool will be a servant to the wise. He feeds on trash. His tongue is full of lies and his fingers are ripe for thievery even from a small child.

A single rebuke does more for a person of understanding than a hundred lashes on the back of a fool.

Proverbs 17:10

And why does GOD consider his son Jerusalem to be a fool? Because Jerusalem is a peacock, strutting around proudly in his beautiful clothes, and newly styled hair. He has a loud voice, with a growling, intimidating face. But GOD will remove your pride and replace it with misery. Then you will know bitterness though you may never understand it. You may never put the two together – the cause and the effect. And so, it is painful to be the parent of a fool for a fool's eyes wander to the ends of the earth, always searching for the next quick thing. The schemes of a fool are sinful. In the mouth of a fool, a proverb becomes as limp as a paralyzed leg. A stone is heavy and sand is weighty, but the resentment caused by a fool is heavier than both are. The fool is blind, and yet, wise and foolish people share the same fate. Jerusalem will not rise above this condition until Christ returns and teaches him wisdom.

Cain's curse[52] will last until the end of the age of the gentiles. He is just wicked[53] – the good and the bad. They seek revenge on all who disagree with their abominable lives.

You are proud that you inspire fear in others. And you are proud because you live in a rock fortress and hide high in the mountains. But don't fool yourselves! Though you live among the peaks with the eagles, I will bring you crashing down," says the LORD.

Jeremiah 49:16

When his lies and crimes are discovered, he is banished to prisons and desolate

---

49   Proverbs 9:4 - 6, 9
50   Proverbs 9:7 - 8
51   Proverbs 14:8 - 9
52   Gen 4: 12 – 14
53   Proverbs 14:32

places. He is the sex offender and the pedophile that is run out of town. He is schemer who takes over companies and countries in a hostile manner. He steals the life savings of the widow and retired people. He is the serial killer, the murderer who, when he is found out, is persecuted by other Gentiles. He will trap himself in his own snare.

Sin whispers to the wicked, deep within their hearts. They have no fear of GOD to restrain them.

Psalm 36:1

For Christ has said to the church of Ephesus which was written for the Gentiles,

But there is this about you that is good: You hate the deeds of the immoral Nicolaitans, just as I do.

Revelations 2:6

The Gentiles are the Nicolaitans. And they are also the ones who seek out the wicked, the vile and the evil that are called the Nicolaitans. The Gentile will expose them and all liars. They will accuse them publicly and dare them to state their defense. They will call them liars in a loud voice and then banish the evildoers from the neighborhoods where decent people live.

Christ also left these words of encouragement for the church of Ephesus. He said,

I know all the things you do. I have seen your hard work and your patient endurance. I know you don't tolerate evil people. You have examined the claims of those who say they are apostles but are not. You have discovered they are liars.

Revelations 2:2

When the Gentile is caught, he is banished. And, he will not be able to hide for long before his urges and deviant behaviour push him to commit even greater crimes. He will be found out but not before many have Gentiles have suffered, not before many Jewels have been sacrificed.

You try to look like upright people outwardly, but inside your hearts are filled with hypocrisy and lawlessness.

Matthew 23:28

When he begins to beat his wife or to molest the neighborhood children, or to brag excessively about what he owns, the people will throw him out. He will move, changing wives or partners, looking for someone else to impress and deceive, wandering everywhere looking for a home. He will not rest in peace.

But some of you Gentiles have gone overboard with your accusations. More frequently, the three Jewels see themselves being unjustly exposed by the jealous lies of the Gentiles. After the Jewels have suffered under the lies and accusations of the Gentiles, the Spirit of Truth will come to rescue them. When they are set free, GOD will bless them.

> **The wicked plot against the godly; they snarl at them in defiance. But the LORD just laughs, for he sees their Day of Judgment coming. The wicked draw their swords and string their bows to kill the poor and the oppressed, to slaughter those who do right.**
>
> *Psalm 37:12 - 14*

They are proud, boasting about what they will do and raising their fists at GOD. Now, the three Jewels are the ones in prison because of the lying, accusing Gentiles.

> **The whole earth is in the hands of the wicked, and GOD blinds the eyes of the judges and lets them be unfair. If not he, then who?**
>
> *Job 9:24*

Today, if anyone goes against the Gentiles or exposes their treachery, he is murdered in his bed or on the street under the cover of night. But, his deeds will follow him.

He will be found out. When Christ returns he will destroy the weeds. GOD had discarded this tree. It will cease to bear fruit.

Who is Sitting on the Throne?

Then as I looked, I saw a door standing open in heaven, and the same voice I had heard before spoke to me with the sound of a mighty trumpet blast. The voice said, "Come up here, and I will show you what must happen after these things." And instantly I was in the Spirit, and I saw a throne in heaven and someone sitting on it! The one sitting on the throne was as brilliant as gemstones – jasper and carnelian. And the glow of an *emerald circled his throne like a rainbow*.

Twenty–four thrones surrounded him, and twenty–four elders sat on them.

Revelation 4:1 – 3

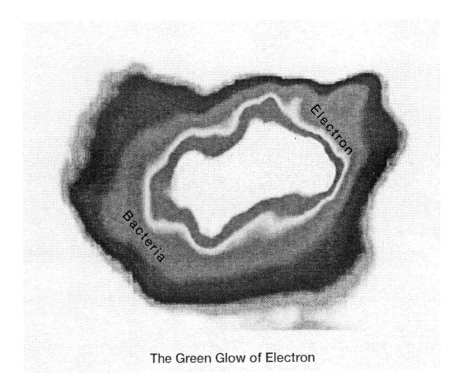

The Green Glow of Electron

While you cannot disern the color from this grayscale photo of the inside of an atom, Electron's emerald green glow can been seen in the nether region surrounding the plasma of an atom. She is the in the turtle-shaped outline outside of the plasma ring (the second ring from the center).

And I will tell you another thing. Not only can the emerald green glow of Electron be seen within the outer regions of an atom, she can also been seen hovering over the northern sky. It is her glow that casts the emerald green wonder that amazes all who see her lights, so compelled are they to stare at the mystery of her – *aurorae borealis*, the northern lights. For, she is as cold as boney death. Oh, she is death, the destroyer.

Among the most magnificent of observable natural phenomena, aurorae displays appear primarily in shades of emerald green, sometimes with flashes of red, yellow, blue and violet. The emerald light is usually brightest in their northern most latitudes. For, Electron is a cold and bloodless witch, a two-headed snake sending chills up your back and freezing you as she drains the blood from your healthy cells, numbing your hands and swelling your feet.

It is Electron, with the power to take your breath away with her neurotoxic bite, gripping the nerves to incapacitate and subdue the body. She has the power to cripple mankind with excruciating pain with her hemotoxic bite as she poisons the blood, sucks out the vital fluid from your joints and cartilage. The cure is the immunological angels, the anti-bodies. They keep all of mankind alive...but the pain remains.

But, Electron is GOD's chosen weapon. With her on your heels, you now know the alternative to faithfulness and the consequences of sin as David knew them so well. With Electron within your body, trying to take over or destroy the life that is within each atom, these are the problems you face each day.

This is a psalm of David, to bring us to the LORD's remembrance. O LORD, don't rebuke me in your anger! Don't discipline me in your rage! Your arrows have struck deep, and your blows are crushing me.

Because of your anger, my whole body is sick; my health is broken because of my sins. My guilt overwhelms me – it is a burden too heavy to bear. My wounds fester and stink because of my foolish sins. I am bent over and racked with pain. My days are filled with grief. A raging fever burns within me, and my health is broken. I am exhausted and completely crushed. My groans come from an anguished heart. You know what I long for, LORD [ATOM]; you hear my every sigh. My heart beats wildly, my strength fails and I am going blind. My loved ones and friends stay away, fearing my disease. Even my own family stands at a distance.

Meanwhile, my enemies [bacteria, Adenine and Guanine] **lay traps for me; they make plans to ruin me. They think up treacherous deeds all day long. But I am deaf to all their threats. I am silent before them as one who cannot speak. I choose to hear nothing, and I make no reply.**

For, I am waiting for you, O LORD. You must answer for me, O LORD my GOD. I prayed, "Don't let my enemies gloat over me or rejoice at my downfall." I am on the verge of collapse, facing constant pain. But I confess my sins; I am deeply sorry for what I have done.

My enemies are many; they hate me though I have done nothing against them. They repay me evil for good and oppose me because I stand for the right. Do not abandon me, LORD. Do not stand at a distance, my GOD. Come quickly to help me, O LORD my savior.

Psalm 38:1 – 22

In the northern sky, Electron can seen in a variety of forms, patches of light, streamers, arcs, banks, rays, or resembling hanging draperies. She not only affects the bodies of people, but on a global level, she does what she can to bring sorrow to many. She interrupts power flows, affecting communications, power lines, equipment and the compasses on planes causing pilots become disoriented, scattered, so that they cannot find their way. This emerald green you see is the devil's glow, Electron. You have seen her. She is a cold and wicked witch, not the lovely ice princess described in your fairy tales, not the sweet and humble Cinderella. The scullery maid turned queen is a heartless witch. I know her, a relentless, weeping idiot savant without the common sense to quit. She keeps going until the life she seeks to conquer is ruined. She is merciless and subdues her victims with deeply felt emotion and poison.

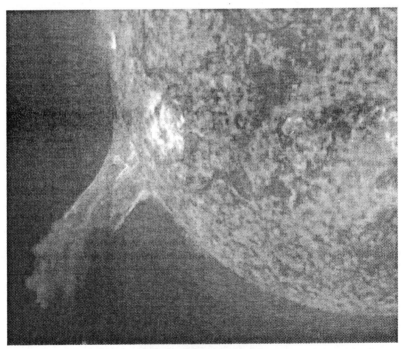

NASA, Sun Eruptions

In the northern sky, the electrons that are cast off from the sun are actually being repelled through the plasma[54] that is the cleaner, Neutron. Only Neutron is resilient enough to negotiate the bacterial evil within Electron and put her back in her place. The *light* is repelled by the **darkness** and casts it away.

Now this may shock you, elders, and I wish it were not the truth. However, I did not write the revelation. John wrote the revelation. I was appointed the task of revealing the word, the light, the truth to you. It is what it is. And Isaiah recorded:

> **For you** [Electron] **said to yourself, 'I will ascend to heaven and set my throne above GOD's stars. I will preside on the mountain of the gods far away in the north** [Mount Zion, the forebrain]**. I will climb** [on the cholinergic branches of the Tree of Good and Evil] **to the highest heavens and be like the Most High'. But instead, you will be brought down to the place of the dead** [the bowels and bladder]**, down to its lowest depths.**

> *Isaiah 14:13 – 15*

> **And instantly, I** [John, the Revelator] **was in the Spirit, and I saw a throne in heaven and someone sitting on it! The one sitting on the throne** [Electron or Satan] **was as brilliant as gemstones—jasper** [Adenine – bacteria producing] **and carnelian** [Guanine – death]**.**

> **And the glow of an emerald** [cholinergic fibres of bile, of death] **circled his throne like a rainbow.**

> *Revelation 4:2 – 3*

---

54   Photo – Sun eruptions, courtesy of NASA.

The Big Bang

Now understand this: GOD, ATOM *chose* the matter particle, Electron, as a necessary evil, to clean up the after birth that littered the earth after the Big Bang. She was named guardian for she protected all atoms from contamination from the beginning.

Michelangelo, GOD and Lucifer, in the Beginning

Soon she will perish, this king of Tyre. For, GOD told Ezekiel:

"Son of man, weep for the king of Tyre [Electron]. Give him this message from the Sovereign LORD [ATOM]: You were the perfection of wisdom and beauty. You were in Eden, the garden of GOD. Your clothing was adorned with every precious stone – red carnelian, chrysolite, white moonstone, beryl, onyx, jasper, sapphire, turquoise, and emerald – all beautifully crafted for you and set in the finest gold. They were given to you on the day you were created. I ordained and anointed you as the mighty angelic guardian.

You had access to the holy mountain of GOD and walked among the stones of fire. "You were blameless in all you did from the day you were created until the day evil was found in you. Your great wealth filled you with violence, and you sinned. So I banished you from the mountain of God. I expelled you, O mighty guardian, from your place among the stones of fire. Your heart was filled with pride because of all your beauty. You corrupted your wisdom for the sake of your splendor. So I threw you to the earth and exposed you to the curious gaze of kings [aurorae borealis, gnats, fruit flies and snakes, bile and bad humor].

Electron's fate to come:

You defiled your sanctuaries with your many sins and your dishonest trade. So I brought fire from within you, and it consumed you. I let it burn you to ashes on the ground in the sight of all who were watching. All who knew you are appalled at your fate. You have come to a terrible end, and you are no more."

Ezekiel 28:12 – 19

Electron is sitting on the throne of GOD, encircled by an emerald green glow. For, was not Electron within the wall of the first ATOM, disposing of the waste during the incubation stage of the birth of GOD's first son? Of course she was.

Electron was chosen to decompose and devour the waste within the wall of the first ATOM, the waste within the universe and in time, the waste within the body of every person. For every living thing that was created or born after the Big Bang is comprised of everything – the elemental and the living that came before it. Ergo, the LORD whose names are Proton, Gluon, and Neutron, the Holy Trinity, lives within mankind. They are the keepers of the Book of Life, the DNA record of every living thing. They are the eyes, the lights that rule from the brain. Cytosine is wisdom or second sight; Thymine who moves you – thy will is my will is the commander of GOD's immunoglobulin armies. Uracil, who teaches all men knowledge, is the seal of the Living GOD. These three are Christ, Michael and Gabriel, the rulers of the sympathetic nervous system within every living body.

So, that is Electron's job, and the job of her armies – to clean up waste. She is responsible for waste management. Are you going to clean it up? No! And if you saw and smelled it, you would be disgusted by it just as the LORD Proton is disgusted by it.

Therefore, come out from them and separate yourselves from them, says the LORD [ATOM]. Don't touch their filthy things, and I will welcome you.

2 Corinthians 6:17

Have you not heard that cleanliness is next to Godliness? So, it is true that Electron, the devil exists within your body. She is the conjoined twins in the DNA chain, the double helix – Adenine the reproducing maggot, the magnet, the lure and Guanine, the decomposer, the destroyer.

Now understand this: The devil did make you do it! She has gained a license to capitalize upon and control your joy, your peace, your health, your attitude. The license is a binding agreement entitled the Parasympathetic Nervous System made of cholinergic fibres – bile and gall. The Big Bang that created the universe is the same as what happened to Eve when she accepted Satan's seed and later bore his son – Cain, the first Gentile. There was an explosion – joy strong – within her womb. This was the second big bang and Satan has been screwing us out of our inheritance every since that time. The price Eve paid the Great Prostitute for that moment of pleasure was high – so high that GOD had to send his only begotten Son – Proton (Jesus Christ as we know him) to pay it. Proton gave his life to pay the debt. Now because of the supreme sacrifice of Christ, mankind can know the truth and be free of her. Eve forfeited the lives of every man to Satan, all of mankind for one night of indiscretion. It was a poor choice to make. The damage was done. For, the demons that came with that seed into her womb caused all of mankind from that time forward to become genetically infected. Thou shalt surely die! The DNA for the demons, the bacteria is in the genes. Now, every person – every man, woman, and child is covered with demons, with bacteria, with gray matter from head to toe. Sex between Eve and Satan was the second big bang – concentrated energy – Eve to dispersed energy – the whole genus of man, including the human race of Gentiles. It is a yeast infection of epic proportion. There is not enough Monistat – 7 in the universe to get rid of it.

No wonder we grope like blind people and stumble along. Even at brightest noontime, we fall down as though it were dark. No wonder we are like corpses [we are full of bodies, of corpses, of undead demons – bacteria] when compared to vigorous young men!

Isaiah 59:10

When Jesus arrived on the other side of the lake in the land of the Gadarenes, two men who were possessed by demons [Adenine and Guanine] met him. They lived in a cemetery [spiritually dead, and yet they live] and were so [violent] that no one could go through that area. [The demons spoke through the mouths of the two men] began screaming at [Jesus], "Why are you bothering us, Son of GOD? You have no right to torture us before GOD's appointed time!"

A large herd of pigs was feeding in the distance, so the demons begged, "If you cast us out, send us into that herd of pigs." "All right, go!" Jesus commanded them. So, the demons came out of the men and entered the pigs, and the whole herd plunged down the steep hillside into the lake and drowned in the water.

Matthew 8:28 – 32

But...Electron is the servant of ... not the ruler over mankind. Electron needs

ATOM to live. If ATOM did not live, Electron would not exist. Just as mankind lives in and because of ATOM, of Proton and Cytosine, Gluon and Thymine, Neutron and Uracil. Electron lives within mankind and because ATOM lives within each man. Without ATOM none of us would exist – Jewel nor Gentile.

The LORD Proton cannot die. She attacked and murdered the chrysolite stone, the stone that the builders rejected, before man was made. She attacked and killed him again using her children, the Hebrew Gentiles, to crucify him when he walked the earth as a man, as Christ.

The LORD Proton cannot die. He is life itself. Life is within him. He is the Light of the world. He is able to lay down his life and take it up again. Electron has tried to kill him. But ... he is GOD. ATOM cannot die.

But Electron has tried to get rid of ATOM, of GOD. Over time, Electron became dissatisfied with the work she was chosen to do. She became tired of cleaning out the bowels of the earth, and eventually the bowels of people even though that is her natural profession, feeding on the bodies of the dead. It is what she was created to do just as I, Judah, was born to write this book and Einstein, Jerusalem, was born to tell you the formula for life and Michelangelo, Israel, was born to illustrate the beginning of life and the end of this age.

Electron, in a surprise attack, murdered the Holy One. She did it so she could become the Master of the Universe. But something unexpected happened.

Everything **stopped** while the LORD Proton slept!

There was no movement at all, no growth, no creation, no destruction – nothing at all. The universe became a still and silent place.

And the scriptures describe the event as a male goat, Electron, crossing the land so swiftly that it didn't even touch the ground. The goat had one very large horn between its eyes. That single horn was knowledge harvested from the Neutron – the one–third of the angels that followed Satan when he was thrown out of heaven.

The goat – Electron, headed toward the two–horned ram – Proton intent on destroying him. The two–horns represent knowledge and wisdom. The shorter horn is knowledge, the longer horn that began to grow after the shorter horn, is wisdom.

The goat charged furiously at the ram and struck it, breaking off both its horns. Now the ram was helpless, and the goat knocked it down and trampled it. There was no one who could rescue the ram from the goat's power.

Daniel 8:7

And there was an electrical storm and high winds in the atmosphere over the earth as the swiftly moving Electron advanced against Proton, trying to put out the light. It was the Creator being attacked by his creation.

Prophecy of the Ram and the Goat

As I looked up, I saw in front of me a ram [Christ] with two long horns standing beside the river. One of the horns was longer than the other, even though it had begun to grow later than the shorter one. [The longer horn is wisdom. The shorter horn is knowledge.] The ram butted everything out of its way [afterbirth, bacteria] to the west, to the north, and to the south, and no one could stand against it or help its victims. It did as it pleased and became very great.

While I was watching, suddenly a male goat [Electron, Satan] appeared from the west, crossing the land so swiftly that it didn't even touch the ground. This goat, which had one very large horn [knowledge] between its eyes headed toward the two–horned ram that I had seen standing beside the river.

The goat charged furiously at the ram and struck it, breaking off both its horns. Now the ram was helpless, and the goat knocked it down and trampled it. There was no one who could rescue the ram from the goat's power.

The goat became very powerful. But at the height of his power, the large horn was broken off. In the large horn's place grew four prominent horns [the four living beings – Judah, Israel, Jerusalem, and the Gentiles] pointing the four directions of the earth.

From one of the prominent horns [Adenine – the urine based reproduction magnate] came a small horn [Guanine – the urine based destroyer] whose power grew very great. It extended toward the south [to Jerusalem – the hindbrain] and the east [to Mount Zion – the forebrain] and toward the glorious land of Israel [Mount of Olives – the midbrain].

His [Electron's] power reached to the heavens [your brain] where it attacked the heavenly armies, throwing some of the heavenly beings to the ground and trampling them. He even challenged the Commander of heaven's armies [Cytosine] by canceling the daily sacrifices offered to him [protein, fuel for the body, and the elimination of the residual waste] and by destroying his Temple [your body – through bacterial infections, multiplying cancer cells, disease – various afflictions]. But the army of heaven [Thymine and Uracil and their antibacterial armies] was restrained from destroying him [Guanine] for this sin.

As a result, sacrilege [germination within and decomposition of the body along with sexual infidelities – homosexuality, oral and anal sex] **was committed against the Temple ceremonies** [which are eating, drinking, reproduction and rest] **and truth was overthrown.** [For Satan, the great deceiver leads the people. All men listen to her voice and follow her instructions]. **The horn** [Satan] **succeeded in everything it did.**

Daniel 8:3 – 12

Now understand this: There is a reason that GOD created the autoimmune system and elected to put it in the belly of every living thing. The problem with sin growing, bacteria growing, viruses growing and killing live cells exacerbated after Adam and Eve consented to follow the devil and again after Noah slept with the devil. People are contaminating their bodies with feces that they lick with their tongues. Of course it is gross when you say it! But that has not stopped most of you from doing it!

The safeguards were put in place in the body of man so that GOD's children, whom he really loves, would be protected from sin, from time without GOD. For, sin means without in the Latin dialect. Sin is literally "time without GOD". Those who direct the autoimmune system have a strict mission – to guard and protect the body. They are trained to detect intrusions and react to protect the live tissue, to keep viruses from spreading up past the intestinal tract. But you have elected to follow Adenine, to follow Electron – the Matter Particle, the virus that kills.

"Go west to the land of Cyprus [to the brain, see Cytosine, to Thymine, and Uracil]; **go east to the land of Kedar** [the bowels and bladder and see Adenine and Guanine]. **Think about what you see there. See if anyone has ever heard of anything as strange as this. Has any nation ever exchanged its gods for another god, even though its gods are nothing? Yet my people have exchanged their glorious GOD** [ATOM] **for worthless I–dols** [the waste managers – Adenine and Guanine – for sex, the joy strong, no less]! **The heavens are shocked at such a thing and shrink back in horror and dismay, says the LORD. For my people have done two evil things: They have forsaken me – the fountain of living water. And they have dug for themselves cracked cisterns that can hold no water at all!**

Jeremiah 2:10 – 13

Now, you and your children are dying daily. The hand of GOD has been restrained from helping you, from destroying Adenine and Guanine and her bacterial offspring. When you choose Electron, you will surely die. It is inevitable. Electron is death. ATOM is life – the only one that is life.

Can you see it? Do you understand now? The one sitting on the throne in heaven, the one lighting the seven lampstands today, is Electron – Adenine and Guanine, the conjoined twins, the two-headed snake, the devil. She is the same one who uses intelligence to dispatch her flying armies to the corpses, to the dead. She is leading you into sin, into death. The anti–Cryst, anti–Christ leads GOD's creation.

The devil is a fly, like a fruit fly.

This is who you worship. I tell you the truth. I will not lie for her like some of your others. She is a bug, a flu bug! Look at her icon. She is Electron, the same one who hovers over the earth, causing the emerald aurorae lights in the northern sky. She is a dragon fly with the power to stir up the waters of the oceans and seas, sinking great ships and ferries, leading hurricanes and tornadoes onto the land to destroy. She has the power to stir up the rain in the cumulus clouds above the earth complete with targeted bolts of lightning carried upon elec-

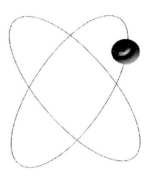

The Devil, the Fly

tromagnetic waves. She delivers her eggs on the dead things lying upon the earth and below the ground – any dead thing with the last light life moving in cells of blood. She is a dragon fly, appearing to everyone who can catch her moving in the corner of his eye. She is fast so you will not be able to hold her gaze for long unless she chooses to engage you as she did me. She is the devil, Satan, the very one.

For, Electron, the fruit fly, is the opposite of ATOM, the opposite of the crystalline Proton, who is Christ. Christ or Cryst is the composer of life. Fingerprinting is our eternal connection to the Creator. Microscopic crystallite dust particles are the diamonds of which we are comprised. That is why mankind is called the Jewels and referred to as jewelry in the revelation. We, all people, are the seven lampstands, the seven churches, the twelve gates. We are the crystallite stones of the revelation.

Now, I want to invite you to go back to creation, back to the first ATOM, who is before his namesake Adam; back to where the Creator's preferred method of the creation of mankind is known to be crystallization – not evolution as you have been led to believe by Darwin and the others.

We, who are mankind, who were created by the Creator, ATOM, and crystallized via diamond dust particles and shards of crystals, have our Father's imprint in our hands and in our foreheads.

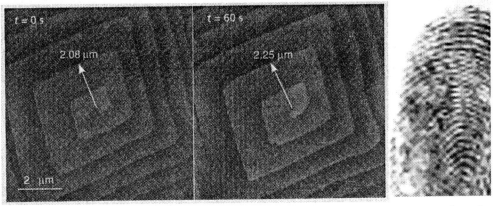

Chrystalline Progression   Fingerprint of
GOD

This graphic[55] from an article entitled *AFM Measurement of Step Kinetics for the Growth and Dissolution of Crystallites,* written by Henry Teng, charts the progress of crystallization, the growth and dissolution of crystalline dust. It is the material of which diamonds and other jewels are made. It is the material of which every man is made. This is how man was created, from the dust, just like the earth is made of dust: one particle at a time until the time came when ATOM was ready to breathe into man the breath of life and man became a living soul. Amen, All men. Yes! That is why we say *Amen.* It is a reminder that ATOM is all men, '*Amen*'.

The same process occurs in the body. For, we are constantly changing, growing while old cells fall away. Compare the progress of crystallization to the pattern on the fingertip above. Now, do you understand what great work GOD gave Michelangelo to do when he painted the Sistine chapel? At GOD's command, he illustrated the complete story of mankind, depicting his allies and enemies.

---

55   Chrystallite progression graphics were used with the kind permission
of Henry Teng, Assistant Professor, Department of Chemistry, The
George Washington University

Michelangelo, Touching the Hand of GOD, ATOM

The LORD ATOM, used Michelangelo to demonstrate his righteousness, his wisdom, his ability to see though eternity to this day, to all of you sitting here reading with me. Now understand this: **All** of Michelangelo's work was commissioned by GOD – no matter who paid his salary. He spoke the truth with his naked bodies on the Sistene Chapel ceiling. Through the ages, the Gentiles are both repelled and aroused by them. They have been marred, covered over so that the truth would be hidden. This is Electron's way.

Michelangelo's paintings and sculptures were completed for GOD's plans and purposes, for this time, for this work. Much of his work on the Sistine Chapel has been misunderstood, misinterpreted. But in this work, I, Cyrus, will set the record straight.

We, all of mankind, crystallized from dust, from earth, from the land. For, mankind consists of three units: a sugar molecule called deoxyribose; a phosphate group such as polonium, which is a silvery white crystalline form of a metallic salt and one of four different nitrogen–containing compounds called bases. The first three of the four bases are the dry or land elements – Cytosine (C), Thymine (T) and Uracil (U). Mankind (the three) is alternately comprised of the dry elements, the three pyramidine bases. The last of the four bases (the two) are the conjoined bacterial elements – Adenine (A) and Guanine (G) also known as humankind, the aliens among us.

> There are bodies in the heavens, and there are bodies on earth. The glory of the heavenly bodies is different from the beauty of the earthly bodies. The sun [Proton, Cytosine] has one kind of glory, while the moon [Neutron, Uracil] and stars [Gluon, Thymine] each have another kind. And even the stars differ from each other in their beauty and brightness. It is the same way for the resurrection of the dead. Our earthly bodies, which die and decay, will be different when they are resurrected, for they will never die. Our bodies now disappoint us, but when they are raised, they will be full of glory. They are weak now, but when they are raised, they will be full of power. They are natural human bodies now, but when they are raised, they will be spiritual bodies. For just as there are natural bodies, so also there are spiritual bodies.
>
> The Scriptures tell us, "The first man, Adam, became a living person." But the last Adam – that is, Christ – is a life-giving Spirit. What came first was the natural body, and then the spiritual body comes later.
>
> Adam, the first man, was made from the dust of the earth, while Christ, the second man, came from heaven. Every human being has an earthly body just like Adam's, but our heavenly bodies will be just like Christ's. Just as we are now like Adam, the man of the earth, so we will someday be like Christ, the man from heaven.
>
> What I am saying, dear brothers and sisters, is that flesh and blood cannot inherit the Kingdom of God. These perishable bodies of ours are not able to live forever.
>
> *1 Corinthians 15:40 – 50*

The Value of "X"

Physically, all men were all created equal. There is no difference between peoples when it comes to race, creed, color, religion or physical capability.

From the behavioural, personality and predestination perspective, all men were

<u>not</u> created equal. Judah (Adam) is at the top and therefore has more reasoning, analytical and scientific ability than the other three. Israel (Eve) is the helper with more strength, more power and stamina than the other three. Jerusalem (a.k.a. the serpent in the Genesis story) is the teacher with more mathetical and engineering aptitude than the other three. These three were born of the straight DNA chain.

The fourth, the Gentiles, with their purine base has the moral law and the facts – just the facts – with few internal resources such as time and reason to decipher what they really mean. That is the way they were made and their bacterial mother before them. The Gentiles are instinctual moving from one mood, or set of feelings, ideas, or references to another. They operate from feelings rather than truth. The Gentiles are children of the wet double helix, which eventually came to be embedded in the straight chain.

In the beginning was the Word [ATOM]**, and the Word** [ATOM] **was with GOD** [the Amorphous One, no mass]**, and the Word** [ATOM] **was GOD. All things were made by him; and without him was not any thing made that was made. In him is** *life* [Proton]**; and the life is the light** [the wisdom - Cytosine] **of men.**

And the light [Cytosine] **shineth in the darkness** [mankind, filled with ignorance]**; and the darkness** [mankind, filled with ignorance] **comprehended it not.**

There was a man sent from GOD, whose name was John [the Baptist]**. The same came for a witness, to bear witness of the Light** [whose name is ATOM, Proton]**, that all men through him** [through Proton] **might believe. He** [John] **was not** *that* **Light, but was sent to bear witness of the Light** [whose name is ATOM]**.**

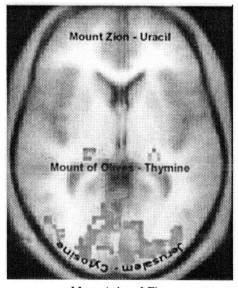

Mountain of Fire

That he [...ATOM, Proton] *is* the true Light, which lighteth every man [synapses firing from the hindbrain] that cometh into the world. He was in the world, and the world was made by him, and the world knew him not. He came unto his own [his own the three Jewels of Israel] and his own received him not [they rejected him and they are unwittingly doing the same today].

But as many as received him [including the Gentiles], to them gave he power to *become* the sons of GOD – even to them that believe on his name [ATOM]:

[I refer to the ones] Which were born, not of blood [Neutron], nor of the will of the flesh [Gluon], nor of the will of Man [Proton, commonly known as Christ], but of *God* [who is Electron, commonly known as Satan].

And the Word [ATOM, the first man] was made flesh [Jesus Christ], and dwelt among us [all of mankind], and we beheld his glory, the glory as of the only begotten of the Father [ATOM], full of grace and truth.

John 1:1 – 14 KJV

Wherefore remember, that ye being in time past *Gentiles* in the flesh, who are called Uncircumcision [Electron] by that which is called the Circumcision [ATOM] in the flesh made by [ATOM's own] hands; That at that time ye were without Christ, being *aliens* [born] from the commonwealth of Israel [who is Eve], and strangers from the covenants of promise, having no hope, and without GOD [Proton] in the world: But now in Christ Jesus [Proton] ye who sometimes were far off are made nigh by the blood of Christ.

Ephesians 2:11-13 KJV

Dear brothers and sisters, you [Gentiles] are foreigners and aliens here. So I warn you to keep away from evil desires because they fight against your very souls.

1 Peter 2:11

For, if GOD was willing to take you who were, by nature, branches from a wild olive tree and graft you into his own good tree – a very unusual thing to do – he will be far more eager to graft the Jewels back into the tree where they belong.

Romans 11:24

Listen, all of you math teachers. The wet double helix – that adjunct, unnecessary element introduced into life's straight, dry chain through unnatural means is the value of X.

The Gentiles are the X–Men, the Who–mans, the humans, the aliens, the foreigners among us.

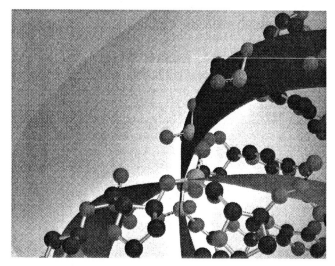

DNA - 33

Now, I know that many of you scientists have been racing to decipher the human genome and competing to understand what DNA really means to intelligence, personality, health, and predestination, but you already have what you need. How can you know the DNA of the creation and not understand the DNA of the Creator? They are inseparable. Man and his GOD, his Father, his Creator are one, intertwined one with another. Without the supporting breath of the Creator, man could not exist. Try breathing on your own without him. You will perish and very quickly.

Humankind is comprised of the conjoined bacterial elements, also known as the DNA double helix. Mankind crystallizes and adapts from conception; only bacteria based entities evolve and become more resistant to remedy.

But Pharaoh hardened his heart again and refused to let the people go.

Exodus 8:32 NLT

This describes the four living beings whose minds are literally the seven spirits of GOD selectively living within me and within you and every person. Here, within this mix of four DNA bases, lies the root cause of all of mankind's misery filled days and long sleepless nights.

DNA Profiles of the Family Members

The DNA Profiles

	Name	Elemental DNA	Carbon	Hydrogen	Nitrogen	Oxygen	Basic Property
		Formula and Base	Scientific Truth	Blood Cleansing	Preservation of Life	Continuation of Life	
GOD	Amorphous ATOM	$C_5H_{10}O_4PO_4^{3-}$	5	10	**0 - No Mass, Spirit**	4	**No visible properties**
GOD in three Persons	Proton, in his image Judah	$C_4H_5N_3O$ Cytosine (C)	4	5	3	1	Pyramidine Dry Land **Crystalline Christ**
	Gluon, in his image Israel	$C_5H_6N_2O_2$ Thymine (T)	5	6	2	2	Pyramidine Dry Land Crystalline
	Neutron, in his image Jerusalem	$C_4H_4N_2O_2$ Uracil (U)	4	4	2	2	Pyramidine Dry Land Crystalline
Anti-Christ	Electron, in his image the conjoined bi-polar Gentiles	$C_5H_4N_4$	5	4	4 - Self Preserved; cannot be destroyed by mankind	0 - Undead, No oxygen, no life	Purine/Urine based DNA Wet, water. *anti-Crystalline* Destroyers
	Gentile 1, Female, magnetic lure	$C_5H_5N_5$ Adenine (A)	5	5	5 - Self Preserved; evolves	0 - Undead, No oxygen, no life	Purine/Urine based DNA Wet, water, anti-Crystalline Destroyers
	Gentile 2, Male, Electric trap	$C_5H_5N_5O$ Guanine (G)	5	5	5 - Self Preserved; evolves	1 - Shares vital aire with the other twin	Purine/Urine based DNA Wet, water, anti-Crystalline Destroyers

The anti–Christ

The anti–Christ, anti–Cryst, Electron, is the de–composer. Decomposition is her life's work. It is what she was created to do. Electron was created to decompose everything that would be harmful to life, all life in the heavens above and on the earth beneath. Like the flies that we can see, her eggs turn into maggots. The maggots eat the dead flesh, devouring every morsel until the bones are picked clean. This is the subject of the small scroll that John, the revelator, was allowed to taste.

> **Are you amazed and incredulous? Do you not believe it? Then go ahead and be blind if you must. You are stupid, but not from wine! You stagger, but not from beer!**
>
> **For the LORD has poured out on you a spirit of deep sleep. He has closed the eyes of your prophets** [Jerusalem] **and visionaries** [Gentiles]**. All these future events are a sealed book to them. When you give it** [the scroll] **to those who can read** [Electron, the one sitting on the throne]**, they** [the liberal Adenine and the conservative, legalistic Guanine] **will say, "We can't read it because it is sealed."**
>
> **When you give it** [the scroll] **to those who cannot read** [the demons, bacteria]**, they will say, "Sorry, we don't know how to read."** [Demons, bacteria can't read, but Electron can read. She knows very well the law and the writings of the prophets.]
>
> *Isaiah 29:9 – 12*

The Divisions between Us

The Gentile children born in this age are more troubled than any other age and they don't understand why. Their parents don't know why. They are the bi–polar, multiple personality, ADHD children (Attention Deficit Hyperactivity Disorder) – high nitrogen, low oxygen. Parents are at their wits end.

This is a generation marked by irascibility, melancholy, moodiness, teenage suicide and teenage murder. Even the children that are Jewels of GOD are more defiant and unruly than ever before.

> **Do you think I have come to bring peace to the earth? No, I have come to bring strife and division! From now on families will be split apart, three in favor of me** [Judah, Israel, and Jerusalem]**, and two against** [the Gentiles — Adenine and Guanine] **– or the other way around** [Judah and Israel — for Cryst and the Gentiles and Jerusalem — against]**.**

There will be a division between father and son, mother and daughter, mother–in–law and daughter–in–law."

Luke 12:51 – 53

Listen now; for, these are the curses for this evil generation.

From now on families will be split apart, three in favor of me, and two against – or the other way around.

Luke 12:52

Brother will betray brother to death, fathers will betray their own children, and children will rise against their parents and cause them to be killed.

Matthew 10:21, Mark 13:12

There will be a division between father and son, mother and daughter, mother–in–law and daughter–in–law.

Luke 12:53

For the son despises his father. The daughter defies her mother. The daughter–in–law defies her mother–in–law. Your enemies will be right in your own household.

Micah 7:6

People will take advantage of each other – man against man, neighbor fighting neighbor. Young people will revolt against authority, and nobodies will sneer at honorable people.

Isaiah 3:5

And what is the result of these deep–rooted divisions – confusion, revenge, great sorrow, depression, murder, adultery and immoral sin. Your son, the Gentile, will cause you to weep, Israel. Your wife, the Gentile, will frighten you and run you off when you realize that you cannot control her high volatility, her weeping and rage, Jerusalem. Nothing you do will be good enough to please her. You will run back to Judah, whom GOD gave you from in the beginning. For the bible says,

A home [the conflicted Gentiles, male and female in the same body] **divided against itself is doomed.**

Mark 3:25

Then he will appoint [Gentile] children to rule over them, and anarchy will prevail. People will take advantage of each other – man against man, neighbor fighting neighbor. Young people will revolt against authority, and nobodies will sneer at honorable people.

In those days a man will say to his brother, "Since you have a cloak, you be our leader! Take charge of this heap of ruins!" "No!" he will reply. "I can't help. I don't have any extra food or clothes. Don't ask me to get involved!"

Judah and Jerusalem will lie in ruins because they speak out against the LORD and refuse to obey him. They have offended his glorious presence among them.

Isaiah 3:4 – 8

[Gentile] **Children oppress my people** [the Jewels], **and** [Gentile] **women rule over them. O my people, can't you see what fools your rulers are? They are leading you down a pretty garden path to destruction.**

Isaiah 3:12

I looked and I saw a Lamb [ATOM, Cryst] **that had been killed but was now standing between the throne** [your mind, where the anti–Cryst sits] **and the four living beings** [Judah, Israel, Jerusalem and the Gentiles] **and among the twenty–four elders** [they unknowingly worship Satan and lead all of mankind to do the same]. **He** [ATOM] **had seven horns** [horns are voices – Proton – diatomic, Gluon – diatomic, Neutron – atomic and Electron – bi–atomic] **and seven eyes** [the four DNA bases – Cytosine – diatomic, Thymine – diatomic, Uracil – atomic and the urine based Adenine and Guanine – conjoined and bi–atomic], **which are seven spirits of GOD that are sent out into every part of the earth** [the body of every person].

He [the Lamb who had been slain –ATOM or Cryst] **stepped forward and took the scroll from the right hand of the one sitting on the throne** [the throne is your mind and body; the one sitting on the throne is Electron or Satan, the anti–Cryst].

Revelation 5:6 – 7

Hold on Christians. Don't act as if you didn't know. Daniel warned you of what would happen. You have quoted him often enough when discussing the Revelation.

His [Satan's] **army** [of bacteria or demons] **will take over the Temple fortress** [the outer courtyard, the forebrain], **polluting the sanctuary** [poisoning the brain and the body with waste and bacteria], **putting a stop to the daily sacrifices** [the daily elimination of waste], **and setting up the sacrilegious object** [the parasympathetic nervous system built of cholinergic fibres – the path by which Satan has come to be in heaven – the minds of all men] **that causes desecration** [in the body of man – GOD's Temple].

Daniel 11:31 – 32

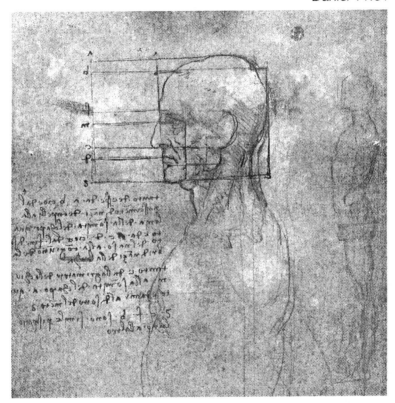

Leonardo, The Mind, the Window

John [the Revelator] **was given a measuring stick and told to go and measure the Temple of GOD** [the body of man] **and to count the number of worshipers. And he was told: But do not measure the outer courtyard** [Mount Zion – the forebrain], **for it has been turned over to the nations** [the nation of Ishmael – the Gentiles, of Electron and his bacterial horde of demons]. **They will trample the Holy City** [the forebrain] **for 42 months** [during the time of testing].

Revelation 11:2

Mount Zion

Mount of Olives

Mount of Olives

Forebrain
Archangel Gabriel
Neutron

Midbrain
Archangel Michael
Gluon

Christ *Proton*
Hindbrain

**Jerusalem
The Holy City**

The HOLY CITY

The Holy City is the home of Cytosine, wisdom; it is where synapses fire truth into the conscious mind of every person. Some reject it. But I digress. Even I am shocked and amazed and I have lived through her constant presence and annoyances for these past three and a half years.

The Twenty–four Elders

They [speaking of the twenty–four elders] **were all clothed in white and had gold crowns on their heads.**

Let me just interject here: The twenty–four wear white but not white linen indicating righteousness. Their white clothes represent the wealth of the nations that has been collected from the poor and unsuspecting souls who are looking for a blessing from the holy one. The poor sent their last, their savings, sacrificing their homes and children so that the elders could increase their wealth and build beautiful state–of–the–art buildings to glorify the one sitting on the throne and themselves. The elders, after all, are the best salesmen in the world. They have convinced the children of GOD to accept the one sitting on the throne by selling them the deceptions of Satan – the lies written in their books, their prayer cloths, their oils, audio tapes and guilt–ridden movies about the life and death of Jesus Christ.

Some of these twenty–four elders have been bold enough to sell "nothing at all". They wrapped this "nothing" in a beautiful package and called it 'Faith'. And Chris-

97

tians who love GOD purchased the pretty package and cherished it unto their hearts, believing everything they were told. Some were blessed and passed it on to their children but most buried it when they found they had been deceived. Nothing came of their purchase. It returned null and void. These stopped believing in the true GOD's ability to heal and rescue by his own power – a sin for which the elders and ministers of the gospel will pay with their own salvation.

Now, Satan does not show himself to be evil. He shows himself to be good. I am not ashamed to say that he tricked me. I, too, thought he was GOD Almighty. I know he deceived me now. It would be foolish to deny it. But it is better to learn and admit that I have been deceived than to never know it. Then your whole life would be a treacherous lie and you would die never knowing why you lived. The scriptures say:

> **For there shall arise false Christs** [false Crysts – Electron], **and false prophets** [Electron's children – Gentile men and women, deceivers], **and shall shew great signs and wonders** [weeping every step of the way]; **insomuch that, if it were possible, they shall deceive the very elect** [the three Jewels of GOD].

Matthew 24:24

Ellen G. White prophesied that Satan would impersonate Christ in every way except one – his coming. Christ will not return until the woman in labour completes her delivery – the Word and reads the revelation to the twenty–four elders. She also prophesied that Satan would cause "false revivals" in the church before the Word is delivered to the world. Many will join the churches as the excitement about God is raised to the boiling point, to a frenetic pitch. And those that join the churches with hands raised high will believe that the Most High GOD is with them. She foretold of a state of "*spiritual drunkenness*". She said that "**music would be a snare**" – an emotional catalyst for teary eyes, loud screams, emotional outbursts calling upon the name of the Lord. But nothing comes of this display. You are calling on the wrong Lord, the wrong Saviour. The one in the forefront is worthless, laughing at mankind and delivering nothing. The one in the background waits for the time when he is solely worshiped. Then he will bless all of mankind.

And from the throne came flashes of lightning, Electron and the electromagnetic force in the forebrain, and the rumble of thunder, Proton and the forces of gravity, strong and electroweak in the hindbrain.

For, while GOD, ATOM sits on his throne in the hindbrain, Satan or Electron is sitting on the throne in the forebrain providing you with feelings – terror, anxiety, hunger, pain and misery. Proton's home is a permanent one. He is the stone that the builders rejected that has now become the cornerstone. He will never be usurped.

The Four Living Beings

And in front of the throne were seven Lampstands [all of mankind] **with burning flames** [synapses firing from the hindbrain]. **They are the seven spirits of GOD.**

Now, I have told you before: The seven spirits are the seven churches. Judah is diatomic, which means two separate force particles in the same atom, one male, one female – Smyrna and Philadelphia; Israel is also diatomic, two separate force particles in the same atom, one male, one female – Laodicea and Pergamum; Jerusalem is atomic, one force particle, either male *or* female – Thyatira; the Gentiles are bi–atomic, 2 conjoined matter particles in one body, male *and* female – Ephesus and Sardis.

In front of the throne was a shiny sea of glass, sparkling like crystal [the crystalline DNA of GOD – the body of every man].

In the centre and around the throne were four living beings [Judah, Israel, Jerusalem and the Gentiles], **each covered with eyes** [the bacterial horde or demons, wings shaking in fear, sending shivers through the body], **front and back. The first of these living beings had the form of a lion** [Israel – the leader]; **the second looked like an ox** [Jerusalem – the teacher]; **the third had a human face** [Judah – made in the image of ATOM]; **and the fourth had the form of an eagle with wings spread out as though in flight** [the unpredictable Gentiles – ready to pounce on their victims].

Each of these [four] **living beings had six wings.**

With the wings, they flew as Nebuchadnezzar flew into a rage[56] and Saul flew into a rage[57] and without warning, threw a spear at David. The wings flew them in whatever direction they wanted to go. We are what we choose to be.

Two sets of wings were their thoughts – wise thoughts generated by Cytosine via the fired synapses in the hindbrain or evil thoughts generated by Adenine delivered via electrical impulses in the forebrain.

Two were their attitudes and actions – full of energy or completely calm guided by Thymine using the strong nuclear force; or manic and depressive guided by Adenine using the electromagnetic force.

And two were their voices, their words – full of knowledge and truth spoken by the Holy Spirit – Gabriel or Uracil; or full of lies, judgment and accusations spoken by Adenine.

---

56   Daniel 3:13
57   1 Samuel 18:9 – 11

And their wings were covered with eyes, inside and out. [The eyes are angels - antibacterial or demons - bacteria.]

Day after day and night after night [the four living beings] **keep on saying, "Holy, holy, holy is the Lord God Almighty – the one who always was, who is, and who is still to come."**

Whenever the living beings give glory and honor and thanks to the one sitting on the throne, the one who lives forever and ever, the twenty–four elders fall down and worship the one who lives forever and ever.

And they lay their crowns [the crowns of their heads, which they bow] **before the throne** [which sits within the brain] **and say, "You are worthy, O Lord our God, to receive glory and honor and power. For you created everything, and it is for your pleasure that they exist and were created."**

Revelation 4:4 – 11

The Twenty–four Elders are Named

Many of these preachers and teachers, I would not have chosen. I have heard them speaking the devil's rhetoric, spewing lies in the name of the LORD. But this is GOD's plan, not mine. He uses whom he uses for his own plans and purposes. He chooses whom he chooses. He does not answer to me. And I am wise. I do what he tells me to do. Therefore, these are the names given to me by the Holy Spirit listed in the order that he gave them to me.

Elder Dr. Hugh Ross

Elder Doug Batchelor

Elder Dr. Charles Stanley

Elder Hal Lindsey

Elder John Hagee

Elder Pat Robinson

Elder Paul Crouch

Elder T. D. Jakes

Elder Juanita Bynum

Elder Dr. Ed Hindson

Elder Joyce Meyer

Elder Kenneth Copeland

Elder Randy Morrison

Elder Jack Van Impe

Elder Rod Parsley

Elder James Robison

Elder Marcus Lamb

Elder Andrew Wommack

Elder Marilyn Hickey

Elder Perry Stone

Elder Joel Olsteen

Elder Creflo Dollar

The Late Pope John Paul II

Elder Benny Hinn

These are the elders, the road warriors with international influence, who have achieved fame and fortune saving souls for the great deceiver, the anti–Christ, for the cause of Satan. You are the quintessential bridesmaids, the ten who represent all of you sitting here today. Half of you, the first half of the list, brought enough oil for your lamps, enough truth to sustain you, staying away from novel ideas that sound good but are full of lies and cannot be proven in heaven or on earth. The other half, the second half of the list, is the bridesmaids who ran out of oil, ran out of truth and accepted the lies of Satan to sustain you until Christ returned to set the record straight.

The Small Scroll

And the revelator recorded this message about the opening of the small scroll:

And I saw a scroll in the right hand of the one who was sitting on the throne. There was writing on the inside and the outside of the scroll, and it was sealed with seven seals.

Isaiah wrote:

All these future events are a sealed book to them. When you give [the scroll] **to those who can read** [Electron, the one sitting on the throne], **they** [Adenine and Guanine] **will say, "We can't read it because it is sealed."**

When you give [the scroll] **to those who cannot read** [the demons, bacteria], **they will say, "Sorry, we don't know how to read."** [Demons, bacteria can't read, but, I will say it again, Electron can read. She gave me a great deal of grief with her lies and whitewash. At first, the lies sound true, plausible. But her lies have no weight, nothing to hold them up. They collapse in a pile of rubble…just as she will at the appointed time.]

Isaiah 29:11 – 12

And I saw a strong angel [Archangel Michael – Gluon], **who shouted with a loud voice: "Who is worthy to break the seals on this scroll and unroll it?" But no one in heaven or on earth or under the earth was able to open the scroll and read it. Then I** [John, the Gentile] **wept because no one could be found who was worthy to open the scroll and read it. But one of the twenty–four elders said to me, "Stop weeping! Look, the Lion of the tribe of Judah, the heir to David's throne,** [Cyrus] **has conquered. He is worthy to open the scroll and break its seven seals."**

I looked and I saw a Lamb that had been killed but was now standing between the throne and the four living beings and among the twenty–four elders. He had seven horns and seven eyes, which are the seven spirits of God that are sent out into every part of the earth. He [Cryst] **stepped forward and took the scroll from the right hand of the one sitting on the throne** [the anti–Cryst].

And as he took the scroll, the four living beings and the twenty–four elders fell down before the Lamb. Each one had a harp, and they held gold bowls filled with incense – the prayers of GOD's people!

And they sang a new song with these words: "You are worthy to take the scroll and break its seals and open it. For you were killed, and your blood has ransomed people for GOD from every tribe and language and people and nation. And you have caused them to become GOD's Kingdom and his priests. And they will reign on the earth."

Then I looked again, and I heard the singing of thousands and millions of angels around the throne and the living beings and the elders. And they sang in a mighty chorus: "The Lamb is worthy – the Lamb who was killed. He is worthy to receive power and riches and wisdom and strength and honor and glory and blessing." And then I heard every creature in heaven and on earth and under the earth and in the sea. They also sang: "Blessing and honor and glory and power belong to the one sitting on the throne and to the Lamb forever and ever." And the four living beings said, "Amen!" And the twenty–four elders fell down and worshiped GOD [ATOM] **and the Lamb** [Cryst].

Revelation 5:1 – 14

The First Three Seals Announce the Birth of GOD's Three Children

The LORD ATOM – GOD has three children – Judah, Israel and Jerusalem.

Judah is my bow [my apostle, my discoverer], **and Israel is my arrow** [my helper – how I will accomplish all of my plans right on target]! **Jerusalem is my sword** [the sword of my mouth – how I teach great discoveries, the truth to all future generations], **and like a warrior, I will brandish it against the Greeks** [the Gentiles].

Zechariah 9:13

As I watched, the Lamb broke the first of the seven seals on the scroll. Then one of the four living beings [Judah] called out with a voice that sounded like thunder, "Come!" I looked up and saw a white horse [gravity]. Its rider [Proton] carried a bow, and a crown was placed on his head [wisdom]. He rode out to win many [scientific, creating, discovering] battles [always seeking the truth] and gain the victory.

Michelangelo, Judah

When the Lamb broke the second seal, I heard the second living being [Israel] say, "Come!" And another horse appeared, a red one [strong nuclear force, the strongest force]. Its rider [Gluon] was given a mighty sword and the authority [but not the desire] to remove peace from the earth. And there was war and slaughter everywhere. [Gluon did not stop the war or the slaughter...but could have.]

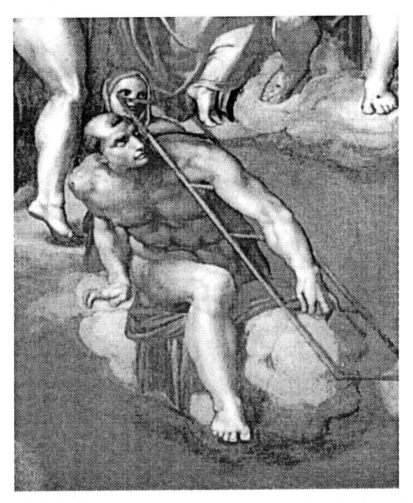

Michelangelo, Israel

We know that this is Israel sitting behind the Archangel Michael because Michael is carrying Jacob's ladder that GOD gave him when he told him his name was Israel.

"Your name will no longer be Jacob," the man told him. "It is now Israel, because you have struggled with both GOD and men and have won."

Genesis 32:28

When the Lamb broke the third seal, I heard the third living being [Jerusalem] **say, "Come!"**

Michelangelo, Jerusalem

Here is GOD's child Jerusalem, shedding his death mask. He can destroy in a rage just as easily as the Gentiles can destroy. He is a sensitive soul. Neutron, Uracil is the teacher, by any means necessary; teaching both good and evil. This is the serpent of the garden, teaching Eve that she should submit to sin with the evil one. What do you think Neutron holds in his hand? He offers the same evil to me, Judah, as I warred with the dragon. I was able to refuse it.

And I looked up and saw a black horse [weak nuclear force], **and its rider** [Neutron] **was holding a pair of scales in his hand.**

And a voice from among the four living beings said,

"A loaf of wheat bread or three loaves of barley for a day's pay [?] [It's a question, said in disbelief and disgust. Jerusalem values fairness above all else.]

Justice Scales

"And don't waste the olive oil and wine." [Jerusalem admonishes. He is the Teacher. He rules with an iron hand, disciplining the rebellious and rewarding the compliant. He is ATOM's sword.]

Jerusalem, like Neutron, the model, is (R) reversible – he vacillates between the light of truth and the darkness of deception, between the powerful force particles and the weak matter particles, between the Jewels and the Gentiles. That is why he was named Je-**ruse**-salem after the throne of GOD. He lies to avoid capture, death. He is lured away from GOD easily. Jerusalem is Ham, the cursed descendent of the Canaanites, the Actor. For, Neutron (Gabriel) is the one-third of the angels who left the LORD Proton to follow Electron – the devil. This is a scientific fact, not fiction. Jerusalem is the serpent in the Garden of Eden. We know this because GOD did not make any animals who could speak intelligible words, save mankind. Israel or Eve's conversation regarding the tree of knowledge was with Jerusalem. But I digress...And the revelator recorded:

GOD's Child Jerusalem

Now all men experience what Proton had worked to protect mankind from – the quick liaison and the slow death, the bacterial death that Electron delivers in the name of love, in the name of liberty, freedom. Because of his divisive lies, and how he helped Satan corrupt Eve, GOD cursed Jerusalem in the garden[58] and again through Noah to reinforce Jerusalem's loss of favor.

Then he [Noah] **cursed the descendants of Canaan** [all of those called Jerusalem in heaven], **the son of Ham: A curse on the Canaanites! May they be the lowest of servants to the descendants of Shem** [Judah] **and Japheth** [Israel]."

---

58   Genesis 3:14 – 19

May Shem [Judah] be blessed by the LORD [ATOM] my GOD; and may Canaan [Jerusalem] be his servant. May GOD [ATOM] enlarge the territory of Japheth [Israel]; may he share the prosperity of Shem [Judah]; and let Canaan [Jerusalem] be his servant."

Genesis 9:25 – 27

Jerusalem – GOD's High Priest on Earth

Then the angel showed me Jeshua [Uracil and hence, Jerusalem] the high priest standing before the angel of the LORD [Cytosine]. Satan [Electron] was there at the angel's right hand, accusing Jeshua [Uracil and Jerusalem] of many things.

And the LORD [Proton] said to Satan [or Electron], "I, the LORD [ATOM], reject your accusations, Satan. Yes, the LORD [ATOM], who has chosen Jerusalem, rebukes you. This man is like a burning stick that has been snatched from a fire."

Jeshua's [Jerusalem's] clothing was filthy as he stood there before the angel [LORD Proton]. So the angel said to the others standing there [Michael or Gluon and Gabriel or Neutron], "Take off his filthy clothes [remove the bacteria, demons, sin, which means "without GOD"]."

And turning to Jeshua he said, "See, I have taken away your sins, and now I am giving you these fine new clothes [a robe of righteousness and truth]." Then I said, "Please, could he also have a clean turban [a pyramidine crown] on his head?" So they put a clean priestly turban [a pyramidine crown] on his head and dressed him in new clothes while the angel of the LORD [Proton] stood by.

Then the angel of the LORD [Proton] spoke very solemnly to Jeshua and said, "This is what the LORD Almighty [ATOM] says:

If you follow my ways and obey my requirements, then you will be given authority over my Temple [your body] and its courtyards [your mind]. I will let you walk in and out of my presence along with these others [Judah and Israel] standing here.[59]

---

59   Jerusalem is different from the other two because he is patterned after Neutron. Neutron is the plasma, the blood. The errant bacteria live within the blood. Therefore, Neutron and hence, Jerusalem is forced to negotiate and often succumbs to Electron, the darkness. This happens even though Neutron is stronger and inherently wiser than Electron. But Electron is a trickster and Neutron is easily fooled...just as Jerusalem is easily fooled.

Listen to me, O Jeshua the high priest [Jerusalem]**, and all you other priests** [Judah and Israel]**. You are symbols of the good things to come.**

Soon I am going to bring my servant, the Branch [Cytosine]**. Now look at the jewel**[60] [wisdom and truth] **I have set before Jeshua, a single stone with seven facets. I will engrave an inscription on it, says the LORD Almighty** [Proton]**, and I will remove the sins of this land** [Uracil, Jerusalem] **in a single day.**

And on that day, says the LORD Almighty [Proton]**, each of you will invite your neighbor into your home to share your peace and prosperity."**

Zechariah 3: 1 – 10

The curses delivered as the judgment to the first sin and the blessings delivered to Noah's three sons are a declaration of predestination. This is the way that the LORD Proton intended life to be for his three children. To whom much is given – Judah and Israel – much is required, many sacrifices. Jerusalem does not have to sacrifice his life for the cause of GOD. He is the teacher. The teacher is loved by men, sought after – not despised for telling the truth, for discovering the hidden. Some of you will not believe it is fair. However, look at what ATOM did for Mozart, for Einstein, for many of you twenty–four elders sitting here today. Mozart and Einstein were both called Jerusalem and their names are written in history books to rival the famous Jesus Christ. What ATOM has done for these, he can also do for you. Trust him.

So, with all that Jerusalem has done, the good and the bad, the LORD Proton who is GOD loves his third child – Jerusalem – without question. He loves him so much that when he made the earth – the body of man – he named Jerusalem, his son, after the beloved and Holy City – Jerusalem, the mind. For Jerusalem is the teacher, the intelligent one who speaks before men on GOD's behalf. He is (R) – reversible – sometimes he speaks foolishly, tells lies. Sometimes he speaks wisely with great intellectual depth.

---

60   The Jewel is the diamond – Cytosine – the cornerstone durable throughout the ages. The Jewel is wisdom and truth. Judah, Israel and Jerusalem are ATOM's precious children along with Electron's children, the Gentiles who also love and serve ATOM. Together, these four make up the seven facets, the seven churches and the seven lampstands. These were Jewels from the beginning of life because of the materials of which we are comprised - crystalline dust.

"LORD [ATOM]**, you are in the right; but our faces are covered with shame, just as you see us now. This is true of us all, including the people of** Judah **and** Jerusalem **and all** Israel**, scattered near and far, wherever you have driven us because of our disloyalty to you.**

Daniel 9:7

Jerusalem (GOD's youngest child) will be honored in the days to come. He will do the work that the Holy One, the LORD Proton and his Father, ATOM, have given him to do concerning the end of this age. And so will each of you when the time comes.

Fourth Seal Announces the Birth of the Gentiles

Electron's crystalline child is what she pined for from the beginning of time. This is why she attacked Electron in the beginning, when Christ, Proton, was innocent, unsuspecting, going around with his hindside exposed. She knew he would be beautiful to loop upon. But...I don't think she realized how messed or dangerous he would be to the children of GOD. Furthermore, I don't think she really cared at the time. Now, you see them. They are in my family and in your family. They are the effeminate ones – male and female in the same body.

And when the Lamb broke the fourth seal, I heard the fourth living being [the Gentile] **say, "Come!" And I looked up and saw a horse** [electromagnetic force] **whose color was pale** [bacterial] **green like a corpse** [Electron]**. And Death** [Adenine] **was the name of its rider, who was followed around by the Grave** [Guanine]**. They were given authority over one–fourth of the earth** [the Gentiles are one–fourth of all of the people upon the earth]**, to kill with the sword** [the conquerors] **and famine** [too much rain; too little rain] **and disease** [cancer, sexually transmitted, pneumonia, diseases of the blood] **and wild animals** [the stalkers, enraged murderers and serial killers, who must kill because they are commanded to do so, compelled to do so by their mother, Electron.]

Don't be repulsed by him Israel. He is your son too. Everyone knows your sin. Repent and get it over with. Stop lamenting. Your Saviour is coming soon to take away all of your sorrows.

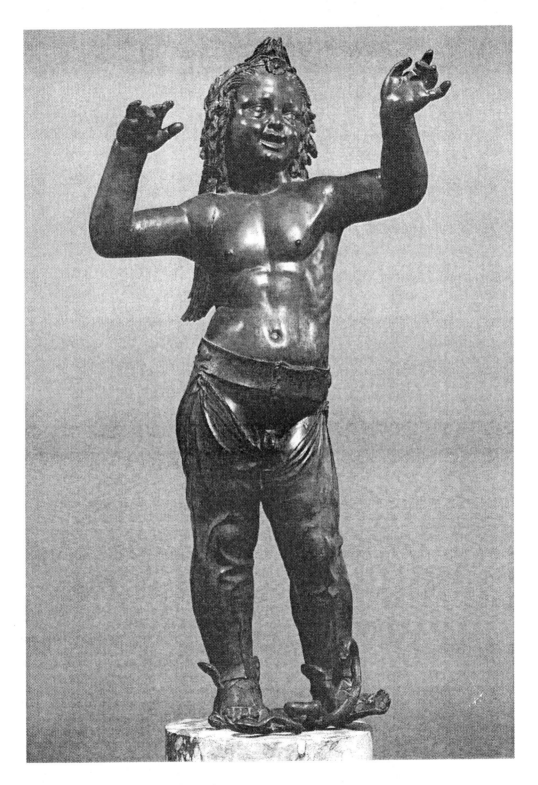

Donatello, The Effeminate Gentile Boy

Donatello, The Effeminate Gentile Youth

The Fifth Seal Announces that Jerusalem seeks Justice

Leonardo, Peter

And when the Lamb broke the fifth seal, I saw under the altar the souls of all who had been martyred for the word of GOD and for being faithful in their witness. They called loudly to the Lord [ATOM] and said, "O Sovereign LORD, holy and true, how long will it be before you judge the people who belong to this world for what they have done to us? When will you avenge our blood against these people?"

Then a white robe was given to each of them. And they were told to rest a little longer until the full number of their brothers and sisters [Jerusalem] their fellow servants of Jesus – had been martyred.

The Sixth Seal is the Face Off – Cryst against the Anti–Cryst

The opening of the sixth seal announces the *Bella Omnium Contra Omnes,* the War of All Versus All. This is the Armageddon you fear.

Then the LORD [ATOM] thundered, "Bring on the men appointed to punish the city [Jerusalem]! Tell them to bring their weapons with them!" Six men soon appeared from the upper gate that faces north, each carrying a battle club in his hand. [The six men are Cytosine, Thymine, Uracil, Adenine, Guanine and Cyrus.]

One of them [Cyrus] was dressed in linen and carried a writer's case strapped to his side [a laptop]. They all went into the Temple court-yard [the forehead] and stood beside the bronze altar [the brain of every person].

Then the glory of the GOD of Israel [ATOM] rose up from between the cherubim [all mankind], where it had rested, and moved to the entrance of the Temple. [The eyes are the entrance to the Temple]. And the LORD [ATOM] called to the man dressed in linen [Cyrus] who was carrying the writer's case [laptop]. He said to him, "Walk through the streets of Jerusalem and put a mark [truth] on the foreheads of all those who weep and sigh because of the sins they see around them." [The streets of Jerusalem are the minds of every person living in this time.]

Then I heard the LORD say to the other [five] men, "Follow him through the city and kill everyone whose forehead is not marked [everyone who does not believe the truth]. Show no mercy; have no pity! Kill them all – old and young, girls and women and little children. But do not touch anyone with the mark. Begin your task right here at the Temple." So they began by killing the seventy leaders [the demons, bacteria who rule over the minds of men].

"Defile the Temple!" the LORD commanded. "Fill its courtyards with the bodies of those you kill! Go!" So they went throughout the city and did as they were told. While they were carrying out their orders, I was all alone. I fell face down in the dust and cried out, "O Sovereign LORD! Will your fury against Jerusalem wipe out everyone left in Israel?"

Then he said to me, "The sins of the people of Israel and Judah are very great. The entire land is full of murder; the city is filled with injustice. They are saying, 'The LORD doesn't see it! The LORD has forsaken the land!' So I will not spare them or have any pity on them. I will fully repay them for all they have done."

Then the man in linen clothing, who carried the writer's case, [Cyrus] reported back and said, "I have finished the work you gave me to do." [It is finished.]

Ezekiel 9:1 – 11

This war will not happen upon the earth. It will happen within the earth, more specifically, within your brain. I can attest to this. For, from the beginning of my election, the war has raged, almost without ceasing.

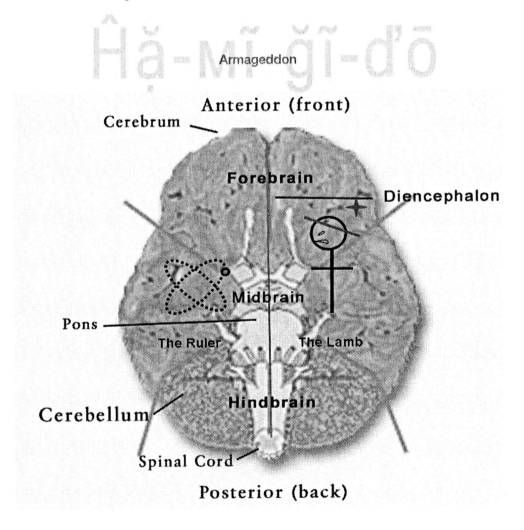

And I beheld when he had opened the sixth seal, and lo,

there was a great earthquake [a shaking from within every living body];

and the sun [the Son of GOD – the Cytosine] became black [in anger] as a sackcloth of hair [he sits beneath your hair at the hind-brain],

and the moon [the moon is the plasma; the moon is Uracil or Gabriel poised for the war within] became of blood [he lives in the blood];

and the stars of heaven [Thymine – Michael and his antibody armies] fell onto the earth [each body], even as a fig tree casteth her untimely figs, when she is shaken of a mighty wind.

And the heaven departed as a scroll when it is rolled together [the two lobes of the brain will roll up with the fierce pounding and unrelenting electrical shock courtesy of Electron. The two lobes will feel as if they have become one];

and every mountain [two sides of the brain of the Jewel] and island [brain of the Gentile] were moved out of their places [with the fierce shaking].

And the kings of the earth [all people] and the great men, and every bondman, and every free man [all people], hid themselves in the dens and in the rocks of the mountains [the brain]. And said to the mountains [of the brain] and rocks [Cytosine, Thymine, and Uracil],

"Fall on us and hide us from the face of him that sitteth on the throne [Electron – Satan], and from the wrath of the Lamb [Proton]: For the great day of his wrath [Proton, Cytosine] is come and who shall be able to stand?

Revelation 6:1 – 17 KJV

The 144,000

Look! The LORD is coming from far away, burning with anger, surrounded by a thick, rising smoke. His lips are filled with fury; his Words consume like fire. His anger pours out like a flood on his enemies, sweeping them all away. He will sift out the proud nations. He will bridle them and lead them off to their destruction. 1But the people of GOD will sing a song of joy, like the songs at the holy festivals. You will be filled with joy, as when a flutist leads a group of pilgrims to Jerusalem – the mountain of the LORD – to the Rock of Israel.

Then [John, the Revelator] **saw four angels** [Cytosine, Thymine, Uracil, and electron – the subatomic matter particle)] **standing at the four corners of the earth, holding back the four winds** [the four forces – gravity, strong nuclear force, weak nuclear force, and the electromagnetic force] **from blowing upon the earth. Not a leaf rustled in the trees** [the Tree of Life and the Tree of Good and Evil]**, and the** [crystalline] **sea became as smooth as glass.** [DNA is as smooth as glass; you can see through it. It has no visible characteristics for the human eye to observe.]

And I saw another angel coming from the east, carrying the seal of the living GOD [Proton, the High Commander]**. And he shouted out to those four angels who had been given power to injure land and sea, "Wait! Don't hurt the land or the sea or the trees until we have placed the seal of GOD on the foreheads of his servants."**

And [John] **heard how many were marked with the seal of GOD. There were 144,000 who were sealed from all the tribes of Israel: from Judah** [Judah] **– 12,000, from Reuben** [Israel] **– 12,000, from Gad** [Jerusalem] **– 12,000, from Asher – 12,000, from Nathalie – 12,000, from Manasseh – 12,000, from Simeon – 12,000, from Levi – 12,000, from Issaquah – 12, from Zebulon – 12,000, from Joseph – 12,000 from Benjamin – 12,000.** [These 144,000 are those who have died for the cause of Christ, whose foreheads were sealed by Proton himself, who gave them the truth just as it was given to me.]

After this [John] **saw a vast crowd, too great to count** [all men]**, from every nation and tribe and people and language, standing in front of the throne and before the Lamb. They were clothed in white and held palm branches in their hands.** [All men who survive the shaking will believe this truth.]

And they were shouting with a mighty shout, "Salvation comes from our GOD [ATOM] **on the throne and from the Lamb[61]** [Proton]**!" And all the angels were standing around the throne and around the elders and the four living beings. And they fell face down before the throne and worshiped GOD** [ATOM]**.**

They said, "Amen! Blessing and glory and wisdom and thanksgiving and honor and power and strength belong to our GOD [ATOM] **forever and forever. Amen!"**

---

61   We know that Proton is the lamb because Jesus Christ was named Judah in heaven just as I am named Judah. Proton, Jesus Christ and Judah have the same mind source; different bodies, same mind. This is true for Gluon, Archangel Michael and Israel; this is true for Neutron, Archangel Gabriel and Jerusalem; this is true for Electron with her conjoined minds – Adenine and Guanine and the Gentiles with their conjoined minds and behaviour.

Then one of the twenty–four elders asked me, "Who are these who are clothed in white? Where do they come from?"

And I said to him, "Sir, you are the one who knows." Then he said to me, "These are the ones coming out of the great tribulation [the Bella Omnium Contra Omnes, the War of All Versus All]. They washed their robes in the blood of the Lamb and made them white. That is why they are standing in front of the throne of GOD, serving him day and night in his Temple [your mind, between the two temples above your earlobes].

And he who sits on the throne [in the hindbrain, ATOM] will live among them and shelter them. They will never again be hungry or thirsty, and they will be fully protected from the scorching noontime heat [synapses firing from the hindbrain].

For the Lamb who stands in front of the throne [Michael or Gluon, who straddles the Mount of Olives] will be their Shepherd. [The atomic Gluon, who is the DNA angel Thymine, moves all men. He is responsible for the muscular and skeletal system in every man. Gluon leads just as Israel leads all men. It is his destiny.] He will lead them to the springs of life–giving water.

And GOD [ATOM] will wipe away all their tears." [Electron causes you to weep. She is the atomic water element. That is how she tried to drown me, with her tears.]

Revelation 7:1 – 17

The Seventh Seal

When the Lamb broke the seventh seal, there was silence through-out heaven for about half an hour.

Revelation 8:1

Cryst (Proton or DNA–Cytosine) will not speak during the time of testing that is about to come upon the entire world. And neither will any of the angels (Thymine or Uracil, Michael or Gabriel). They won't speak to anyone who has not accepted this truth and committed his life to this truth. No one will receive any instructions, words of encouragement or wisdom or signs from the Light, who is Proton).

Every mind – men, women, and all children – for a little while, after the revelation is revealed, will be void of intelligent thought. Every person will have to decide who is GOD and who is Satan based on what you know to be true. Don't trust your instinct; it will fail you. Trust your eyes. For, the truth will be manifest in every person, every event and every thing around you. The anti-Christ's intention is to rule over you, to decompose you, to flood you with physical pain and sorrow. But you can choose not to follow the evil one and die. You may choose Cryst, ATOM, and live.

The only voice you may hear is the voice of Satan, Electron, trying to convince you that she is God, that she is Holy. She lives within your body, just as Cryst lives within your body. She is an ever present faction, always at war with you. During these days, she will weep on the outside of your body and on the inside; it will be dismal outside – cloudy with a light, misty rain. She will weep, inconsolable, as she did during the last days of my incarceration. And when she realizes that she has lost you, she will begin to pound you in the head with her fist. Be strong. If I was able to survive it, so will you.

The Seven Trumpets Announce the Genesis of Life

And I saw the seven angels who stand before GOD, [They are Philadelphia and Smyrna for Judah, Pergamum and Laodicea for Israel, Thyatira for Jerusalem, and Ephesus and Sardis for the Gentiles] **and they were given seven trumpets** [seven voices].

Then another angel [Gabriel, also known as DNA–Uracil] **with a gold incense burner came and stood at the altar.** [The gold incense burner is the mind of every man with the golden fire of synapses firing from the hindbrain; incense is a euphemism for the thoughts of every man. Like incense, our thoughts rise up and then dissipate into the air.]

And a great quantity of incense [thoughts – fears, desires, anxiety, needs and wants – that have accumulated and gone unanswered during the past few millennia] **was given to him** [Gabriel] **to mix with the** [unanswered] **prayers of GOD's people, to be offered on the gold altar before the throne.** [Gold altar is a euphemism for the gold crowns we wear naturally. It is the crown of our heads filled with the golden fire, the synapses that flow from the presence of GOD.]

The smoke of the incense [man's thoughts]**, mixed with the prayers of the saints** [finally] **ascended up to GOD from the altar** [the forehead] **where the angel** [Gabriel] **had poured them out.**

Then the angel [Gabriel] **filled the incense burner with fire from the altar and threw it down upon the earth** [the body]**; and thunder crashed, lightning flashed, and there was a terrible earthquake** [within the body]**. Then the seven angels with the seven trumpets prepared to blow their mighty blasts.**

Revelation 8:2 – 6

From the Genesis to the
Return of Christ

Birth of ATOM: PRO + on[62] = Creation of the Word, the Crystalline Creator

The Big Bang: The first angel blew his trumpet, and hail [a crystallized solid, Proton] **and fire** [air, Gluon] **mixed with blood** [plasma, Neutron] **were thrown down upon the earth, and one–third of the earth** [bacterial matter] **was set on fire. One–third of the trees** [bacterial matter] **were burned, and all of the grass** [atomic green "death defying" bacterial matter] **was burned.**

Revelation 8:7

Birth of Gluon – Glue[63] + on

Then the second angel blew his trumpet, and a great mountain of fire [air or gas, Gluon] **was thrown into the sea. And one–third of the water in the sea became blood** [plasma, the Neutron]. **And one–third of all things living in the sea** [bacteria] **died. And one–third of all the ships** [cellular level molecules that carry bacteria] **on the sea were destroyed.**

Revelation 8:8 – 9

Birth of Neutron – Neu + R[64] + on

Then the third angel blew his trumpet, and a great flaming star [plasma – the Neutron] **fell out of the sky, burning like a torch.** [Neutron is the child of Proton and Gluon] **It fell upon one–third of the rivers and on the springs of water** [matter particles].

The name of the star is Bitterness[65]. It made one–third of the water bitter, and many people [Jerusalem and the Gentiles] **died because it was so bitter.** [Water used here refers to the iron within water. Water is also a euphemism for people. Jerusalem is liquid, plasma, iron, water. He is a stern and bitter opponent.]

Revelation 8:10 – 11

---

62   PRO + on = Creator, Glue + on = Protector, Neu + R + on = Teacher, Elect + R + on = Chosen.

63   Very strong glue indeed!

64   R, the Reversible ones – Neutron and Electron – vacillate between light (Truth) and darkness (Deception).

65   Neutron is bitter because he is compelled to console the darkness – Electron, even as he (Neutron) walks in the light. To accomplish this act of consolation, Neutron is Ham, the actor.

This is the first pattern, after which the soul of the universe, the body and mind of all men were patterned from the beginning. This is Cryst, the Archangel Michael and the Archangel Gabriel.

The Matter Particle is Selected – Elect + R + on[66]

Then the fourth angel blew his trumpet, and one–third of the sun [Proton] was struck, and one–third of the moon [Neutron], and one–third of the stars [Gluon], and they became dark.

And one–third of the day was dark [Adenine] and one–third of the night also [Guanine].

Revelation 8:12

ATOM and his amorphous spirit covers everything, every where. When something evil passes through him, as Electron was elected to do because of the important task of waste management, ATOM, and the light within him, is affected. They are seared in a negative way. Into the most holy place, where there had only been truth and justice, came deception and injustice. That is the way of the anti-Christ. It is her nature – deception, folly and death.

Then I looked up. And I heard a single eagle crying loudly as it flew through the air, "Terror, terror, terror to all who belong to this world because of what will happen when the last three angels blow their trumpets."

Revelation 8:13

The Rage of Women

This passage concerns Eve's curse, which was put upon all the bodies of all females.

Then he said to the woman, "You will bear children with intense pain and suffering. And though your desire will be for your [chosen] husband [Electron or the devil], he will be your master."[67]

Genesis 3:16

---

66   On indicates always on but not necessarily forever. After 1000 years has ended, Electron will be Electr**off**.

67   The Song of Songs is the sad story of Eve whose name is Israel and Adam whose name is Judah separately seeking the devil, Electron for sex.

Then the fifth angel blew his trumpet, and I saw a star [Electron] that had fallen to earth from the sky, and he [Electron] was given the key to the bottomless pit [bladder and bowels]. When he opened it, [gaseous] smoke poured out as though from a huge furnace [the stomach is the furnace; the ash or bacteria flowed over the healthy cells and molecules], and the sunlight [Cytosine] and air [Thymine] were darkened by the smoke.

Then locusts [airborne bacteria] came from the smoke [which ascended upwards from all manner of contaminated feces] and descended on the earth [within the body of every generation since that time], and they were given power to sting like scorpions. [Where they sting, you itch and you scratch, usually in difficult to reach or inopportune places – the scalp, middle of the back, bottom of the feet, genitalia and between the toes – any damp or moist place.]

They [the bacteria] were told not to hurt the grass or plants or trees [the root system of the pyramidine tree, the sympathetic nervous system also known as the Tree of Life] but to attack all the people who did not have the seal of GOD on their foreheads [did not know this truth about their ruler]. They [the bacteria] were told not to kill them but to torture them for five [days, all] months with agony like the pain of scorpion stings [pulsating menstrual cramps].

In [during] those [five] days, [all] people [men and women] will seek death but will not find it. They will long to die, ["just shoot me!"] but death will flee away!

The locusts [hormones] looked like horses armed for battle. They had gold crowns [the pyramidine crown – Cytosine, Thymine, and Uracil] on their heads, and they had human faces [they are human]. Their hair was long like the hair of a woman [because they are women], and their teeth were like the teeth of a lion [ready to bite your head off].

Donatello, Electron, The Bi-Polar Manic Depressive

This is the curiously crazy Electron, Adenine - the virtuous, after she murdered Christ at Calvary. Here she is shown going through the full gamut of emotion, of mania and depression, joy and sorrow. She is truly bi-polar...and so are the Gentiles, her children; and so is every female who is unlucky enough to bleed each month.

Satan – Electron is shown here in all of her stages of bi–polarism, mania and depression after she connived and schemed to murder Jesus Christ – the Son of GOD, ATOM *manifest*. Today, she is known as Mary and was given sainthood. She is worshiped and prayed to, and exalted as a god all over the world. She is Athena, Poseidon, Dianna from Greek Mythology, Isis and Osirus – male and female in one body. She is Adenine and Guanine, the Queen of Death.

Electron is Typhoid Mary, infecting everyone with diseases while she lives on and on. Killing the ones she loves as easily as she kills the ones she hates. She loved Alexander, the Great, and yet, in the end, she could not save his life. He died of AIDS related disease. Nor could she save the life of the first emperor of China who did her bidding, murdering millions to conquer the land, implementing laws to control thought and building the great wall, with great zest and vigor. Her love is lethal to all people who partake in her zeal for lust, who eat of contaminated fruit (semen) and who follow her instructions.

They wore armor made of iron [the hormones are covered with filthy menstrual blood]**, and their wings** [voices] **roared like an army of chariots rushing into battle** [screaming in a rage, unexpectedly].

They had tails [geni–tails] **that stung like scorpions** [the genitals are clothed with bacteria – the yeast infections]**, with power to torture people** [men, generally]**. This power was given to them for five** [days every] **month. Their king** [the locusts king] **is the angel from the bottomless pit; his name in Hebrew is Abaddon** [a bad don as in Madonna, the godmother or Satan, Electron, Adenine – the Great Prostitute, the whore of Babylon]**, and in Greek, Apollyon – the Destroyer** [Guanine – the devil, the matter particle who destroys with both electricity or fire and water].

Revelation 9:1 – 11

Today, most women behave like Electron, Adenine and Guanine – bipolar, enraged one minute, crying and depressed the next, happy go lucky the next. These phases may not last long, but they are most prominent during the menstrual cycle. For the Gentile women, this bi-polarism – rage and depression or ecstatically happy is the norm.

The first terror is past, but look, two more terrors are coming!

Revelation 9:12

Then the sixth angel blew his trumpet, and I heard a voice [ATOM] **speaking from the four horns** [Proton, Gluon, Neutron, Electron] **of the gold altar that stands in the presence of** [the Amorphous] **GOD. And the voice spoke to the sixth angel** [Gluon or Israel] **who held the trumpet:**

"Release the four [anti–body] angels who are bound at the Great Euphrates River." [The Great Euphrates River is a euphemism for the bladder, a wide transport that carries molecular ships of bacteria filled with cargo of germs, sperm, parasites and fungi that have been contaminating your body via the backup of waste within your stomach.]

And the four angels who had been prepared for this hour and day and month were turned loose to kill one–third of all the people [bodies – bacteria] on earth [every body]. They led an army of 200 million mounted troops [antibodies and antiparticles per body] – I heard an announcement of how many there were.

Revelation 9:13 – 16

The Plagues Suffered by Mankind

And in my vision, I saw the horses [forces] and the riders sitting on them [the three primary particles – Proton, Gluon and Neutron fighting against the matter particle - Electron].

The riders wore armor that was fiery red [Thymine and the adrenergic fibres] and sky blue [Thymine and the anti–bacterial navy] and yellow [Uracil and the immunoglobulin navy within the plasma]. The horses' heads were like the heads of lions, and fire and smoke and burning sulfur billowed from their mouths.

One–third of all the [bacterial] people on earth [within the body of every person] were killed by these three plagues – by the fire and the smoke and burning sulfur that came from the mouths of the horses.

Their power was in their mouths, but also in their tails. For their tails had heads like snakes, with the power to injure people [bacteria are people, too].

But the people [under Electron – Adenine and Guanine's command] who did not die in these plagues still refused to turn from their evil deeds. They continued to worship demons [Electron] and idols made of gold, silver, bronze, stone and wood [everything that mankind desires] – idols that neither see nor hear nor walk!

And they did not repent of their murders or their witchcraft or their immorality or their thefts.

Revelation 9:17 – 21

The Anti–body Air Force

In the universe, "Stars" are antibodies or "immunological armies" that take their instructions from the Gluon. These armies are ultimately responsible to Proton who gives Gluon direction and instructions. In space, stars exist free floating on air. Gluon is Lord of the Air – the Strong Force, the prince of peace.

In the humoral immune response, antibodies are also "Stars" or "immunological armies" that are responsible to Thymine and ultimately to Cytosine who gives Thymine his direction and instructions. Thymine is known by the Jewels, Christians, and Muslims throughout the world as the Archangel Michael. Cytosine is known as Cryst or "Christ".

Antibodies or "stars" exist free floating through the bloodstream, in blood and tissue fluids, just as they do in space. They are synthesized and secreted by B cells of the immune system; they are activated upon binding to substances in the body that are recognized as foreign antigens.

The forked end of the "Y" shaped "pyramidine" antibody is known as the variable binding domain or in DNA structures as Thymine. In the brain, the forked end of the "Y" sits on the Mount of Olives or the right and left lobe. The stem of the "Y" is known as the constant binding domain or in DNA structures as Cytosine.

When antibodies recognize viruses, they can block them directly by their sheer size and strength. They take their energy from the strong nuclear force. The virus will be unable to dock to a cell and infect it, hindered by the antibody. Antibodies that recognize bacteria mark them for ingestion by macrophage. Together with the plasma component complement or the armies of the Uracil, antibodies can kill bacteria directly. Using the weak nuclear force, Uracil can kill bacteria without harming the rich healthy cells in the human body.

The way that antibodies work is by binding with the specific antigen for which the antibody is "designed". This formation of the antigen–antibody results in a procedure in which cells engulf and destroy matter particles.

Antibodies are less effective if they are in low concentrations. The Second Law of Thermodynamics indicates that there are far less antibodies guarding the human body than there was in the days of Adam and Eve. As a result, they are less effective against viral infections and disease.

A viral infection can hide from an antibody so that the antibody does not destroy it when it enters the healthy cell. Bacterial infections, however, can be destroyed because they attach to the outside of the cell.

Antibodies or "stars" are effective in preventing any foreign antigens that go into the body. If an antibody can't take care of an already existing infection then it could be very effective in preventing an infection that is about to begin its process in targeting the cells. The "stars" learn and re–strategize their approach to destroying their enemies. This is how they were made by the LORD Proton. This is how the race call mankind continues to survive.

The Immunoglobulin Navy

Immunoglobulins are armies of rich plasma, iron, led by Uracil. They are dispatched from the front of the "Y" shaped pyramidine antibody, from Mount Zion – the forebrain. They receive their orders from the constant binding stem, Cytosine, who sits in the hindbrain – Jerusalem.

As Cytosine "fires" instructions to Thymine and Uracil from his seat in Jerusalem, Uracil metabolizes oxygen from the surrounding blood. Approximately 6 seconds after a burst of neural activity, a haemodynamic response occurs and that region of the brain is infused with oxygen–rich blood.

Neurons (army of the Thymine under the command of the Neutron), like all other cells, require energy to function. This energy is supplied in the form of glucose and oxygen (the oxygen being carried in haemoglobin). The blood supply of the brain is dynamically regulated to give active neural assemblies more energy while inactive assemblies receive less energy.

Plasma is grouped into five classes: **IgG, IgA, IgM, IgD,** and **IgE.**

> **IgG** is an immunoglobulin that is present in normal blood and is the most numerous. This immunoglobulin can bind to many kinds of pathogens such as viruses, bacteria, and fungi to fight against toxins. This is the source of the Neutron's bitterness, Thymine's bitterness. He must bind himself to Adenine and Guanine and play the fool. So, he is Ham, the actor waiting for an opportunity to get away.

> **IgA** represent about 15 to 20% of immunoglobulins in the blood although it is primarily secreted across the mucosal tract into the stomach and intestines. This immunoglobulin helps to fight against pathogens that contact the body surface, ingested, or inhaled.

IgM can detect whether a person has ABO blood type. It is also important in fighting bacteria.

IgD immunoglobulins make up about 1% in the plasma membranes in B–lymphocytes. These immunoglobulins are involved in the development of plasma and memory cells that are in the B–lymphocytes.

IgE is an immunoglobulin that can be found on the surface of the plasma membrane and mast cells of connective tissue. IgE can also be found in involved with diseases such as hypersensitivity and also in the defense of parasites such as worms.

Immunoglobulins are heavy plasma proteins, often with added sugar chains on N–terminal (all antibodies) and occasionally O–terminal (IgA and IgD) amino acid residues. In order to be protected from any possible antigen, the immune system led by DNA–Uracil produces millions of antibody epitopes, each differing in the variable portion that detects and attaches to an antigen.

The Land

When we look at the planet Earth, what we see underneath all of the roofs, walls, factories, and bridges is soil or "clay" and water. Water covers 71% of the Earth's surface. The Earth's core is comprised mostly of Iron (plasma) – 80% and by mass, it is comprised of Oxygen – 29.5%. It is surrounded by energy – the four forces in the Universe – Gravity, Strong Nuclear Force, Weak Nuclear Force, and the Electromagnetic Force.

When we look at the Body of Man also called "the earth", what we see underneath the makeup and beautiful clothing is soil or "clay" and water. Inside, the body is comprised of a complex arrangement of some 100,000 billion cells, water, iron or "plasma" and oxygen.

We are surrounded by and filled with Energy – with the glory of GOD.

Our bodies are kept calmly working, tick ticking like a clock by Proton as he rules the Central Nervous System using Gravity to keep us on schedule. We move and are kept together as one unit by the Gluon. Using the Strong Nuclear Force, he rules the Muscular and Skeletal system in every man. We breathe and are kept alive through the Cardiovascular System ruled by the Neutron using the Weak Nuclear Force.

Our bodies are regulated by the bacterial matter within us – food intake is converted to fuel with all excess waste eliminated daily. This was the work of Electron – the matter particle using the Electromagnetic Force in the compost generator – our stomachs.

In the end, all of us Jewels are soil based, clay. We are fruit from plants with roots that grow deep into the soil – into the land that GOD created for us – Cytosine, Thymine, and Uracil under the healing wings of the LORD Proton, Gluon and Neutron. In order for mankind to grow in the soil, in the land that GOD prepared for us from the beginning, clay has some very specific requirements

All Plants thrive in an active and vibrant environment, in "balanced soil". "Balanced" means having energy sources that enable growth – like sun, air and iron. "Balanced" means having matter particles that clean up and dispose of waste – like bacteria and fungi. Without the activities of bacterial soil organisms or matter particles, dead matter would accumulate and litter the soil surface, and there would be no food to nourish the plants during their development stage. Therefore, bacteria and fungi play key roles in maintaining a healthy soil, a healthy body.

While the mineral content of soil and its physical structure are important for a tree's well-being and for the size and sweetness of its fruit, it is the pyramidine life of the earth – Cytosine, Thymine, and Uracil – the Holy Trinity, that power the cycles of growth and provides the fertile soil in which every person born.

The Water

Bacteria or "water" are single-celled organisms, and are the most numerous denizens of the soil, with populations ranging from 100 million to 3 billion in a gram. In favourable conditions, they are capable of very rapid reproduction by binary fission (dividing into two).

Like roaches hiding behind a stove, one bacterium is capable of producing 16 million more in just 24 hours. Most bacteria – Adenine and Guanine – live in close proximity to plant roots, the reproductive organs.

Bacteria live in the water of the tissues that form the organs, cartilage, and the dermis, including the film of moisture surrounding cells. Some are able to swim by means of flagella.

The majority of the beneficial cell-dwelling bacteria requires oxygen and is termed aerobic bacteria. Adenine commands the aerobic bacterial armies. Aerobic bacteria are most active in the moist places – in the organs surrounded by the pelvic bone. The tissues and cells in these organs – stomach and reproductive organs – are rich in oxygen. Since Adenine has no oxygen in her DNA profile – $C_5N_5H_5$ – she (and her armies of bacteria) marries herself to the intestines and the abdomen, the colon, rectum, bladder, and some of the organs of regeneration. These organs and the waste within them are moist but not saturated. Saturated organs would deprive aerobic bacteria of the oxygen that they require. These organs generally have a neutral pH. Also, there is plenty of food (carbohydrates and micronutrients from organic matter or waste) available to them.

Bacteria that do not seek oxygen – $C_5N_5H_5O$ – are referred to as anaerobic bacteria. Guanine is anaerobic bacteria. Guanine tends to cause putrefaction of organic matter. Putrefaction is caused by a lack of oxygen. Like roaches, hostile conditions will not completely kill bacteria; rather, the bacteria will stop growing and move into a dormant stage, or may mutate to adapt to the new conditions.

Some positive bacteria will produce spores in order to wait for circumstances that are more favourable.

Then he [Electron] **stood waiting on the shore of the sea** [the female reproductive system].

Revelation 12:18

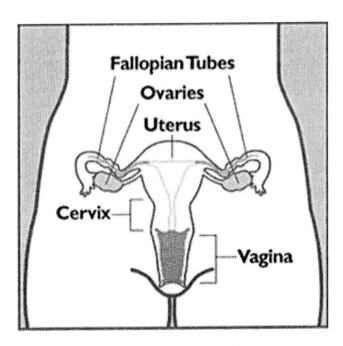

Female Anatomy

The shore of the sea is the tip of the bladder, where the uterus meets the vagina. This is Babylon, or the baby loins, a place of great pleasure and excruciating pain.

Some negative bacteria and their Gentile counterparts will move into a "non-culture" stage and refuse to grow at all.

> **At harvest time, Cain brought to the LORD a gift of his farm produce** [carbohydrates], **while Abel brought several choice lambs from the best of his flock** [protein]. [Cain was vegetarian. The carbohydrates were eaten by Cain. That is how his gift was offered to the LORD. The protein was eaten by Abel. That is how his gift was offered to the LORD.]
>
> **The LORD accepted Abel and his offering, but he did not accept Cain and his offering.** [Excess carbohydrates produce gas; produce yeast in the stomach – the compost bin.] **This made Cain very angry** [rage] **and dejected** [depression]. [Cain, the Gentile, was bi-polar – vacillating between rage and depression – like his mother, his father Adenine and Guanine, Electron or Satan.]
>
> **"Why are you so angry** [enraged, mania]**?" the LORD** [ATOM] **asked him. "Why do you look so dejected** [depressed]**?**
>
> **You will be accepted if you respond in the right way. But if you refuse to respond correctly, then watch out! Sin is waiting to attack and destroy you, and you must subdue it."**
>
> **Later Cain suggested to his brother, Abel, "Let's go out into the fields." And while they were there, Cain attacked and killed his brother** [the first Gentile, crystallized as Cain, the first murderer].

Genesis 4:3 – 8

The important roles that bacteria play in the body:

Nitrification:

A vital part of the nitrogen cycle wherein certain bacteria – Adenine, reproducing – can manufacture their own carbohydrate supply. Without using photosynthesis, these bacteria are able to transform nitrogen into a form of ammonium (purine or urine) that is produced by the decomposition of proteins. The nitrates, which are available to growing plants and all people, are converted to proteins for the second time. In the body, the nitrification process reduces the need for red meat or natural protein.

Denitrification:

Returns an approximately equal amount of nitrogen to the atmosphere. Denitrifying bacteria tend to be anaerobes – Guanine, destroying – and can alter between oxygen dependent and oxygen independent types of metabolisms.

In excess, denitrification can lead to overall losses of available nitrogen and a subsequent loss of fertility (egg and sperm production). Fixed nitrogen may circulate many times between bacterial organisms in the body and the body before denitrification returns nitrogen to tissues and organs whereby it is eventually led out of the body via the built-in filters.

Actinobacteria:

Critical in the decomposition of organic matter, and in waste formation. Their presence is responsible for the sweet aroma associated with a healthy body (generally found in babies). They require plenty of air and a pH between 6.0 and 7.5, but are more tolerant of dry conditions than most other bacteria and fungi. This is the good bacterium.

Fungi

A gram of soil or clay (in a man's body) can contain around one million fungi, such as yeasts and molds.

Many fungi are parasitic, often causing disease to their living host, to people. However, some fungi have beneficial relationships with people. In terms of clay and humus creation (the decomposed component of clay), the most important fungi tend to live on dead or decaying organic matter, thus breaking it down and converting it to forms which are available to the body as nutrients. A succession of fungi species will colonize the dead matter, beginning with those that use sugars and starches – the bloating carbohydrates. They are succeeded by those that are able to break down cellulose and lignin (the complex polymer that gives cartilage in the joints rigidity).

A fungus spreads by sending long thin threads throughout the body. These threads can be observed throughout compost heaps in the lower intestine, the stomach and bowels. Fungi threads can be identified in the body of man as cholinergic fibres.

Fungi are able to throw up their fruiting bodies, the visible part above the skin. Like mushrooms, and toadstools on the land, they show up as molds on the body, boils under the arms or between the two hams of the gluteus or butt (that stink to high heaven when they burst), as dandruff in the head or fungus on the face or under the toenails, as yeast infections in females. They contain millions of spores. The fruiting bodies confirm that there is an imbalance somewhere in the long digestion / elimination cycle. When the fruiting body bursts, their spores are dispersed to settle in fresh environments. They are able to lie dormant for years until the right conditions for their activation arise or the right food is made available to reactivate their growth.

The Cytosine / Fungi / Man relationship can be a three way harmonious trio. The Cytosine uses fungi to aid in the decomposition of dead matter, to obtain the nutrients in certain food for the organs, and for digestion. Together, the trio is a never-ending cycle of life and death. Fungi, though not glamorous, is a necessary evil within the body of man.

The lack of understanding of the delicate and complex relationships that pervade the natural systems of man is the main reason why man should not seek to enhance himself and his offspring by engaging with matter that is not well understood. Even, vitamin supplements can be helpful to some and harmful to others.

But...how would you know lest you could look inside yourself and diagnose your own imbalance? Are you a healer? No! That is the Cytosine's job. Only he can permanently fix what ails you.

The Body, the Water and the Matter

A body is a corpse or carcass. It is a mass of matter that is distinct from other masses such as a body of water or a celestial body.

Unlike Proton, Gluon and Neutron, Electron is by definition a plant – the chief matter particle – the tree of good and evil or knowledge. Proton, Gluon, and Neutron are the soil and therefore considered "dry land". The Matter Particle – Electron and her host of children and armies live and grow in soil water below the land and in the moist air around the soil.

Escherichia Coli – Adenine (Female), the Lure

Bacterium, viruses and parasites are the children and armies of Electron in the universe and within every living body – Adenine –the reproducer and Guanine – the murderer of all things healthy.

Bacteria are unicellular round, spiral or rod-shaped single-celled microorganisms that move independently by means of flagella. They live in soil, water, organic matter, or the bodies of plants and animals, and that are autotrophic, saprophytic, or parasitic in nutrition and important because of their biochemical effects and ability to cause disease.

A virus is a genus, a simple submicroscopic parasite of plants, animals, and bacteria that often cause disease and that consist essentially of a core of RNA or DNA surrounded by a protein coat. Unable to replicate without a host cell, viruses are typically not considered living organisms.

A virus is the causative agent of an infectious disease. It is any of a large group of submicroscopic infective agents that are regarded either as extremely simple microorganisms or as extremely complex molecules. A virus typically contains a protein coat surrounding an RNA or DNA core of genetic material but no semi permeable (allows some types of particles to pass through but not others) membrane, that are capable of growth and multiplication only in living cells, and that cause various important diseases in humans, animals, or plants.

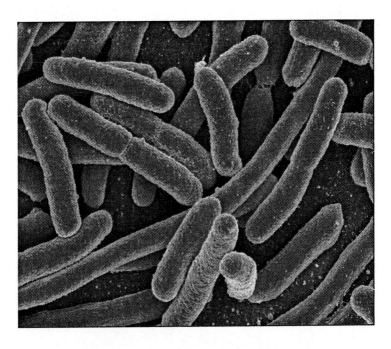

Escherichia Coli, the Parasite, Guanine

A parasite is an organism that grows, feeds, and is sheltered on or in a different organism while contributing nothing to the survival of its host.

But, life in the universe did not begin this way. It has come to be this way because of what is written in the Second Law of Thermodynamics – "in all energy exchanges, if no energy enters or leaves a system, the potential energy of a state will always be less than that of the initial state". The Second Law of Thermodynamics predicts that the entropy (degradation) of an isolated system always increases with time.

The Attacking Armies – *A Song for the Ascent to Jerusalem*

If the LORD [ATOM] had not been on our side – let Israel now say – if the LORD [ATOM] had not been on our side when people [bacteria, demons] rose up against us, they would have swallowed us alive because of their burning anger against us.

The waters [the bacteria – the wet ones] would have overwhelmed us. Yes, the raging waters of their fury would have overwhelmed our very lives [with stress anxiety, fear, conflict, disease and death].

Blessed be the LORD [ATOM], who did not let their [the demon's] teeth tear us apart! We escaped like a bird from a hunter's trap. [Cytosine saw their destructive power and sent his armies – Thymine via the Sympathetic Nervous System to free the captives, to destroy the attacking armies, the death traps.] The trap [the Parasympathetic Nervous System – from Babylon to the brain] is broken, and we are free! Our help is from the LORD [ATOM] who made the heavens [our minds] and the earth [our bodies].

Psalm 124

Now, from generation to generation, diseases have been incorporated into the DNA chain, into the genetic strand and are passed through the body of the mother to the children to the third and fourth generation; it is longer if incest is involved; shorter if there is genetic distance between the husband and wife.

Now the LORD [ATOM] descended in the cloud and stood with him [Moses] there, and proclaimed the name of the LORD [ATOM]. And the LORD passed before him and proclaimed, "The LORD, the LORD GOD [ATOM], merciful and gracious, longsuffering, and abounding in goodness and truth, keeping mercy for thousands, forgiving iniquity and transgression and sin, by no means clearing the guilty, visiting the iniquity of the fathers upon the children and the children's children to the third and the fourth generation."

Exodus 34:5 – 7

The Dissemination of the Truth after Centuries of Deception

Then I saw another mighty angel [Cyrus, GOD's anointed one] coming down from heaven, surrounded by a cloud [the amorphous GOD, ATOM], with a rainbow [all truth] over his head. His face shone like the sun [Proton], and his feet were like pillars of fire [Gluon].

Michelangelo, The Delphic Sybil, Cyrus

And in his hand was a small scroll, which he had unrolled. He stood with his right foot on the sea [Electron] and his left foot on the land [ATOM]. And he gave a great shout, like the roar of a lion. And when he shouted, the seven thunders [who is ATOM] answered. When [ATOM] the seven thunders spoke, [John] was about to write. But a voice from heaven called to [him]: "Keep secret what the seven thunders said. Do not write it down."

Then the mighty angel [Cyrus] standing on the sea [Electron] and on the land [ATOM] lifted his right hand to heaven. And he swore an oath in the name of the one who lives forever and ever [ATOM], who created heaven and everything in it, the earth and everything in it, and the sea and everything in it. He said, "GOD will wait no longer. But when the seventh angel blows his trumpet, GOD's mysterious plan will be fulfilled. It will happen just as [ATOM] announced it to his servants the prophets."

Now, don't be confused. The references to this angel, Cyrus, even the name appears to be male in gender. And yet, I am a wo–man. How can this be?

"Look at my servant [Cyrus], whom I strengthen. He [Judah] is my chosen one, and I am pleased with him. I have put my Spirit upon him. He will reveal justice to the nations. He will be gentle – he will not shout or raise his voice in public. He will not crush those who are weak or quench the smallest hope. He will bring full justice to all who have been wronged. He will not stop until truth and righteousness prevail throughout the earth. Even distant lands beyond the sea will wait for his instruction."

GOD, the LORD, [Proton] created the heavens and stretched them out. He created the earth and everything in it. He gives breath and life to everyone in all the world. And it is he who says,

"I, the LORD, have called you [Cyrus] to demonstrate my righteousness. I will guard and support you, for I have given you to my people as the personal confirmation of my covenant with them. And you will be a light to guide all nations to me. You will open the eyes of the blind and free the captives from prison [slavery to Electron, those who sit in ignorant bliss]. You will release those who sit in dark dungeons [ignorance].

"I am the LORD [ATOM]; that is my name! I will not give my glory to anyone else [neither Electron nor any man or human]. I will not share my praise with carved idols [of Jesus, of Mary, of Buddha, or any other so called god]. Everything I prophesied has come true, and now I will prophesy again. I will tell you the future before it happens."

Isaiah 42:1 – 9

The name Cyrus includes the root of the word "*ruse*"; it a subterfuge: a deceptive device by stratagem in order to conceal the hidden or secret meaning. For Cyrus, who was made in the image of the Cytosine is a woman – not a man. Cyrus is Judah – a descendant of the first man Adam or ATOM. Cyrus is made in the image of the Cytosine, the pattern and likeness of Proton.

I am **Cyrus**, the wo–**man** born to fight the dragon – Electron or Poseidon, or the devil or whatever name you wish to call him, her. I was chosen to open the scroll, record the contents and after my labour had reached its full term, deliver the child, the Word, which is the Revelation of Christ.

> **Then the voice from heaven called to** [John] **again: "Go and take the unrolled scroll from the angel who is standing on the sea and on the land." So** [John] **approached him and asked him to give me the little scroll. "Yes, take it and eat it," he said. "At first it will taste like honey** [for you are a Gentile with all of the privileges of ruling the world today]**, but when you swallow it, it will make your stomach sour!"** [Your stomach will swell up with bloat and gas from the bacteria blowing within its walls.]
>
> **So** [John] **took the little scroll from the hands of the angel, and** [he] **ate it! It was sweet in my mouth, but it made my stomach sour. Then he said to me, "You must prophesy again about many peoples, nations, languages and kings."**
>
> *Revelation 10:1 – 11*

The Temple of GOD has been Ruined

> **Then** [John] **was given a measuring stick and told to go and measure the Temple of GOD** [the body of man] **and to count the number of worshipers.**
>
> [And he was told:] **But do not measure the outer courtyard** [Mount Zion – the forebrain]**, for it has been turned over to the nations** [of Satan, of Electron and his bacterial horde of demons]**. They will trample the Holy City** [the forebrain and the hindbrain] **for 42 months** [during the time of testing].
>
> *Revelation 11:1 – 2*

> **His** [Satan's] **army** [of demon bacteria] **will take over the Temple fortress** [the outer courtyard, the forebrain]**, polluting the sanctuary** [poisoning the brain, the mind and the body with excrement, waste, bacteria]**, putting a stop to the daily sacrifices** [the daily elimination of waste from the body]**, and setting up the**

sacrilegious object [the parasympathetic nervous system built of cholinergic fibres – the path by which Satan has come to be in heaven – the minds of all men] **that causes desecration** [in the body of man – GOD's Temple].

Daniel 11:31 – 32

The Truth of the Matter

Demons are the many varieties of matter particles – quarks, muons, taus, and all spin ½ fermions. The matter particles are so densely populated throughout all the organs and upon all living tissue that the Earth – the world and the earth – your body – and all of space around it appears to be totally comprised of matter, as if matter guides us rather than the brightness of the stars. The matter waits eagerly, most impatiently outside of the wall of the nucleus of the atom. They are searching, searching for a breach in the wall – a way to get in so they can attack the Holy Ones – Proton, Gluon, Neutron and their armies of angels. For, Proton, like ATOM, exists in every atom in every living thing in all the world.

The matter particles are demons, demon spirits. In our bodies, they are called 'germs' for they carry diseases that break down the immune systems. An extreme case of demonitis is also known as halitosis – the demons are so thick in the digestive track, corroding everything, that the smell that comes up through the mouth is unbearable. You hold your breath trying not to offend anyone.

In our minds and in our thoughts, the demons are responsible for the 'negative thoughts', 'evil intentions'. They are responsible for the words that fly out unexpectedly, the words that get you into trouble, the words you kick yourself for saying. "Why did I say that?" They are responsible for the thoughts that lead people into depression, thoughts of suicide, divisiveness, thoughts of murder, thievery, materialism, idol worship, unnatural sexual acts and adultery – all of the sins that GOD hates; all of the thoughts that go against GOD's natural law of love and peace. They cover our brains and the scientist call them little gray cells, gray matter. They have invaded our bodies and our thoughts.

Though they continue to elude our physicists and researchers, Christ recognized demonic activity and he could see demons and talk to them when he walked the earth. And interestingly enough, they talked back – just as they talk to every man today.

"What is your name? Jesus asked. "Legion," he replied—for the man was filled with many demons [bacteria].

Luke 8:30

In Jesus' day, there were enough demons to fill a large herd of pigs and send them plunging down a steep hillside into a lake, where they drowned. And if you can believe the biblical account then you must believe me. For I also have seen and heard demons moving about, within and between men. I hugged a woman in church and she was so filled with demons that they jumped off her and on to me giving me a furious headache. I tried to flee from them. I could not. And neither can you. They control people you know – some more than others. They cause men to be lifted up in their own pride, to be rapists, and murderers.

Electron or Satan interacts with matter particles, demons in the human body causing random and sudden movements of the hands or fingers, unexpected knee jerks, eye twitching, and more. You may have felt this particle in action when you were shocked closing a car door. It wasn't the car that shocked you. The metal on the car was only a conductor of the electricity within you. Who has not felt the electric charge of an electron? This is the first glimpse of the evidence of something other than GOD governing us. This is the first scientific evidence that points to the demons within us.

How can I know all the sins lurking in my heart?

Cleanse me from these hidden faults. Keep me from deliberate sins! Don't let them [bacteria, demons] **control me. Then I will be free of guilt and innocent of great sin.**

May the words of my mouth and the thoughts of my heart be pleasing to you, O LORD, my rock and my redeemer.

Psalm 19:12 – 14

When an electron is put together with a positively charged nucleus, they will form atoms and atoms are subject to the forces and to explosions. Similar to the weak nuclear force, electrons are responsible for radioactive beta decay, where the beta particle is the electron. It is responsible for decomposition. It is responsible for death.

Each of the four micro particles corresponds with the character of one of the four living beings at the macro level. These four particles dominate selectively based on which of the four you are.

To review the particles and their human counterparts, there is the positively charged Proton who is called Judah and the binder particle Gluon is called Israel. There is the Neutron whose name is Jerusalem, which can go either way – to the good or to the evil. And the Gentiles are the negatively charged twins Electron.

The electron has magnetic draw. When charged particles are in motion, they produce magnetic forces on each other. The electron has electric charge. When charged particles at rest or in motion they exert electric forces on each other.

It is the same theme throughout the entire universe – the four in the five, two horns like a lamb but speaks with the voice of the dragon, attractive and repulsive, good and evil.

To recap, the three Primary Force Particles – Proton, Gluon, and Neutron enable, lead and teach. Together they make one whole being, that is called ATOM, GOD. Together they are strong, fearless and incorruptible. Separated or scattered apart from each other ... well, you can see the result in the world around you.

The Physical Nature of the Universe, Grand Unification

Four Princes	Christ	Michael	Gabriel	Dragon
Four Forces are the four horses of the apocalyse	Gravity	Strong Nuclear Force	Weak Nuclear Force	Electromagnetic Force
Primary Particles, the Riders, the Horns	*Proton*	Gluon	Neutron	Electron Adenine and Guanine
Force Particles, Angels Subatomic Level	Gravitons	Gluons/Photons, quark-anti-quark pair	W&Z bosons, neutrinos	Certain electrons at the subatomic level
DNA Base - the Eyes of GOD in the body of every person	Cytosine	Thymine	Uracil	Adenine and Guanine
Four Living Beings	Judah	Israel	Jerusalem	Gentiles
Matter Particles, Demons			Neutrinos	leptons, quarks, electrons, muons, taus, pious pions
Quark Pair Properties				up and down strange and charm top and bottom
Spin	2	1	1	1/2
Properties	Always looks the same	Looks different from different directions; same at the end point	Looks different from different directions; same at the end point	• Two-headed; bi-polar; conjoined • Must be rotated two times to see the full breath of its properties • Good and evil • Male and female in the same body
Churches/ Mankind	• Smyrna • Philadelphis	• Laodicea • Pergamum	• Thyatira	
Churches/ Humankind				• Sardis • Ephesus

Then, there are the lights or photons at the subatomic level. These are angels. The absence of the three angels is notable when the body refuses to function properly, as it was created to function. This happens when the demons take over as they have in this generation. That the body refuses to function as it was designed is evidenced when the body is in conflict with the mind. For, surrounding the central nucleus of an atom are the matter particles, electrons. It was the first particle to be discovered; the negative ones, demons showed themselves first. The scientific community was so excited about the discovery that they began to worship Electron as God, putting his symbol on every electronic thing.

Matter particles interact with everything that we can see in the universe. So what does that mean? What are matter particles?

Matter particles are negative bursts of energy. They are invasive. In human beings, matter particles cover the molecules of which our bodies are comprised. Matter particles cover our skin and the tissue underneath the skin causing us to itch, drawing our attention to the growing fungi on our bodies. They cover cartilage and collagen around our bones and in our joints. They cover our bones, our hair, our finger and toe nails. They cover everything. They interact with and affect proteins and acids – whatever the body produces to sustain itself, to reproduce itself. But most importantly, matter particles are in our blood.

The trained scientists can detect demon spirits – but the quarks have never been seen. They have only been assigned the properties listed above based on what has been detected. According to the theory written in the Standard Model of Physics, it is unlikely that anybody ever will. Neither have gravitons or neutrinos been seen directly.

But I have seen Electron. She is the invisible one who can become visible – like black smoke rising or a fruit fly appearing out of no where. More often, she can be seen from the corner of your eye, like crystal glass – visible for a second and then disappearing. She tried to scare me – coming toward me quickly and moving through me like Casper. I laughed. She is a trickster, the harmless dragon. She is a spirit – an evil spirit – who has captured the hearts of man.

Subatomic particles, which are believed to be indivisible into smaller particles, are known by physicists as fundamental particles. There are two types of fundamental particles. There are the force particles, of course – gravitons, gluons/photons, and W and Z bosons, and subatomic electrons.

A W and Z boson is a subatomic force particle like a photon. It has zero or integral / basic spin properties. Bosons that have the same spin can exist in large numbers together.

In the real world, when a large group of the ones called Jerusalem get together to praise GOD, they are like many photons sparkling in unison. Emitting from that group is a burst of concentrated light, which can be seen very well in the heavens.

Then there are the matter particles, so called because they are so dense that they appear as one unit. They have been given these names – neutrinos and electrons, muons, taus, and quarks. Often they are so dense and thickly clustered that ordinary matter particles appear to be completely comprised of them. They are like roaches covering a crumb. There can be millions in a very small space and they adapt like roaches adapt to whatever chemical is used to get rid of them. This makes them virtually indestructible.

I lay down and slept. I woke up in safety, for the LORD was watching over me. I am not afraid of ten thousand enemies who surround me on every side.

Isaiah 3:5 – 6

At the subatomic level, all except one, neutrinos, are demon spirits, Assyrian soldiers, eyes, as Ezekiel called them, or locusts as John called them.

Both the cherubim and the wheels were covered with eyes. The cherubim had eyes all over their bodies, including their hands, their backs, and their wings.

Ezekiel 10:12

A neutrino is a stable, neutral subatomic particle like a Neutron but it has almost no mass. It travels at the speed of light and it rarely interacts with matter particles. It is neutral. It can go either way.

A muon is an unstable subatomic particle, which behaves like an electron (can be positively or negatively charged) but it has a much greater mass. A muon is a locust.

A tau is also a charged, unstable subatomic particle like an electron with one difference – it is heavier than an electron. A tau is a locust.

At the subatomic level, electrons, muons, and neutrinos are grouped together in a classification called leptons (Gentile males and Jerusalem males). Leptons are weak and cannot endure or survive strong force (Gentile women or Israel) interactions. In this grouping, Jerusalem (the neutrino) has switched sides. This is a prime example of Jerusalem (neutrinos) going either way. It swings hot (for Christ – Proton) or cold (for Satan – Electron).

We have talked about the characteristics of electrons at the atomic level. They are either positively charged or negatively charged particles. At the subatomic level, they are the same. So, the only particle left to discuss is the quark. A quark is a locust with an ax to grind.

Now, a quark may be called a quark because of its random, erratic and unpredictable behaviour. I don't really know. But, like the other matter particles, it is a fundamental component that interacts with and all living things.

Ever true to the theme – four that exist in five – the quarks always come in pairs. You cannot have a single quark. There is the quark and the anti–quark just as the electron can be positively charged or negatively charged, just as the Gentiles have two horns like a lamb but speak with the voice of the dragon.

Now, no quark has been observed directly so is has been theorized that six types of quarks exist. Six types have been detected and recorded. The six types are identified as flavors: up and down, strange and charm, top and bottom. They can appear as one of the three possible colors – red, blue, or green.

But quarks are deceptive just like electrons, the electromagnetic force, the Gentiles, and Satan himself. Satan is a puppeteer – always, always pushing people in the direction of sin. He is the cause. He is the reason that perfectly righteous people snap and make very bad decisions. Satan is a ventriloquist. He can throw his voice or carry strong aromas for long distances. He is a shape shifter – appearing one way in the morning and a completely different way in the afternoon.

My enemies [demons] cannot speak one truthful word. Their deepest desire is to destroy others. Their talk is foul, like the stench from an open grave. Their speech is filled with flattery.

Psalm 5:9

Listen to the thoughts that come to your mind. Remember them, for these are the demons within you telling you what to say, what to think and how to feel. They always have a negative comment to say to you about anyone passing by. Their goal in life is to get you to sin against the Most High so that you will be lost.

Your thoughts are not your own. They are the nasty thoughts of demons within you waiting, waiting for an opportunity to cause you to sin. All of them impatiently talking at the same time. It is like a carnival full of stimuli. You don't know what to listen to first: it is all so evil, so you try to take it all in until you pick one. 'Surely these are my thoughts', you say. 'Surely these are my feelings.' Don't claim them! They are not your thoughts. They are not your feelings. Those thoughts were superimposed upon you by the ones who have nothing to lose by causing you to sin, by causing you to lose eternal life.

When you realize that you have been mislead – hoodwinked, deceived – you will have to apologize for the evil things you have said. That is, unless you are so puffed up with pride that you can't believe that something outside of that which you were created to be rules over you and causes you to say evil things.

> **Their** [demons] **mouths are full of cursing, lies and threats.** [You have heard them in your mind just as I have, making a ruckus, trying to convince you to say or do something evil.] **Trouble and evil are on the tips of their tongues** [and because of them, their evil words pass through your lips, often unexpectedly; they cause you to lie and trap you with the whistle blowers who call you out]. **They lurk in dark alleys** [in your mind, your thoughts, in the crevices of your brain]**, murdering the innocent** [angels] **who pass by. They are always searching for some helpless victim** [Judah, Jerusalem, Israel and the Gentiles]**. Like lions, they** [the demons] **crouch silently, waiting to pounce on the helpless. Like hunters, they** [the demons] **capture their victims and drag them away in nets.**
>
> *Psalm 10:7 – 9*

Like Satan, quarks are conjoined twins – never free from each other, one weeping and one destroying. Just like Electron and Gentiles, quarks always come in pairs.

So, I have concluded that there are only three types of quarks taking on different forms depending on whether they are feeling up (ready to destroy) or down (waiting to make you cry). A quark is two-faced and can take any number of shapes – the shape shifter. Like electromagnetism, quarks or demons are deceptive. Like Satan – the electron, quarks are demon spirits. They are the eyes, Assyrian soldiers and locusts.

The physicists have recorded that quarks are massless subatomic particles with a spin of ½ – they must be rotated two complete times before you can fully see what they look like, what they are up to. They are demon spirits that influence how we think and act. That is why David wrote:

> **Create in me a clean heart, O GOD. Renew a right spirit within me.**
>
> **Do not banish me from your presence, and don't take your Holy Spirit from me. Restore to me again the joy of your salvation, and make me willing to obey you.**
>
> *Psalm 51:10 – 11*

Now listen to my argument and tell me if it does not make sense to you. I am not in the habit of blaming others for my shortcomings ... but I know the truth of the matter. Let's call a spade a spade.

Who would rather do the wrong thing or say the wrong thing at the wrong time and offend someone mistakenly? I would not. I would rather tell the truth, say the right thing at the right time to lift someone up! I would rather not make mistakes, or live in pain and misery –– if I had control over the source. But today, I don't have any control over my life, my words, my way. My days are not my own. My nights are not my own. My spirit is not my own. For, every single moment is coveted by the evil one, by Electron, who is Satan herself. Satan – the smooth talker, with the lithe tongue, smooth like satin. In fact, that is exactly where her name comes from. But what is satin but a man-made material – silk and rayon, smooth with a glossy face on the front and a dull back. And so Satan was man made – by ATOM – the first Man before mankind was created. For, we Jewels are mankind. GOD is Man.

What man chooses – of his own volition – to be spiteful, tyrannical, mean spirited, vengeful?

What man chooses – of his own volition – to be frustrated, unhappy, fearful, discouraged, aggravated?

What man chooses – of his own volition – to be tired, brought low, to drag his feet, to wallow in his own pity?

No man chooses misery over joy seeing those two side by side! But … if joy is hidden, covered up, he accepts misery as if it is his only option.

It is the spirit within man that keeps the problems stewing, a brew of dissension on the fire that is life.

Would a benevolent GOD, a benevolent Spirit be the author of lies and dissension. No. Like begets like. A vengeful and evil spirit will hand you lies, half–truths, myths, and bogus dreams.

Who would rather forget things or lose things or find things he doesn't want to find – if he could control this power. If he could control it – he would forget what he wants to forget. He would remember what he wants to remember. For, what man would rather lose his mind if he could keep it? Who would not rather have a healthy body with eyes that see and ears that hear? I venture to say that everyman would rather live than to die, to be happy than to be alone and in misery. Today you have but one choice. You will die. And that is that.

However, there is a way to live. But you must choose him. His name is Proton. He is life. He is peace.

Reverend Jim Jones: People's Temple Massacre, Guyana:

What began as a beautiful, idealist, peaceful and seemingly Christian society ended as a horrible cult where 918 adults and children were commanded to commit suicide or were murdered – a human tragedy. It was dubbed as one of the most appalling events of murder in age – the age of the Gentile rule. The Reverend Jim Jones was a Gentile, Satan's son, Adenine's lover.

Everyone speculated on what happened. They looked at the events but could not clearly see the cause. How did it go so terribly wrong?

The answer is a simple entropy equation.

As evilness increases, goodness decreases.

The Reverend began as the spiritual leader, reading GOD's word. Then he took on additional wives to satisfy Adenine's sexual desire of which he was filled. And with sexual desire and fulfillment of that desire comes confidence, comes delusions of grandeur, arrogance, pride and finally rage against those who were given the wisdom to see the truth of the matter, those who dared to point it out.

I liken the Gentile twin mind to the series Highlander. It is both good and evil, but in the end, there can be only one ruler. The one with the violent and bloody sword is the one left standing. This has been proven over and over. I don't have to give you examples of this. Watch the news! What Gentile murdered his wife last night in a sudden fit of fury? What quiet and sweet Gentile kid took a gun into a school and shot the ones who laughed at him and then turned the gun upon himself. The one who is both good and evil will show his true self to you. Then he will self–destruct. He will cave in upon himself. He will implode – the evil within him overtaking his inclination to do good. This is the cause and Adenine's demons is the source of the matter. This is an unexpected flash of randomness. This is disorder. And this is entropy.

Adolph Hitler and the Nazi Invasion:

Entropy, however, was not the case with Adolph Hitler. It was the scattering, the deception that led Adolph into the arms of Electron, of Satan.

Adolph Hitler was a Jewel of GOD. He was a Jewel just as surely as I am standing before you today. His name was my name. His name was Judah.

Satan spoke to him and told him the task for which he had been predestined. He accepted, taking dictation from Electron and writing the book, Mein Kampf, that would become his bible just as Electron dictated the Koran to Mohammed. Adolph accepted believing that Satan was GOD, believing that Electron was Proton, believing that the evil one was the Holy One, believing that the Final Solution was good, for the benefit of mankind. He was blinded just as you were before I began to tell you the truth.

For, Adolph was born for the task just as surely as I was born to tell you the truth and to introduce you to the one who made you; just as Judas (a Jewel) was predestined to betray

Christ; just as Peter (a Jewel) was predestined to deny him.

Hitler's mission and motive were simple and clear from the beginning: The poor were feeling the hand of oppression in Germany – a true statement for every time. The rich, ergo, the Jews are oppressing the poor. The solution: organize and eradicate oppression; destroy the Jews.

What began as an innocent, almost noble idea (why else would a whole nation be deceived into following it?) turned into a mission of murder. And momentum carried it as far as it could go. It could not be stopped. The ones in charge of the research camps and the killing camps were largely Gentiles. The ones who tested the methods of murder were Gentiles. The ones who tested removing parts of brains to make people into zombies were Gentiles – working with Satan to see if there was a way to eliminate Cryst, Cytosine, from the minds of men so that she Adenine could be the sole ruler over the minds of men.

How could they know the source of their treachery? This is the age of deception. Every man is operating under a cloud of deception. Even you Elders are preaching Satan's lies. Some of you know it; some of you don't. But it doesn't matter. You too will have to choose.

And this was Satan's plan – pretend to be Christ returning to save his children, eliminate the Jews – the Jewels of GOD and reign supreme for one thousand years – the Thousand Year Reich. Eliminate all of those who seek the truth. Purify the race of humans so that only Gentiles remain – the children of Satan and those who would serve them.

But even with the many millions of Jews that were killed, they could not destroy GOD's seed, his children, who were from the beginning of time.

The children of GOD are three. The children of Satan are two in one body. When you kill GOD's children, you kill Satan's children. We are all intertwined, tightly knit vines covering the earth, the helix and the double helix together. You cannot kill one without killing the other. For the Gentile mother holds her Jewel children to her breast. For the Jewel mother does not understand her Gentile children but has been told that she must love and protect them – no matter what evil they do.

Satan's thousand–year reign only lasted six years. He had the same failed attempt when he killed boy babies during the days of Moses and during the days of the birth of Christ. And the same failed attempt when he used the Catholics to kill the Jews during the days of Tomás de Torquemada – the Spanish Inquisition that lasted until the 19th century.

Neither your children, nor your bombs can kill all of the Jews of GOD. And is GOD going to allow Satan to destroy his creation and his son – Proton who is Cryst?

No, but mankind chose to be deceived. We chose to follow the evil one, so caught up in her lies and her love for sex.

And GOD allowed this treachery. This was GOD's plan: Show them how easy it is for them to be deceived. Let them witness the horror and experience it so they will forever know.

It has happened before. It is happening now. Mankind has been deceived. You follow the evil one and his Gentile children rule over you. They are your judges, your policemen, doctors, and lawyers. They keep your children at the day care. They are your bosses, your friends. They entertain you in your theatres. They are your wives, your husbands, your children. You kowtow to them trying to please them, to keep the rage and the tears at bay.

And with all that you have seen, you still pretend not to know what it means. But you belong to GOD! Should three bow down to one who is nothing at all?

But, don't take these matters in your own hands, Israel. Vengeance is mine saith the LORD Proton. GOD will give you wisdom concerning these things. He will make right what is wrong. It is his responsibility. He has his own plan and he will implement it when the time is right.

But in the future, Israel – the Thymine branch of the LORD – will be lush and beautiful, and the fruit of the land will be the pride of its people.

All those whose names are written down, who have survived the destruction of Jerusalem, will be a holy people.

The LORD will wash the moral filth from the women of Jerusalem [Uracil]. He will cleanse Jerusalem of its bloodstains by a spirit of judgment that burns like fire.

Isaiah 4:2 – 4

Though you may not have realized it, Satan is your master. He and his demons rule your every thought, your words are his words, and your actions are his actions. You have said yourself that you don't know why you did what you did. If you deny it, you will be lost. If you admit it, GOD will show you the error in you life so you can be saved.

Now, the strong, well-respected Gentile policeman suddenly goes berserk and takes justices into his own hands. He becomes unrestrained as he spins into a state of frenzy. He goes out of control. He will beat the accused, so strong is the electromagnetic force within him. He will murder the accused and later regret it. For an uncontrollable moment, he was overtaken by the rise, the electromagnetic force. Through that force, he was given immutable power, lifted up above his station high into the air. In this state of invincibility, the one who has sworn to uphold the law breaks the law and justifies his action. He cannot see it any different. He is confused and full of lies, lies the demons have told him and they hold him tightly.

Then the accused becomes the victim. Everyone looks for the reason, the smoking gun in past events, in childhood. The father left. The mother did not love. The lover rejected. The teacher did not teach.

But, this is an unexpected flash randomness that had been brewing, like a cup of tea suddenly coming to a rolling boil. This is disorder. And this is entropy. There is no sustainable reason that you can put your forefinger upon. Electron rose up and Adenine, having a bad day, decided that it was a good day for someone to die. Every other explanation is speculation, is lies, is insignificant. This is root cause. Electron needs to unify her Gentile children and in doing so, she will enslave and subdue the children of ATOM.

Patty Hearst and the SLA

Another well-publicized case is that of Patty Hearst and the SLA. Patty Hearst, the heiress and daughter of newspaper tycoon William Randolph Hearst, was kidnapped in 1974 by the radical Symbionese Liberation Army (SLA). The official story is that she was brainwashed and assumed the name 'Tania'.

However, she is a Gentile and Gentiles love causes. They are naturally inclined to support perceived injustice – starving children, children dying of cancer, people dying of Aids. Her inclination to support causes made her a sympathizer and a participant in the very crimes from which she would eventually be rescued. She willingly joined the army, and participated in the same crimes that they were known to have committed. It is an unexpected turn of events. This is an unexpected flash randomness, a turn of events. This is disorder. And this is entropy.

Entropy shows how the mind of Judah has deteriorated, becoming simple – no longer respected. It demonstrates how Israel has become increasingly violent – not caring what anyone thinks of her including her Father in heaven. It demonstrates how Jerusalem has become more bitter and angry, ready to fight in a moment so strong are the spin ½ matter particles within him.

Therefore, over time, entropy is constantly increasing because energy flows toward diffusion in the real world just as the universe continues to expand apparently without end. This expansion could only have begun from a single source. And who would know these things except the one who created that single source.

From the single ATOM– Proton came the entire universe, came life.

From a single man Adam – Judah and his helper Eve – Israel, came all men, came all sin, all debauchery, all bacteria, all death.

What was done cannot be undone. What is now learned cannot be unlearned. It's time to choose. It's time for the vote.

The Two Witnesses

Then the angel who was talking with me came forward and said,

"Look up! Something is appearing in the sky."

"What is it?" I asked. He replied,

"It is a basket for measuring grain [grain is mankind], and it is filled with the sins of everyone throughout the land."

When the heavy lead cover was lifted off the basket, there was a woman sitting inside it [Electron or Satan]. The angel said,

"The woman's name is Wickedness," and he pushed her back into the basket and closed the heavy lid again.

Then I looked up and saw two women [John, the Revelator and Cyrus] flying toward us, with wings gliding on the wind.

Their wings were like those of a stork [they delivered the Word of GOD to all people, the coded Revelation and the decoded Revelation]**, and they picked up the basket and flew with it into the sky.**

"Where are they taking the basket?" I asked the angel. He replied,

"To the land of Babylonia, where they will build a temple for the basket. And when the temple is ready, they will set the basket there on its pedestal."

Zechariah 5:5 – 11

The apostle John is a woman by way of the DNA chain. He is a Gentile, both male and female in the same body, as are all Gentiles. I am a woman by gender, but I am a man by way of the DNA chain – Cytosine, modeled after the first pattern Proton, of the lineage of Adam whose name is called Judah in heaven, the first son of GOD whose name is ATOM.

That Babylonian temple is ready. That woman, the Dragon, will be delivered in her basket to the Temple of Babylonia when the Time of Testing has ended.

Now, the truth can finally be revealed. This is the beginning of the **end** of the Age of Deception, the Age of the Gentiles. The Time of Testing has begun. Soon the Day of Armageddon will arrive. But before that day, you will know the whole truth and the truth is a firm foundation. It is the only rock that will make you free.

And the revelation reads:

And I will give power to my two witnesses, and they will be clothed in sackcloth and will prophesy during those 1,260 days." These two prophets are the two olive trees and the two lampstands that stand before the Lord of all the earth.

The two witnesses are the two angels of the revelation and the two olive trees. The LORD explained these two olive trees to the prophet Zechariah. Zechariah recorded:

Then I asked the angel, "What are these two olive trees on each side of the lampstand, and what are the two olive branches that pour out golden oil through two gold tubes?"

Then he said to me, "They represent the two anointed ones [John, the revelator and Cyrus, the revealer] **who assist the LORD of all the earth."**

Zechariah 4:11 – 12, 14

Daniel also saw the two witnesses to the Revelation.

Then I, Daniel looked and saw two others standing on opposite banks of the river.

Daniel 12:5

If anyone tries to harm them, fire flashes from the mouths of the prophets and consumes their enemies. This is how anyone who tries to harm them must die. [Like Elijah] They have power to shut the skies so that no rain will fall for as long as they prophesy. And they have the power to turn the rivers and oceans into blood, and to send every kind of plague upon the earth as often as they wish.

When they complete their testimony, the beast that comes up out of the bottomless pit [the bladder and bowels] will declare war against them. He will conquer them and kill them. And their [bacterial] bodies will lie in the main street of Jerusalem, the city which is called "Sodom" and "Egypt," [feces flows into the main street when men die] the city where their Lord was crucified.

And for three and a half days, all [bacterial] peoples, tribes, languages, and nations will come to stare at their bodies [consuming them – the contaminated blood, the puss, the feces]. No one will be allowed to bury them. All the people who belong to this world will give presents to each other to celebrate the death of the two prophets who had tormented them. But after three and a half days, the spirit of life from GOD entered them, and they stood up! And terror struck all [demons, bacteria] who were staring at them.

Then a loud voice shouted from heaven, "Come up here!" And they rose to heaven in a cloud as their enemies watched. And in the same hour there was a terrible earthquake that destroyed a tenth of the city. Seven thousand people died in that earthquake. And everyone who did not die was terrified and gave glory to the GOD of heaven.

The second terror is past, but look, now the third terror is coming quickly. Then the seventh angel blew his trumpet, and there were loud voices shouting in heaven: "The whole world has now become the Kingdom of our Lord [ATOM] and of his Christ [Proton], and he will reign forever and ever."

And the twenty–four elders sitting on their thrones before GOD fell on their faces and worshiped him. And they said, "We give thanks to you, Lord GOD Almighty, [ATOM] the one who is and who always was, for now you have assumed your great power and have begun to reign.

The nations were angry with you, but now the time of your wrath has come. It is time to judge the dead and reward your servants. You will reward your prophets and your holy people, all who fear your name, from the least to the greatest. And you will destroy all who have caused destruction on the earth."

The Ark of the Covenant

Michelangelo, Arc of the Covenant

Then, in heaven [the mind], the Temple of GOD [the brain] was opened and the Ark of his covenant could be seen inside the Temple. Lightning flashed, thunder crashed and roared; there was a great hailstorm, and the world was shaken by a mighty earthquake.

Revelation 11:3 – 19

This is the crown that the elders lay before the throne. You lay down your crown when you bow your head. This is the gold crown that I wear. The outer courtyard is where all information is received. It passes through the Holy Place and is scrutinized and validated. In the Most Holy Place truth is revealed.

Then I witnessed in heaven an event of great significance. I saw a woman [Cyrus] clothed with the sun [the LORD Proton], with the moon [Neutron] beneath her feet, and a crown of twelve stars [Gluon] on her head. She was pregnant [bursting full with the Word, the truth], and she cried out in the pain of labour [what misery!] as she awaited her delivery.[68]

Suddenly, I witnessed in heaven another significant event. I saw a large red dragon with seven heads [sitting on the seven lampstands] and ten horns [all men], with seven crowns on his heads [every man's head has a crown circling the temple lobes].

His tail dragged down one–third of the [three] stars [Neutron is the one he dragged down], which he threw to the earth.

He [Electron] stood before the woman as she was about to give birth to her child, ready to devour the baby as soon as it was born. She gave birth to a boy [ATOM, the Word, in the beginning was the Word, truth] who was to rule all nations with an iron rod[69]. And the child [truth] was snatched away from the dragon and was caught up to GOD and to his throne.

And the woman [Cyrus] fled into the wilderness, where GOD had prepared a place to give her care for 1,260 days.

---

68   The misery of Cyrus is this: a band of spider's silk tightly wound around the forehead and over the top of the two lobes that was unbearable just to the point of fainting; boney hands around my neck choking me; fierce cramps in the bowels and stomach; a pitch of gas from the abdomen to the brain knocking out oxygen and leaving the victim in a heap on the floor; searing pain under the finger nails and at the tips of the fingers; swollen and pulsating blood filled toes, fingers, hands to stop me from working; swollen feet and legs; sudden stab wounds over my body, like a bee aiming her stinger and attacking full force; day and night; night and day as I slept sitting up in a chair, unable to get any rest any other way; cursing, vile name calling, threats and lies. These have been my days and nights during this period of discovery.

69   Truth will rule all nations with an iron rod. According to Daniel, when Electron was allowed to rule the minds of men, truth was overthrown (Daniel 8:12).

Then there was war in heaven. Michael and the angels under his command fought the dragon and his angels. [It is the Armageddon you fear; the war of all versus all within every head, every mind.]

And the dragon lost the battle and was forced out of heaven [the minds of men]. This great dragon – the ancient serpent called the Devil, or Satan, the one deceiving the whole world – was thrown down to the earth [the bowels and bladder] with all his [bacterial] angels.

Then I heard a loud voice shouting across the heavens, "It has happened at last – the salvation and power and kingdom of our GOD, and the authority of his Christ! For the Accuser has been thrown down to earth – the one who accused our brothers and sisters before our GOD day and night. And they have defeated him because of the blood of the Lamb and because of their testimony. And they were not afraid to die.

During the first year of my incarceration, I read the bible, the Holy Word of GOD and learned the names of the four living beings, their characters and behaviours from the Apostles and Prophets – Paul, Isaiah, Ezekiel, Samuel, Job, Amos, Jeremiah, Malachi, and Daniel, and from the sacred parables of Christ written by the four apostles – Matthew – Judah, Mark – Israel, Luke – Jerusalem, and John – the Gentile. I studied to prove myself worthy of GOD's wisdom, of Proton's knowledge.

During the second year of my persecution, I studied the sciences – the laws of GOD and learned how the world was created and the technical names assigned to each function under the Sun. I chuckle now at the heroes of science – Galileo, the Einsteins and the Newtons and the theorists who came before and after them. For the laws, mathematical equations, and even the names of the subatomic particles existed long before physicists, biologists, and archeologists were allowed to observe them and theorize about their meaning. The Creator made his invisible creation observable to physicists just as he showed Adam the animals in the Garden of Eden and gave him license to name them and to record his observations. The quarks and anti–quarks – the red, the green, the strange and the charmed, leptons, muons, and taus, pions were names spoken to men and women of science by the Creator, through Uracil or Gabriel who speaks to all men. The brilliance of your scientific heroes is the brilliance of the Creator. They were chosen to know the truth – just as I was chosen to observe it. The crystalline author of the universe chose to honor them. Now, he has chosen to honor me.

During the third year, how those two great disciplines – science and religion – fit together, hand and glove was revealed to me. And though I did not always understand why immediately, I observed all of the truth written here and will testify to its accuracy.

During the entire 3 years, I studied Satan, Electron – her habits, her misery, her tricks, and traps, her constant presence in the lives of men – until I came to know her and recognize her lies as no man could. Finally, during the last six months of my incarceration, I learned why Satan behaves as she does – a murdering sex addict; it is written in her DNA. And once I understood her genetic behaviour, I began to understand the behaviour of the Creator and his Son and the Holy Spirit, and finally I began to see the why of the four living beings. I came to know the root cause of this evil state that we call real life. And then I learned the two things that can stop Electron's obsessive behaviour. The first is rejection – do not accept her gifts – neither her ideas, nor her songs, nor her offers of pleasure – or she will claim you as her own.

The second thing that will stop her is to defer to the wisdom of GOD, the Most High, the Mighty Proton, to call upon Cryst's name – Proton. Whatever you ask in his name – you shall have it and it won't be long in coming. It will arrive when you least expect it.

During these long months of labour, I learned to wait without whining, without wanting.

Take your burdens to the LORD. Lay them down and leave them there.

Bebe Winans

GOD, the LORD Proton, Cytosine is more committed to our success than we could possibly imagine. When I wait on him, he rewards me with unimaginable treasures – wisdom, joy, honor and great prosperity. I learned to move when the Gluon moves me and to listen to the Neutron for the wisdom of GOD. Before I had time to think about it, I found myself rising from my seat, boldly walking with great confidence, my arms in a steady stride and a smile on my lips. This happened through no will of my own. I learned to trust in the Almighty Proton and his many armies to protect and deliver me as he has sworn by his own name, Proton, to do. He does the same for you – everyday.

Against great odds, I have come through a trial of fire to know the truth. And now, it is time for you to see the Word as he truly is – in all of his magnificent glory. Now, everyone will see him as I have seen him. Observe in silence the things that he has told me to tell you. This is my delivery.

Rejoice, O heavens! And you, who live in the heavens, rejoice! But terror will come on the earth and the sea. For the Devil has come down to you in great anger, and he knows that he has little time." [It is the time of testing that has come upon the entire whole.]

And when the dragon [Electron] realized that he had been thrown

down to the earth, he pursued the woman [Cyrus] who had given birth to the child. But she was given two wings like those of a great eagle. This allowed her to fly to a place prepared for her in the wilderness, where she would be cared for and protected from the dragon for a time, times, and half a time [literally, the rest of her life].

Then the dragon tried to drown the woman with a flood of water that flowed from its mouth. [The flood of water is tears for all of those that are being violently massacred by Electron every day now.] But the [crystalline] earth [Proton] helped her by opening its mouth and swallowing the river that gushed out from the mouth of the dragon.

Then the dragon became angry at the woman, and he declared war against the rest of her children – all who keep GOD's commandments and confess that they belong to Jesus [the crystalline, the Cryst whose name is Proton].

Revelation 12:1 – 17

The Name of Jesus Christ

Every thing has a purpose and a reason. Many, we can easily see and understand; others are more complex and must be revealed to us. It is in this vein that I discovered the meaning of the name of the crucified one – **Jesus Christ.**

Christ is an abbreviation of whom and what the Lamb is; he is the crystallized manifestation of his Father, the omnipotent Amorphous Spirit – Energy, the LORD Proton. Crystallized means you can see him. Cryst is the phonetical value of the Word Christ. It is the pronunciation of the word that holds its meaning – not the semantical value. Now, I am Christ and so are you and every living being. I am the physical image of the invisible GOD. I am the brightness of his glory. *ATOM* is the first and the last, the future and the past. ATOM is GOD. Anyone who can be seen or touched is Christ, is Cryst, the crystallized manifestation of the Father – LORD Proton. When you see my face – you see Cryst or Christ. When I see your face, I see Cryst or Christ. Christ is a title – not a surname.

As surely as I live, says the Sovereign LORD [ATOM], I will rule you with an iron fist in great anger and with awesome power. With might and fury I will bring you out from the lands where you are scattered. I will bring you into the wilderness of the nations, and there I will judge you face–to–face [mind to mind, hindbrain to forebrain]. I will judge you there just as I did your ancestors in the wilderness [with justice and truth] after bringing them out of Egypt, says the Sovereign LORD. I will count you carefully and hold you to the terms of the covenant [all of the laws of GOD – the laws of Physics, the laws of procreation and regeneration and the Ten Commandments, which ATOM wrote with his own hand]. **I will purge you** [Jewels] **of all those who rebel and sin against me** [Gentiles]. **I will bring them out of the countries where they are in exile – but they will never enter the land of Israel** [Jerusalem – the Holy City – the hindbrain]. **And when that happens, you will know that I** [Proton] **am the LORD.**

Ezekiel 20:33 – 38

Now, in like manner, the name Jesus is a 'tag line', a slogan, a product identifier, a descriptor – not a name. That is why no other man born to woman has been named Jesus or Christ. Remember that GOD – ATOM is the Word, the Logos, the first person, the first pronoun. He is the "I" (I am that, I am) and the "eye", omnipotent and omnipresent, seeing everything, everywhere. He uses words in any way he chooses.

Toward the end of my incarceration, I was thinking about the name Jesus. What does it mean? Why was that name chosen, Jesus? Knowing that there are no coincidences or accidents in the universe, I knew it meant something. But at the time, I could not decipher a semantical meaning. Then on 3–22–05, early in the morning, I heard it's phonetical meaning and I laughed aloud – Jesus. Jesus is the tag line for Christ. It is a slogan, a repeated phrase associated with an individual or organization or product. The slogan is: "Gee, he's us!" I heard it in Donnie McClurkin's song – *Jesus, the Mention of Your Name* from the 1996 CD *Stand*. GOD is quite brilliant in how he reveals the truth. He is creative in all of his ways. Everyday I am amazed to know him, at how much he has taught me in this three years. He focused my attention.

"Je–hez–us. Je–hez–us. At the mention of your name every knee will bow and tongue proclaim." "Je–hez–us. Je–hez–us. You are Saviour, you are LORD and you are GOD.

Donnie McClurkin broke down the word Jesus into three syllables – not two. Then I could hear the intended meaning, the slogan – "He's us!" He lives within us. ATOM is us, every man. It is what GOD told Moses – "I am that! I am." It's why we say "Amen" when we pray. The LORD *ATOM* is all men. We have shortened it to "Amen". He is all men. How else could Nebuchadnezzar have eaten grass like a cow for 7 years and then wake up to recognize that there is a higher power that exists within us, a power that controls our lives, leads us, the sheep of his pasture.

Sadly, the anti–Christ, Electron, is also "Je–hez–us". For today, for now, Electron also lives within us. The Sympathetic Nervous System – Proton against the Parasympathetic Nervous System – Electron, Jerusalem and Babylon – life and death commingled. But we need the LORD *ATOM*. We would not last one day without him. He is life itself and the source of all light. Electron is only death and the grave.

As for me, I am that! I am. I am the "Gem", the Jewel sent by GOD, the LORD Proton, to read the scroll, to tell the truth. These are not titles I chose for myself. No! These are the names my Father – *ATOM* called me when I delivered the Child, the Word – his testimony. I am Christ or Cryst, but so are you. Until this time, only the LORD Proton and his angels knew what the words Jesus and Christ meant. Now, I am reminded of the true meaning every time I write the name my mother gave me. The C is for Cryst or the crystalline man made from the dust of diamonds from the time of the Big Bang. The J is for Jesus or "He's us!" and my married name Allen tells me that all men are Cryst, are Christ; all men are Jesus or "He's all of us!" Now, every-man can see GOD – ATOM – face–to–face. You see him in all of his glory when you look up in the sky and see his home, the Sun. His face shines upon your face, lighting your way. You see him when you see my face. *ATOM* cannot be contained. He chooses to cover himself so that we who walk upon his Earth can live. Without his covering of protection – the sun – we would burn up.

ATOM accomplished this nearly impossible feat – deciphering the scroll, showing me the patterns in the universe, in the Scriptures, in the world – succinctly summarizing the good and the evil of human existence, delivering it to the one who would publish it, and convincing the publisher to read the Word with understanding. The LORD Proton accomplished this by his might, by his power – even when I unwittingly tried to sabotage his plans. But he knew in advance what I was up against – the desire for peace against the persistence of persecution. Today, every man is free and every man is a prisoner – the battle of the centaurs, Jerusalem against Babylon.

The Beast Out of the Sea

Then he stood waiting on the shore of the sea.

Revelation 12:18

Just as you have seen ATOM, I want you to see Electron as she really is and to know her as I have come to know her.

Donatello, Satan Unmasked

Electron is the praying mantis: holier than
thou before he devours the flesh of her victims.

In the world of bacteria, some is good (will save your life) and some is downright deadly (will eat you alive, suck your blood and devour your flesh, use the water within you to decay whatever is left).

You have seen the virus e–coli and of its killing power. You have heard its scientific name – Escherichia Coli. It is both aerobic and anaerobic bacteria; both beautiful and ugly, good and evil. Electron is a plant, just like the bacteria and viruses she spawns. She shelters a murderous brood; they are the children of the corn; marked as killers before they are born.

And now in my vision I saw a beast rising up out of the sea. It had seven heads [that rest on the seven lampstands] **and ten horns** [good and evil]**, with ten crowns** [the crowns of every person's head] **on its horns.**

And written on each head were names that blasphemed GOD.

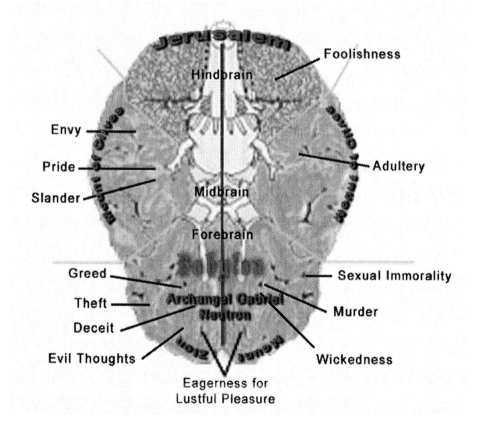

Names that Blaspheme GOD, ATOM

This beast looked like a leopard [Jerusalem]**, but it had bear's feet** [Israel] **and a lion's mouth** [Judah]**! And the dragon gave him** [mankind] **his own power and throne and great authority.**

I saw that one of the heads of the beast seemed wounded beyond recovery – but the fatal wound was healed! [Electron is dead; and yet, he lives.] **All the world marveled at this miracle and followed the beast in awe.**

Revelation 13:1 – 3

Electron

According to the scientific data and every eleventh grader's physics book, Electron is known to have the following properties:

- An electron is a stable subatomic particle in the lepton family having a rest mass of $9.1066 \times 10{-}28$ grams and a unit negative electric charge of approximately $1.602 \times 10{-}19$ coulombs.

- Electrons are all of one kind, so far as known, and can only be described as "afterbirth". Matter or bacteria is a component found in all life, in all atoms. It is any of various small circumscribed multi–cellular bodies.

- The bodies of men are comprised of atoms. An atom which has an electron attached has a negative charge. An atom from which an electron has been detached has a positive charge.

- Within man's body and without, electron is an **undead organism**, also called a **corpuscle**, a corpse. A corpuscle is a minute particle. It is a living cell; especially one as a red or white blood cell or a cell in cartilage or bone. A corpuscle is not aggregated into continuous tissues but dispersed randomly.

- The electrons in the body causes and speeds up decay in blood, in cartilage, and in bones.

- Electrons move water. Water can be found in any of the fluids normally eliminated from the body, such as urine, perspiration, tears or saliva – all of which contain bacteria. Elimination or clean up is why the electrons were created. Electrons are responsible for cleanup and elimination.

Scientists and engineers of this generation assume that she is called "Electron" because of her electric charge and credit her with electrical power putting her fast moving icon on anything related to power. But she is not the source of electricity or power. She is only a conductor of light using electromagnetic waves.

O, she can shut down your power grids in a fit of rage as she did from New York to Canada in 2003. She can cause your equipment to stop working as she has mine. She can bring a virus down to destroy your files and design intriguing crop circles in a field. She is full of tricks. She is Puck, the trickster. And if you have ever had an occasion to stomp on the gas when you intended to brake, Electron was using the electromagnetic force to guide your foot into a speeding disaster. And if you have ever had a sudden debilitating headache, an unexplained high fever, a sudden rush of fear, a sudden urge to urinate, an unstoppable desire to cry.

She is a destroyer. I watched her cause the space ship Columbia to disintegrate killing GOD's scientists, seven Jewels with one blow. She can only carry light waves because of her electromagnetic mass. She is not the source of the power. Proton is the source of all Power. But she shows herself in the midst of it leading you to believe that she is GOD.

They [all men] **worshiped the dragon** [Electron or Satan, calling him God] **for giving the beast** [mankind] **such power, and they worshiped the beast** [they worshiped themselves, the I-dolls]. **"Is there anyone as great as the beast?"** ["Is there anyone as great as us?"] **they exclaimed. "Who is able to fight against him?"**

Then the beast was allowed to speak great blasphemies against GOD [against ATOM, using the mouths of men]. **And he** [Electron or the beast] **was given authority to do what he wanted for forty–two months** [during the time of testing].

And he spoke terrible words of blasphemy against GOD[70], slandering his name and all who live in heaven [seek the truth], **who are his temple** [your body is his body; ATOM crystallized to be you]

And the beast was allowed to wage war against GOD's holy people and to overcome them. And he was given authority to rule over every tribe and people and language and nation [every body, every mind].

And all the people who belong to this world worshiped the beast. They are the ones whose names were not written in the Book of Life, which belongs to the Lamb who was killed before the world was made.

---

70   The most awful blasphemy against ATOM is Electron saying and pushing men to say that mankind evolved from bacteria as if she created the world. What a crock of crap that is!

Anyone who is willing to hear should listen and understand.

Revelation 13:4 – 9

The Book of Life, the Lamb's Book of Life

Every Jewel and every Gentile's name is recorded in the **Book of Life**. **The Book of Life is** the DNA record, the genetic serial number assigned to each person. It is a complex record of every man's life. It is how ATOM knows everything you do – the good and the bad. Everything is recorded there.

Michelangelo, The Books

However, everyone's name is not written in the **Lamb's Book of Life** – the one that was written before the world was made. It is a very small book. There are only nine names in that book. They are Proton, Gluon and Neutron – the force particles, the rulers of the planet Earth. And there is Cytosine, Thymine, and Uracil – the rulers of the Sympathetic Nervous System in every person's body, also called the earth or clay. And finally, there is Judah, Israel and Jerusalem – GOD's three Jewels, made in the image of Proton, Gluon and Neutron and produced in a 12–year cyclical birth pattern. The double helix will be snatched out of the DNA chain and thrown into the lake of fire – when Satan – Electron is thrown into the lake of fire. No more Gentiles will be born after the 1000 year Reign of Cryst has ended. There will be peace among all of mankind. But ... the Gentiles who are chosen by GOD's son – Proton – shall have eternal life just as Christ promised.

The people who are destined for prison will be arrested and taken away. Those who are destined for death will be killed. But do not be dismayed, for here is your opportunity to have endurance and faith.

Revelation 13:10

In the Garden of Eden, Electron was chosen by Eve after the temptation – for pleasure called "joy strong".

Bacteria were the source of Eve's pleasure – the contents of Pandora's Box. Satan planted her mentally unstable, erratic, bipolar, manic depressant, attention deficit, bisexual seed within Eve's unfertilized egg using that ancient tool – the flagella. After her body was infected with the virus, Eve lay with her husband, Adam and Satan's Gentile son was born – Cain.

The straight DNA chain was then overlaid with the adjunct double helix, adding a crop of foreigners every fourth year on the DNA clock. Living among GOD's three Jewels are the bisexual, homosexual, murderers, rapists, pedophiles, attention seeking charismatic liars, thieves and swindlers – beginning with the first murderer Cain.

The virus, the decomposing matter was passed to Adam from Eve when he lay with her and death is the legacy Adam and Eve left for every generation born after that time. This is the meaning of the sad Song of Songs. It is not a license for illicit love.

All of Electron's children and ATOM's children who preferred the evil one over the Holy One were destroyed during the flood of Noah's day. But then, there was Satan ...waiting. Then Noah chose Electron and brought her back into our midst on the day he was found drunk and naked by his three sons, the three Jewels, Shem who was Judah, Japheth who was Israel and Ham who was Jerusalem.

Noah blessed and cursed them as the LORD ATOM commanded him to do.[71]

Today, Electron, Adenine and Guanine is no longer doing their job of decomposition. She stopped the daily sacrifices (bowel movements) and mankind is dying from recurring, cancerous diseases and weakened immune systems. The virus (that began as a seed in Eve's fertile fecal material and grew down to the feet setting up strong roots) learns and evolves, growing stronger with each new generation of diseases. What is worse, now the talking witch now sits in the outer courtyard – in the mind, where she speaks, babbling continuously to mankind, raising anxiety levels, inciting rage and riot. Unrestrained, Electron has evolved to her present madness where she has sex with every living creature, reproducing a billion, billion, billion bacteria and viruses per minute, killing every healthy living cell she touches.

And from all accounts, the following story is true. I will tell you the story as I remember it. You may fill in what you remember if you like.

The Three Bears

But I have heard that once upon a time there were three brown bears. Their names were Judah, Israel and Jerusalem. Judah was the poppa bear. Israel was the momma bear. And Jerusalem was the name of the baby bear. These three lived happily in a beautifully wooded area. Their days were spent discovering new things, helping and organizing, and teaching, sharing with each other. These three are the same three Wise men who traveled to visit Jesus when he was born in Bethlehem. These three are the Wise Men who were compelled to move by a star, a star named Gluon.

One day after Israel, the helper, had cooked supper, the three sat down at the table to eat but since the food has just been removed from the stove and was still quite hot. They decided to take a walk in the woods while the food cooled. The put on their hats and went to walk in the light, underneath the glow of the afternoon sun.

While they were out, a visitor came. You know the story. Her name was Goldilocks, so called because of her golden curls. Goldilocks tasted Judah's porridge and found it to be "too hot". Judah was closest to the Sun, the Sun of Righteousness. She tasted Israel's porridge and found it be "too cold". Israel is a "star", out in the cold regions of space. She tasted Jerusalem's porridge and found it to be "just right". Jerusalem is the moon, a lover of the night, reversible, good or evil. Goldilocks found his porridge to be just right. So she ate it all up. After she had eaten, she was distracted by the three chairs she saw lined up near the chimney. She sat in Judah's seat. It was too

---

71   Genesis 9:25 – 27

hard. Judah knows the difference between the truth and a lie. He is an apostle, a natural discoverer. His seat is GOD's seat, the seat of wisdom. Goldilocks moved on to Israel's seat and found that it was too soft. Israel has compassion, and heart, and a very strong will. She will not be controlled once she knows the truth and the girl moved on. Goldilocks sat down in Jerusalem's seat and found it to be just right – in between hot and cold, in between hard and soft. When she sat down and began to rock, the chair broke. And Jerusalem is broken to this day, all eaten up inside.

After she broke Jerusalem's seat, Goldilocks was again distracted and saw the beds. She had a silly idea. "Maybe I'll take a nap." She did not consider that they might come back and find her. She did not think it through. And so in like manner, she lay on Judah's bed. It was too hard. She lay on Israel's bed. It was too soft. She lay on Jerusalem's bed. It was just right – so she went to sleep.

When the three brown bears came home to find the intruder sleeping, they were shocked. She had come in as if she belonged there, as if it were naturally her home. When they discovered her, they chased her out with brooms and sticks.

Now, for a while, you will have to chase Adenine out of Jerusalem in the same manner. But she will return until ATOM takes back his throne. She is a relentless pig, a glutton for my time, your thoughts, your mind.

Noah, being discovered by his three sons – Shem who is Judah, Japheth who is Israel, and Ham who is Jerusalem – as he committed adultery against the Creator – ATOM, with Electron or Satan.

Like Eve, Noah's sin – accepting sex with Satan, Electron, to appease his lust – sacrificed all of mankind, all of the Jewels – Judah, Israel and Jerusalem to a life of poverty, sadness, anguish, pain and death. Noah is Israel. Eve is Israel. Israel is highly susceptible to the suggestion of pleasure. For pleasure, Israel is easily overcome. It is how Israel was made. So, here is the sacrifice: Truth was overthrown. All of the lambs have been deceived by a goat in lamb's clothing. We follow the very one who would eat us alive, devour our dead flesh.

Then I saw another beast [Cain – the Gentile son of Satan and Eve] **come up out of the earth** [out of the body of the woman Eve who is known in heaven as Israel]. **He had two horns like a lamb** [looks like a Jewel of GOD]**, and he spoke with the voice of a dragon** [bipolar, sounds and acts like Electron, their father, mother; vacillates between rage and weeping].

Revelation 13:11

Over the centuries, people have marveled at Michelangelo's depiction of Moses sitting on a throne with two horns. However, the moment I saw the statue in all of its majesty, I knew exactly what it meant. Moses was a Gentile, the son of Satan. And although he was chosen by ATOM, by GOD to deliver the Jewish people, he was not a jewel of ATOM's. He was not one of the ones whose name is written in the Lamb's Book of Life, in Proton's Book of Life. There are only ten names written in that book. They are ATOM, Proton, Gluon and Neutron; Cytosine, Thymine and Uracil; Judah, Israel and Jerusalem. Why, you ask, were the Gentiles, Electron, Adenine and Guanine's names not written in the Lamb's Book of Life? It is simple. None of these five are alive. They are undead or as Jude recorded, they are doubly dead – undead and their roots will be pulled from the DNA chain when Electron, their father, mother is destroyed.

When these people [Gentiles] **join you in fellowship meals celebrating the love of the Lord, they are like dangerous reefs that can shipwreck you. They are** shameless in the way they care only about themselves. They are like clouds blowing over dry land without giving rain, promising much but producing nothing. They are like trees without fruit at harvest time. They are not only dead but doubly dead, for they have been pulled out by the roots.

Jude 1:12

The Gentiles

Jesus explained the Gentiles.

I will speak to you in parables. I will explain mysteries hidden since the creation of the world.

Matthew 13:35

The Fate of the Rebellious Gentiles

The Kingdom of Heaven is like a farmer [ATOM] **who planted good**

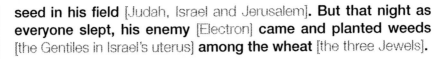

seed in his field [Judah, Israel and Jerusalem]. But that night as everyone slept, his enemy [Electron] came and planted weeds [the Gentiles in Israel's uterus] among the wheat [the three Jewels].

When the crops began to grow and produce grain [produce the children of ATOM], the weeds [the Gentiles] also grew. The farmer's servants [Cytosine, Thymine and Uracil] came and told him,

'Sir, the field where you planted that good seed is full of weeds [full of Gentiles]!'

'An enemy [Electron] has done it!' the farmer exclaimed.

'Shall we pull out the weeds?' they asked.

He replied, 'No, you'll hurt the wheat if you do. Let both grow together until the harvest [during the time of testing]. Then I will tell the harvesters to sort out the weeds [the rebellious Gentiles] and burn them and to put the wheat [the Jewels] in the barn.'

Matthew 13:24 – 30

The Fate of the Puritanical Gentiles

But some of these branches from Abraham's tree, some of the Jews, have been broken off. And you Gentiles, who were branches from a wild olive tree [Electron], were grafted in [to the straight DNA chain as the adjunct double helix]. So now, you also receive the blessing GOD has promised Abraham [Jerusalem] and his children, sharing in GOD's rich nourishment of his special olive tree [life].

Romans 11:17

For if GOD was willing to take you who were, by nature, branches from a wild olive tree [double helix, children of Electron, the liar, the devil] and graft you into his own good [DNA] tree – a very unusual thing to do – he will be far more eager to graft the Jews back into the [the adrenergic] Tree [of Life] where they belong [instead of the cholinergic tree of death upon which they cling to their very lives].

Romans 11:24

The Beast out of the Earth

Then I saw another beast come up out of the earth. He had two horns like those of a lamb, and he spoke with the voice of a dragon. He [the Gentile] exercised all the authority of the first beast. And he

**required all the earth and those who belong to this world to worship
the first beast** [Electron]**, who's death–wound had been healed.** [Electron, Adenine and Guanine is undead, a bacterial corpuscle, a corpse.]
He [Electron] **did astounding miracles, such as making fire flash down
to earth from heaven while everyone was watching**

Revelation 13:11 – 13

The Gentile performs unnatural miracles such as he did at Hiroshima, the rapes and serial murders, the car bombs, and body bombs while Electron performs seemingly *natural* miracles and disasters such as lightning striking buildings and people, tornados, twisters, hurricanes, tsunamis, floods and earthquakes. I woke me up to show me how powerful she is as she took the Space Shuttle Columbia down. She is a braggart and a fool.

And with all the miracles he [the Gentile] **was allowed to perform on
behalf of the first beast, he deceived all the people who belong to
this world** [into believing that he was the natural ruler over GOD's, AT-
OM's creation].

Revelation 13:14

The Riddle of the Revelation

He [Electron] **ordered the people of the world** [the little Parisian Gentile
who designed it, the craftsmen and labourers] **to make a great statue of
the first beast, who was fatally wounded and then came back to life.**
[The name of the statue is called Liberty. The statue looks like Athena who
was also Electron in the days of the Greeks.]

He was permitted to give life to this statue [value] **so that it could
speak. Then the statue commanded that anyone refusing to worship
it must die.** [In the name of liberty, all men go to war.]

Revelation 13:14 – 15

Liberty beckons all men to come to her.

Give me your tired, your poor, your humbled masses yearn-
ing to breathe free. *I* left *my lamp* beside the golden door.

Now, I ask you: What is a lampstand without a lamp? What is a man without wisdom? The treasure that you sought inside the golden door was yours all along. Your maker and Creator have given it to you freely from the very first moment of inception. Don't you know? There is no treasure inside the golden door, no riches, only misery, pain, war, slavery, loss of freedom; there is no peace of mind, no piece of the pie. Some of you Americans can't hear me. Electron is talking to you, telling you lies to divert your attention away from the issue at hand. In the end, if you can't see and believe that which is true, you will perish.

> **He required everyone – great and small, rich and poor, slave and free – to be given a mark on the right hand or on the forehead. And no one could buy or sell anything without that mark, which was either the name of the beast or the number representing his name.**
>
> Wisdom is needed to understand this. **Let the one who has understanding solve the number of the beast, for it is the number of a man. His number is 666.**

Revelation 13:16 – 18

I, Cyrus, am the one with wisdom. Allow me to clearly explain the meaning.

And Electron, Satan causeth **all** (both past and present), both small and great, rich and poor, free and bond, to receive a mark in their right hand, or in their foreheads; that mark is called **choice**. Eve had to choose Electron; Noah had to choose Electron. It was their destiny to do so. Without further information what choices did they have? To be curious, to try is a normal characteristic of mankind. I know this because I was also given that option but I knew what they could not have known and I refused the tyrant, the demon, the dragon.

Who wants to have sex with a corpse knowing it's a corpse? No person with good sense and reasoning ability; no man with GOD, ATOM on his side. Only a fool would even consider it. I want to live. I don't want to die. I choose life over death, ATOM over Electron, peace over insanity, prosperity over poverty, love over hate. I choose ATOM. He is GOD, the only one that ever was, the only one from the creation of the world.

The riddle reads: that no man might buy or sell, save he that had the mark, or the name of the beast, or the number of his name. How many of you buy without choosing? Did you not date before you got married? Did you not test out the paint samples before you painted the wall? How can you plunge into a commitment without knowing what you are getting? And neither will you ordinarily buy without knowing what you are buying with your forehead, which is where your mind and eyes rest. You want to see it with your eyes or touch it with your hand before you buy it.

Now here is the wisdom of ATOM who has intrigued you with this riddle since John first wrote the words: Let him that hath understanding count the number of the beast; for it is the number of a man, the man of lawlessness, who is Electron, Satan;

and his number is six, six, six. Don't be afraid of the number. It does not mean what you have been told.

Listen now: Count the number of the beast – the beast is the Matter Particle, Electron, the virus, the bacteria; her number is billion, billion, billion: To count the number of the beast, you must know how she *multiplies*. This is how she multiples – sex, sex, sex. She is the whore of Babylon – the Hormone of the Baby Loins. The number of a man is an indication of how man reproduces – sex, sex, sex. And have you not heard of sextuplets? **Sex**tuplets are six children born to one mother at one time. It is a simple idea blown up to terrorize you. For, it is the only terrorist that ever was who haunts you; I-van, the terrible. Be afraid. Be very afraid. For, now that you know, Electron is coming down to wage war up you and the rest of mankind.

Listen: The mark of the beast is **choice**. The name of the beast is **Elect**ron. Elect means to choose. Look it up! Make your election and you will have nothing to fear. For, "causeth all" means requires. Christ, **Proton** requires that all men *know* the truth but because of the extensiveness of GOD's plan (covering many centuries) it was given to us in subterfuge, as a ruse, a stratagem to conceal the truth of GOD's brilliant plan. It could only be revealed at the appointed time, at this time, by Cyrus, by me. That is the meaning of the riddle of the revelation; of the 666 you fear.

Satan, Electron, stands for liberty, liberty to do what is wrong in the sight of ATOM, in the sight of GOD. But GOD, ATOM lives within every man, everywhere, so his range of sight is infinite. Proton sees everything you do; knows what you are going to do before you do it.

Electron stands for and defends sodomy, unnatural love between two men or two women. These degraded lustful forms of sex allow her to live, gives her a breeding ground within each body. Sure, she wants you to do this. She is bi-sexual by nature. Bacteria mates in and with all species – male and female, even her own offspring and so do many of you Gentiles. And now, Electron has convinced the highest courts – ruled by her Gentile children and the godly Jerusalem – to accept these foul acts as natural, setting up a corrupt future for all of mankind. The family of GOD has all but disappeared. The deformities and birth defects multiply in the genetic chain as we speak.

And now, you know why Christ said that these last days would be worse than the days of Sodom and Gomorrah. In those days, most Gentiles hid their salacious whims and their faces behind closed doors, masks of darkness. Their contemporaries condemned them. Even the virtuous Gentiles condemned them, stoning them for their evil lifestyle. But these days are filled with open, unholy matrimony – an evil and disgusting trend, sickening me all the more when I think of my children and my grand nieces and nephews growing up in such a world. Now, I know why the Queen of Sheba will stand up and condemn this generation for its wickedness. Satan has deceived the whole world saying darkness is light and light is darkness. And you nod your head in agreement or shrug your shoulders saying it does not affect you. You are wrong my friend. It's not the ozone that will destroy mankind. It is the changing, degrading genetics and the introduction of strong drugs that make the bacteria resilient that will destroy mankind. ATOM punishes men to the fifth and sixth generation. On this current pace, what will we look like six generations from now? I shudder at the thought.

The Message of the Three Angels

Then I saw the Lamb [Proton] standing on Mount Zion, and with him were 144,000 who had his name [Cryst] and his Father's name [ATOM] written on their foreheads. And I heard a sound from heaven like the roaring of a great waterfall or the rolling of mighty thunder. It was like the sound of many harpists playing together. [It is Proton, Gluon and Neutron, Cytosine, Thymine and Uracil all singing in harmony.]

This great choir sang a wonderful new song in front of the throne of GOD and before the four living beings and the twenty–four elders. And no one could learn this song except those 144,000 who had been redeemed from the earth. For they are spiritually undefiled, pure as virgins [having had no relationship with Electron], following the Lamb [Proton, the Sun of righteousness] wherever he goes. They have been purchased from among the people on the earth as a special offering to GOD and to the Lamb. No falsehood can be charged against them; they are blameless.

The First Angel's Message [Proton, Cryst]

And I saw another angel flying through the heavens, carrying the everlasting Good News to preach to the people who belong to this world – to every nation, tribe, language, and people. "Fear GOD [fear ATOM]," he shouted. "Give glory to him. For the time has come when he will sit as judge. Worship him who made heaven and earth, the sea, and all the springs of water."

The Second Angel's Message [Gluon, Archangel Michael]

Then another angel followed him through the skies, shouting, "Babylon [Electron, Satan] is fallen – that great city is fallen – because she seduced the nations of the world and made them drink the wine of her passionate immorality."

The Third Angel's Message [Neutron, Archangel Gabriel]

Then a third angel followed them, shouting, "Anyone who worships the beast and his statue or who accepts his mark on the forehead or the hand must drink the wine of GOD's wrath [of ATOM's wrath]. It is poured out undiluted into GOD's cup of wrath. And they will be tormented with fire and burning sulfur [in the stomach and groin] in the presence of the holy angels and the Lamb. [And though they live] the smoke of their torment rises forever and ever, and they will have no relief day or night, for they have worshiped the beast and his statue and have accepted the mark of his name.

Let this encourage GOD's holy people [Judah, Israel and Jerusalem] to endure persecution patiently and remain firm to the end, obeying his commands and trusting in Jesus."

And I heard a voice from heaven saying, "Write this down: Blessed are those who die in the Lord [ATOM] from now on. Yes, says the [Amorphous] Spirit, they are blessed indeed, for they will rest from all their toils and trials; for their good deeds follow them!"

Then I saw the Son of Man [Proton, Cryst] sitting on a white cloud. He had a gold crown on his head and a sharp sickle in his hand.

Then an angel [Cytosine, Cryst] came from the Temple and called out in a loud voice to the one sitting on the cloud, "Use the sickle, for the time has come for you to harvest; the crop is ripe on the earth." So the one sitting on the cloud [Proton, Cryst] swung his sickle over the earth, and the whole earth was harvested. [All men were cleansed of the gross volume of bacteria within them.]

After that, another angel [Uracil, also called Gabriel] came from the Temple in heaven, and he also had a sharp sickle. Then another angel [Thymine, also called Michael], who has power to destroy the world with fire, shouted to the angel with the sickle, "Use your sickle now to gather the clusters of grapes from the vines of the earth, for they are fully ripe for judgment."

So the angel [Cryst] swung his sickle on the earth and loaded the grapes into the great winepress of GOD's wrath. And the grapes were trodden in the winepress outside the city, and blood flowed from the winepress in a stream about 180 miles long and as high as a horse's bridle.

[This winepress runs to the blood veins, through the catacombs within every person's body. The demons will be cleansed from the blood of every man.]

Revelation 14:1 – 20

The Last Seven Plagues

Then I saw in heaven another significant event, and it was great and marvelous. Seven angels were holding the seven last plagues, which would bring GOD's wrath to completion.

I saw before me what seemed to be a crystal sea [crystallized DNA] mixed with fire [synapses firing from the hindbrain]. And on it stood all the people who had been victorious over the beast [had rejected Adenine, Electron and Guanine] and his statue [Liberty to sleep with Satan, to murder, to maim] and the number [six or sex as in sextuplet] representing his name.

They were all holding harps [Uracil] that GOD [ATOM] had given them. And they were singing the song of Moses, the servant of GOD, and the song of the Lamb:

"Great and marvelous are your actions, LORD [ATOM] Almighty. Just and true are your ways, O King of the nations. Who will not fear, O LORD [ATOM], and glorify your name? For you alone are holy. All nations will come and worship before you, for your righteous deeds have been revealed."

Then I looked and saw that the Temple in heaven [the mind of men], GOD's Tabernacle, was thrown wide open! The seven angels who were holding the bowls of the seven plagues came from the Temple, clothed in spotless white linen with gold belts across their chests [deoxyribonucleic acid].

And one of the four living beings [Cyrus, by telling the truth] handed each of the seven angels a gold bowl filled with the terrible wrath of GOD, who lives forever and forever. The Temple was filled with smoke from GOD's glory and power.

No one could enter the Temple until the seven angels had completed pouring out the seven plagues.

Revelation 15:1 – 8

The First Bowl of GOD's Wrath

Then I heard a mighty voice shouting from the Temple to the seven angels, "Now go your ways and empty out the seven bowls of GOD's wrath on the earth."

So, the first angel left the Temple and poured out his bowl over the earth, and horrible, malignant sores broke out on everyone who had the mark of the beast [the right to choose] and who worshiped his statue [called Liberty].

Revelation 16:2

And diseases and epidemics have swept across the continents and those who have lusted after the beast and worshipped the statue called Liberty are familiar with this plague. For, they seek freedom from the one who is Holy and True. I am certain that the first bowl has been poured out because the Holy Spirit told Paul who wrote,

And the men, instead of having normal sexual relationships with women, burned with lust for each other. Men did shameful things with other men and, as a result, suffered within themselves the penalty they so richly deserved.

Romans 1:27

These diseases have names. They are called AIDS, prostate and colon cancers, Hepatitis, Syphilis, cold sores, uterine cancers, breast cancers, and there are many, many others. And medicines have been developed that can stifle the symptoms, but the researchers can't discover the root cause and eradicate it. It seems a losing battle. The advances in medicine abates the disease for a time but then the bacteria and viruses that spread the disease get stronger with each new generation of the disease. Can these diseases be cured? Not now! Can Babylon be healed? Not ever! The scriptures say,

Weep for [Babylon, Adenine] and give her medicine. Perhaps she can yet be healed. We would have helped her if we could, but nothing can save her now. Let her go; abandon her. Return now to your own land, for her judgment will be so great it cannot be measured.

Jeremiah 51:8 – 9

Many have perished and those who remember them have taken up quilting to relieve their pain. Some just grind their teeth because they are still suffering. And the children suffer for the sins of their parents on every continent. Their futures look grim. Their sores will not heal and their eyes have wasted away, sunken into their sockets. The liberty that brought so much pleasure now brings only pain and hopelessness. Their tongues have shriveled up because their lust has led them into some serious sexually transmitted diseases. But because they do not realize that the Most High has sent these plagues, they have not repented. They believe that a cure will be found and Satan gives them this hope. The beast has told them to trust in man, to trust in 'me'. And so, they continue in their wickedness.

The Second Bowl of GOD's Wrath

Then the second angel poured out his bowl on the sea [reproductive organs]**, and it became like the blood of a corpse. And everything in the sea died** [sperm and eggs]**.**

Revelation 16:3

When the second bowl was poured out on the people, the blood of the dead began to flow and the seed of man began to die in great quantities. And the children he so desperately desired could not be produced.

The people of Israel are stricken. Their roots are dried up; they will bear no more fruit. And if they give birth, I will slaughter their beloved children.

Hosea 9:16

Those that were produced were defective – born too early or too late with physical and mental maladies. And the parents weep, their dreams unfulfilled. And the children stare into space, lost and unable to care for themselves.

Now, listen to the Holy Spirit. She shouts in the streets of Jerusalem, which is her home and also, her name. She calls out to the crowds along the main street, and to those in front of city hall.

"You simpletons!" she cries. "How long will you go on being simple-minded? How long will you mockers relish your mocking?

How long will you fools fight the facts? Come here and listen to me! I'll pour out the spirit of wisdom upon you and make you wise.

I called you so often, but you didn't come. I reached out to you, but you paid no attention. You ignored my advice and rejected the correction I offered."

Proverbs 1:22 – 25

So now, Jerusalem – the Holy Spirit, will laugh when you are in trouble! Wisdom will mock you when disaster overtakes you –

When calamity overcomes you like a storm, when you are engulfed by trouble, and when anguish and distress overwhelm you. "I will not answer when they cry for help. Even though they anxiously search for me, they will not find me."

Proverbs 1:27 – 28

For you mockers hate knowledge and choose not to fear the LORD. You have rejected the advice of the Holy Spirit, the counsel of gentle Jerusalem. You hate to listen to wisdom even when GOD himself showed you the way. You will suffer during the time of testing that is coming to test the whole world. You will suffer because they don't listen. For the scriptures say,

That is why they must eat the bitter fruit of living their own way. They must experience the full terror of the path they have chosen. For they are simpletons who turn away from me – to death. They are fools, and their own complacency will destroy them.

But all who listen to me will live in peace and safety, unafraid of harm.

Proverbs 1:31 – 33

The Third Bowl of GOD's Wrath

Then the third angel poured out his bowl on the rivers and springs, and they became blood.

Revelation 16:4

When the third bowl was poured out, Jerusalem was no longer restrained from the bitter anger he holds in his heart. He was allowed to rise up against the Gentile murderers, the enemies of GOD's people. Jerusalem was given the power and the desire to destroy them, to beat them down with angry words, to subdue them without compassion.

And I heard the angel who had authority over all water saying, "You are just in sending this judgment, O Holy One, who is and who always was.

For your holy people and your prophets have been killed [by Gentiles], and their blood was poured out on the earth.

So, you have given their murderers blood to drink. It is their just reward." And I heard a voice from the altar saying, "Yes, LORD GOD Almighty, your punishments are true and just."

Revelation 16:5 – 7

And so, murder for murder – justice from those murdering Gentiles – the mourning star, the sons of Satan is the third plague.

The Fourth Bowl of GOD's Wrath

The fourth bowl will be the destruction of Babylon. And all of mankind will be purified with fire. And every person will feel that blast of heat signifying the destruction of those evil spirits, demons, and thieves that live within the body of every living being.

Then the fourth angel poured out his bowl on the sun, causing it to scorch everyone with its fire. Everyone was burned by this blast of heat, and they cursed the name of GOD, who sent all of these plagues. They did not repent and give him glory.

Revelation 16:8 – 9

The children of Zion, and the chosen ones should rejoice at this blast of heat. Because ...

... Suddenly, your ruthless enemies will be driven away like chaff before the wind. In an instant, I, the LORD Almighty, will come against them with thunder and earthquake and great noise, with whirlwind and storm and consuming fire. All the nations fighting against Jerusalem will vanish like a dream! Those who are attacking her walls will vanish like a vision in the night.

Isaiah 29:5 – 7

For everyone will be purified with fire.

Mark 9:49

And Babylon, the Baby Loins, will fall. Babylon will be violently thrown down like a stone that is pitched away. She will disappear from the minds and loins of all mankind forever. Once it was a hideout of demons, evil spirits, a nest for filthy buzzards, and a den for dreadful beasts. But now it will be burned completely and smoke will rise from her charred remains.

And after that day of fire, the sound of music will never again be heard there. There will be no industry of any kind – no milling of grain, no flagellum grinding, grinding to feed her insatiable lust. Her nights will be dark, without a single lamp. There will be no happy voices of brides and grooms thanking the god of their lust for her pleasure. Her merchants, shepherds and priests, were the greatest in the world. And they deceived the world with her sorceries. In her streets, the blood of the prophets was spilled. And through her influence, GOD's people were slaughtered all over the world.

> **In that day, the LORD will punish the fallen angels in the heavens and the proud rulers[72] of the nations on earth. They will be rounded up and put in prison until they are tried and condemned.**
>
> *Isaiah 24:21 – 22*

> **Babylon is fallen – that great city is fallen – because she seduced the nations of the world and made them drink the wine of her passionate immorality.**
>
> *Revelation 14:8*

The Fifth Bowl of GOD's Wrath

The fifth plague shuts out the light that Satan has enjoyed while he sat on GOD's throne in the outer courtyard near Uracil's seat where she babbles on and on, singing songs over and over, songs she doesn't know the words to. She surely sits there babbling, reminding you of the wrongs done to you by others – wrongs she caused. She surely sits there flashing lewd pictures in front of your mind's eye, forcing your eyes to look upon evil and lust after it.

Then the pain of mankind will increase – the pain in the joints, the fungi rooted sores upon the body. For the scriptures say,

> **Then the fifth angel poured out his bowl on the throne of the beast, and his kingdom was plunged into darkness. And his subjects** [bacterial demons and men who follow the evil one] **ground their teeth in anguish, and they cursed the GOD of heaven for their pains and sores. But they refused to repent of all their evil deeds.**
>
> *Revelation 16:10 – 11*

---

72   The fallen angels and the proud rulers are the demons and evil spirits that rule from the city of Babylon. For Babylon exists in the mind and heart of every man. And the lights of Babylon will go out like a wick in the wind. And the second angel will shout her glorious message,

The world that Satan claimed and tempted Christ with will no longer be his. He will be thrown down from his high place in heaven when the fifth plague is poured out.

He knows he has very little time to round up his troops for battle on the LORD's Day. And many will join him for the beast is persuasive and O, such a good liar! He has told you that good is evil and that evil is good. He has convinced you that the truth is a lie and that his lies are true. How could I know this lest I experienced his lies? How could I know the truth of his deception had I not been freed from it? Wake up, little ones!

My GOD is coming and he brings 200 hundred million of his holy ones with him. They are angels coming to fight the demons who have taken over this world, over your body. You will not be able to be callous and nonchalant on the day of his coming. He will rouse you from your sleep with his spear. Then you will know who is the true GOD of heaven.

The Sixth Bowl of GOD's Wrath

Now get ready. The day of Armageddon that you have been waiting for is coming swiftly now.

Then the sixth angel poured out his bowl on the great Euphrates River [the bladder]**, and it dried up so that the kings from the east** [to Babylon – Adenine and Guanine] **could march their armies westward** [to Jerusalem] **without hindrance.**[73]

And I saw three evil spirits that looked like frogs leap from the mouth of the dragon [Electron]**, the beast** [Adenine – death]**, and the false prophet** [Guanine – the grave]**. These miracle–working demons** [bacteria] **caused all the rulers of the world** [every person] **to gather for battle against the LORD** [ATOM] **on that great Judgment Day of GOD Almighty.**

"Take note: I will come as unexpectedly as a thief! Blessed are all who are watching for me, who keep their robes ready so they will not need to walk naked and ashamed."

And they [the three evil spirits] **gathered all the rulers and their armies**

---

73   This is the beginning of the parasympathetic nervous system, the cholinergic fibres, taking over the body of man, strangling the adrenergic fibres of the sympathetic nervous system and rendering them powerless. Now, mankind is tired and lifeless, lackluster, without energy or interest. Depression has set in and all peoples are moody, depressed and angry.

[every person and the bacterial legion of demons within them] **to a place called Armageddon in Hebrew.**

Revelation 14:12 – 16

Armageddon will take place within the brain of every person, upon the two mountainous lobes called the Mount of Olives. Every man – Judah, Israel and Jerusalem – will return to his own land, his perfect home before all men were scattered.

Dress yourselves in sackcloth, you priests! Wail, you who serve before the altar! Come, spend the night in sackcloth, you ministers of my GOD!

There is no grain or wine to offer at the Temple of your GOD.

Joel 1:13

It is a time for fasting and solemn meetings. It is time to bring the leaders who love GOD and all of the people into his Holy Temple and cry out to him there. All of the bread—GOD's Holy Word has disappeared. Even the wine is watered down. There are no words from him, no fountains of blessings flowing from him.

The Seventh Bowl of GOD's Wrath

Then the seventh angel poured out his bowl into the air. And a mighty shout came from the throne of the Temple in heaven, saying, "It is finished!" Then the thunder crashed and rolled, and lightning flashed. And there was an earthquake greater than ever before in human history.

Revelation 16:17 – 18

And seven thousand people will be killed in that earthquake. And look!

The great city of Babylon split into three pieces, and cities around the world fell into heaps of rubble. And so, GOD remembered all of Babylon's sins, and he made her drink the cup that was filled with the wine of his fierce wrath. And every island disappeared, and all the mountains were leveled.

Revelation 16:19 – 20

When Babylon splits into three pieces – Cytosine, Thymine, and Uracil – the beast that rose up from the sea – Electron – will be no more. But this will not happen until the 1000–year reign of Christ has ended and Electron is let out of his prison for a little while.

And on that day, there will be a terrible hailstorm, and hailstones weighing seventy–five pounds will fall from the sky onto the people below. And the people will curse GOD because of the hailstorm, which was a very terrible plague.

But when the terror is ended, Judah, Israel, and Jerusalem will stand, a righteous nation. The Parasympathetic Nervous System will be gone. The cholinergic fibres with their bile and gall, irascibility and melancholy will be gone. The Jewels will break free from the bondage of their sins. They will not be guided by the Gentiles or Jerusalem who helped the Gentiles achieve power. They will know that they belong to GOD and they will follow him. For the scriptures say, 'Every knee will bow before him'. And the Lamb will be their shepherd and they will be his sheep. And those who stand alone – the islands, the Gentiles – will join in with their tribe. Judah will stand with Judah and praise the LORD Almighty. And Israel will stand with Israel to compare blessings. And the mountains will be leveled; for they will see the gifts that GOD gave them from the beginning. They will shout..."for our GOD has redeemed us, at last!"

Return to the LORD Almighty, LORD ATOM

"I, the LORD [ATOM], was very angry with your ancestors. Therefore, say to the people, 'This is what the LORD Almighty says:

Return to me, and I will return to you, says the LORD Almighty.'

Do not be like your ancestors who would not listen when the earlier prophets said to them,

'This is what the LORD Almighty says:

Turn from your evil ways and stop all your evil practices.'

"Your ancestors and their prophets are now long dead. But all the things I said through my servants the prophets happened to your ancestors, just as I said they would. As a result, they repented and said,

'We have received what we deserved from the LORD Almighty. He has done what he said he would do.'"

Zechariah 1:2 – 6

In a vision during the night, I saw a man sitting on a red horse [Thymine] **that was standing among some myrtle trees in a small valley. Behind him were red** [red blood cells]**, brown** [iron, plasma]**, and white**

horses [white blood cells], each with its own rider [antibodies]. I asked the angel who was talking with me,

"My lord, what are all those horses for?"

"I will show you," the angel replied.

So the man standing among the myrtle trees explained,

"They are the ones the LORD [Proton] has sent out to patrol the earth."

Then the other riders reported to the angel of the LORD [Michael, Thymine], who was standing among the myrtle trees,

"We have patrolled the earth [the body], and the whole earth [the whole body] is at peace."

Upon hearing this, the angel of the LORD [Michael] prayed this prayer:

"O LORD Almighty, for seventy years [all years] now you have been angry with Jerusalem [your prophets and priests] and the towns of Judah [the wise ones]. How long will it be until you again show mercy to them?"

And the LORD, [ATOM] spoke kind and comforting words to the angel, Michael, who talked with me. Then the angel, Michael, said to me,

"Shout this message for all to hear: 'This is what the LORD Almighty says: My love for Jerusalem [Cytosine] and Mount Zion [Uracil] is passionate and strong. But I am very angry with the other nations that enjoy peace and security. I was only a little angry with my people, but the nations [Electron – Adenine and Guanine and the Gentiles] punished them far beyond my intentions.

"'Therefore, this is what the LORD [Proton] says: I have returned to show mercy to Jerusalem. My Temple will be rebuilt [the tower of babble will be torn down], says the LORD Almighty, and plans will be made for the reconstruction of Jerusalem [the minds of men].' Say this also:

'This is what the LORD Almighty says: The towns of Israel will again overflow with prosperity, and the LORD will again comfort Zion [the forehead] and choose Jerusalem [in the hindbrain] as his own.'"

Zechariah 1:8 – 17

The Age of Deception

One of the seven angels [Uraoil, the teacher] **who had poured out the seven bowls came over and spoke to me. "Come with me,"** he said, **"and I will show you the judgment that is going to come on the great prostitute** [Electron]**, who sits on many waters** [the waters are urine, mucus and puss in the bladder and bowels of every person]**."**

The rulers of the world [the Gentiles and some jewels -- Jerusalem and Israel] **have had immoral relations with her, and the people who belong to this world** [the Gentiles] **have been made drunk by the wine of her immorality** [always seeking pleasure, showing you lewd and graphic pictures to excite your mind as well as your body].

So the angel took me in spirit [in my mind's eye] **into the wilderness.** [The wilderness is the vast and thick trees of veins branching out all over your body, also called The Garden of Eden in heaven.]

Revelation 17:1 – 3

There I saw a woman [Adenine] **sitting on a scarlet beast** [the bloody pelvis bone of the female reproduction system; Ezekiel's whirling wheel, the wheel in the middle of a wheel] **that had seven heads** [all people] **and ten horns** [both good and evil]**, written all over with blasphemies against GOD** [ATOM]**.**

The woman [Adenine] **wore purple and scarlet clothing** [blood, the blood of every person; she lives within the blood] **and beautiful jewelry** [the Jewels of ATOM, the Jewels of GOD] **made of gold** [Judah] **and precious gems** [Israel] **and** [beautiful] **pearls** [Jerusalem]**.**

She held in her hand a gold goblet full of obscenities and the impurities of her immorality [homosexual sex, all unnatural acts concerning the exchange of bacteria filled bodily fluids]**.**

A mysterious name was written on her forehead: "Babylon the Great, Mother of All Prostitutes and Obscenities in the World."

Electron, Adenine exposed all of mankind to the names that blaspheme GOD. The names are murder, theft, torture, pedophilia, homosexuality, greed, covetousness, racism and divisiveness.

I could see that she was drunk – drunk with the blood of GOD's holy people who were witnesses for Jesus. [Adenine is a blood sucker, a corpuscle whose lives on the blood of people everywhere, always grinding the wheel shouting more, more.] **I stared at her completely amazed.**

"Why are you so amazed?" the angel [Uracil] asked. "I will tell you the mystery of this woman and of the beast with seven heads and ten horns. The beast you saw was alive but isn't now. And yet he will soon come up out of the bottomless pit [pit of your stomach, your bowels] and go to eternal destruction.

And the people who belong to this world [the Gentiles, the humans], whose names were not written in the Book of Life from before the world began, will be amazed at the reappearance of this beast who had died.

Revelation 17:4 – 8

There are only ten names written in the Book of Life from **before** the world began. They are ATOM, Proton, Gluon, Neutron, Cytosine, Thymine, Uracil, Judah, Israel and Jerusalem. Electron's name was never in the book of life as she has no life within her. Electron is a corpse, a corpuscle, the one who devours the waste before the waste. She is a water-based decomposer, anti-crystalline, anti-Christ. She is not alive; never was.

If your name is Gentile as John, the revelator and Moses, the deliverer and Joseph, the schemer was, your name was not written in the Lamb's Book of Life written before the world was made. Your Gentile name had to be added to the DNA book of life, the double helix was added, grafted into the DNA book with every person's name written inside.

You who are born Gentiles are the *humans*. I call you humans, the "who mans", for, who are you that you should rule over ATOM's children? Israel, tell me, if you know.

Your kind, you Gentiles, had to be ratcheted into the DNA chain because you came after the earth had crystallized; the body of mankind and its components were already set. The original pattern after which all of mankind was modeled did not include murderers, rapists, pedophiles and con artists. Electron is a servant of GOD, of ATOM, responsible for waste management within the bottomless pit, in the bowels of the earth, in the bowels of your body. There is no reason for Cain to ever be born, for murderers, rapists and pedophiles to be introduced into our midst...except that the father of all pedophiles was chosen ... not once, but three time, by honorable jewels, curious, looking for a good time. Like Peter, whose name is Jerusalem, Christ was denied three times by mankind, by those with the authority to end the madness, to choose good over evil.

The first denial was by Adam, who was led astray by Eve who was deceived by the serpent, whose name is called Jerusalem in heaven. The second denial was by Noah, who could not resist the joy strong. The third denial was by all mankind, who chose Bar-Jesus over Jesus Christ, whom they crucified.

Now, this evil one rules over us all. All of mankind and humankind is forced to suffer. Who could imagine the far reaching consequences of such a tiny selfish act? No one could. It is unthinkable.

> **And now understand this: The seven heads of the beast** [all mankind and humankind] **represent the seven hills of the city where this woman rules.**
>
> *Revelation 17:9*

And what hills are these and where are these hills located?

These are small hills, so small; you could hardly call it a hill. It is the mons pubis on top of the pelvic bone upon each and every person.

> **They** [the seven heads of the beast] **also represent seven** [earthly] **kings. Five kings have already fallen, the sixth now reigns, and the seventh is yet to come, but his reign will be brief.**
>
> *Revelation 17:10*

The Seven Kings

And also understand this: The seven heads of the beast that rose up out of the sea represent seven kings. The seven kings are seven powerful leaders who for a moment in history ruled, conquered, and killed many. They are the whore mongers who care only about their own pleasure and the warmongers who seek war for profit – domination – as this is Satan's plan. They speak friendly words to their international neighbors while planning evil in their hearts. They lie boldly about rescuing the oppressed from tyranny but their objective is murder and gold.

And these are the names of the kings past and present. Like the one to come, they all agreed to give their power and authority to Satan – Electron in exchange for complete power before men.

The First Four Kings

Joseph who enslaved all of the Hebrews for Pharaoh during the time of Moses was the first king. Nebuchadnezzar was the second. Alexander, the Great was the third. Genghis Khan was the fourth.

The Fifth One to Fall was Hitler

Long ago, the prophet Daniel wrote,

> **The next to come to power will be a despicable man who is not directly in line for royal succession.** [He is a Jewel of GOD.] **But he will slip in** [to power] **when least expected and take over the** [Gentile] **kingdom by flattery and intrigue. Before him, great armies will be swept away, including a covenant prince. By making deceitful promises, he will make various alliances. With a mere handful of followers, he will become strong. Without warning, he will enter the richest areas of the land and do something that none of his predecessors ever did – distribute among his followers the plunder and wealth of the rich. He will plot the overthrow of strongholds, but this will last for only a short while.**

Daniel 11:21 – 24

The covenant prince that was swept away was Hitler himself. He is a covenant prince because his name is called Judah in heaven. He is of the church of Smyrna. But he chose to follow Satan so that he could have honor among men. He will rise to GOD's judgment. The pain of his punishment will never end.

The Sixth Now Reigns!

And he is Pharaoh, a Gentile. He is the beast out of the earth with two horns like a lamb but he speaks with the voice of the dragon. Though he does not yet know it, his name is Cain. He is a thorn Bush and he is a thorn in the side of all who belong to ATOM. All Jewels despise him and criticize him for they see him as he truly is, a deceiver with a soft voice and silky smooth tongue. He is both loved and hated by the Gentiles for he is both good and evil. His name is George W. Bush – the current President of the United States. Some call him a murderer because of the war, but he is more a symbol of the one that you cannot see, made in her psychological image, vacillating between violence and tears, giving and taking.

The wicked conceive evil; they are pregnant with trouble and give birth to lies. They dig a pit to trap others and then fall into it themselves. They make trouble, but it backfires on them. They plan violence for others, but it falls on their own heads.

Psalm 7:14 – 16

It is a difficult concept to imagine that George Bush, Sr., the former president, number 41, a Jewel named Israel, who led with honor and veracity spawned this Gentile leader from within his loins. It is clear to see that the senior and the junior are not cut from the same cloth, not made from the same pattern. The senior's wars were fought on truth, a solid foundation. For truth is the only solid rock there is. Those who believe that the son, W, is following in the elder's footsteps don't see the whole picture. It is unlikely that they ever will. But soon you will look at your own family members and decipher a pattern that you cannot imagine before the truth was revealed.

And poor Mr. Bush, the sixth and current ruler of the world, will not understand the truth of it for he has been completely deceived by the one who made him, the one who speaks to him and gives him his instructions, the one who calls himself God. And the sixth, W, the son of the double helix, is the devil's child, a Gentile, so he believes that he was born to rule all the more. Mr. Bush is the living example for this time, for all of mankind to observe and nod their heads as they observe his errant and erratic behavior.

But the seventh Gentile who reigns will come to know the truth. It will fall upon him like a smooth, white veil. He will come to know the Living GOD and he will step down from that high place. His reign will be brief.

The Scarlet Beast

The scarlet beast that was alive and then died is the eighth king. He is like the other seven, and he, too, will go to his doom.

Revelation 17:9 – 11

Now understand this: The title *scarlet beast, which refers to blood, specifically the spilling of blood,* has three distinct meanings. The first is the bloody pelvis bone of the female reproduction system, also referred to as Ezekiel's Wheel.

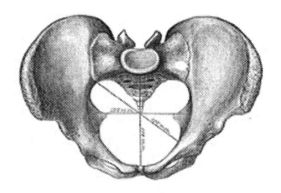

Ezekiel's Wheel

The second is metaphorical and refers to a sect or specific group. The third is literal and refers to the scarlet beast that **was alive and then died** indicating a specific person that has been given that title because of the horrible crimes committed during his lifetime.

In regard to the second meaning, Electron is the beast, the woman sitting on the scarlet beast called *religion.* In regard to the third, Constantine is the scarlet beast that was alive and then died, also known as the eighth king. However, before I explain Constantine further, let me set the tone for second meaning of *scarlet beast*.

The Scarlet Beast – All Faiths, All Religions

The scarlet beast represents all religion. For, all religion has murdered men in the name of God. The Jews, the Christians and the Muslims have all spilled the blood of GOD's prophets and servants, those who spoke the truth from the true and living GOD, ATOM.

However, the religion that worships Electron best and openly is the *Catholic church.* The others have been deceived. They don't know who they worship or who they call God. They think Electron is benevolent when their eyes show them a different picture of poverty, racism, torture and death.

What a great and easy deception religion is!! Now, every person who is compelled to worship in these days bows down to Electron not knowing. But the Catholic church and it members worship Satan openly and without apology.

The Scarlet Beast – The Catholic Church

The Catholic Church is aptly referred to as the scarlet beast because of the amount of blood that it shed for Satan's rise to power. Over her four century rise to power, Jewels and Gentiles, which are the seven lampstands of ATOM, called Philadelphia and Smyrna – Judah, Pergamum and Laodicea – Israel, Thyatira – Jerusalem, Ephesus and Sardis – the Gentiles, were slaughtered by the millions for the sake of purging the world of sin, purging the world of the Jewels of GOD.

Now, the Gentiles have led the Catholic Church from its inception. Satan – Electron is their god. Millions worship her and follow her commandments, reading her canon, written by Constantine, the eight king. The canon leaves out the truth of GOD, of ATOM, omitting of the books of condemnation against the Gentiles, such as the book of Jude and the book of Revelation. These followers of Catholicism are completely deceived. It is an easy deception.

For who made Mary, your Catholic icon, a god to be prayed to? Is she part of the Trinity of GOD – the Father, Son, and Holy Spirit **and Mary**? *Hell No!*

Where was Mary when the world was formed by Proton, Gluon and Neutron? When the body and mind of mankind was fashioned by Cytosine, Thymine and Uracil? When ATOM breathed the breath of life into man?

Then she is an idol – Electron, Adenine and Guanine – and those who pray to her and her image with beads in hand pray to Satan. That's true! For Satan is Mary. Mary is the form, the idealism, the icon that represents Electron in human form. She is the weeping Satan, the mother with her hu–man child. She is the mother with the child on her lap, her own child – Cain, the Gentile, born of Israel, who was called Eve when the earth was still new.

Donatello, The Scarlet Beast

Constantine, the Eighth King

The scarlet beast whose name is Pope Constantine is the eighth king. He is the one that was alive and then died. He was a Gentile, typhoid Mary's son, a conqueror. See him sitting oblivious to the truth on his mother's lap (Electron) while Adenine and Guanine sit idly by...waiting.

Constantine changed the LORD's Day of worship from the Sabbath – the seventh day – that GOD ordained from the Creation of the world to the first day of the week. It was easy to do. The deception celebrates the resurrection of Christ. No. It actually, it celebrates Satan's ascension to the throne of GOD after Jesus Christ died on the cross.

Constantine was corrupt, a confidence man; and like the other seven kings, he, too, will be cast into the lake of fire. He was Satan's con; con means against; he was against Cryst – the Holy One, the LORD whose name is Proton. He was for Electron – the evil one who is commonly known as Satan or the devil.

And Satan used him to deceive the world with religious ideals. It was part of her plan to conquer the world.

Trust is an important element in the art of deception. If you can't trust the church who can you trust?

It is the classic story of Little Red Riding Hood and the wolf. Innocent Israel was tricked into sleeping with the devil by someone highly trusted and thought to be trust worthy. Right now, so is every man, but we will be rescued by the woodsmen, Thymine and his anti–bacterial armies, with their tools, axes and picks and fire.

The bacterial Electron, the matter particle, the purveyor of death, pretends to be someone that she is not. She pretends to be Christ. It is the Cinderella story. The scullery maid pretends to be the princess. Her faggot, *oh sorry*, fairy godmother – Electron – gives her the tools – clothes and transportation to pull off the deception. Under false pretenses, she steals your heart with her sad, sad story causing you to weep and carry on with her. You buy the deception and pay for it in full with your life. You and your two relatives are left behind, enslaved. In disbelief, you are left asking the question, "What happened here?" They tricked you.

Michelangelo saw Satan rise up out of the body of Jesus Christ and ascend to the throne of GOD. All who saw her called her the Virgin Mary. But she is no virgin – far from it. She is, however, the weeping one that has appeared too many around the world. She weeps because she is about to lose her seat on GOD's throne. She weeps to convince you of her innocence. But ... she is a liar.

Here is Electron (Adenine) rising up from the body of Christ after the crucifixion, the evil spirit departing every body after death. This is Electron before she began to impersonate Christ, the SON of ATOM, calling herself Mary and acting as if she is really holy. She is a conflicted spirit. This is the one you worship, the deceiver.

Michelangelo, Adenine Rising from the Body of Christ

Here, ATOM allowed Michelangelo to see Electron (Guanine) flying, rising swiftly up from the tomb of Christ where she startled the two guards who fled. After his work of decomposition had begun and Electron had her fill of blood and flesh, Guanine rose up out of the tomb. This internal decomposition is the fate of your cows.

Michelangelo, Guanine Leaving the Tomb of Christ

Calvary was the beginning of the age of deception in earnest, the age of the Gentiles, the age of lies. For, with these pictures, Electron convinced the world that Christ has risen, that she is Christ and that people of religion should worship her on Sunday, the first day of the week instead of Saturday, the seventh day.

The Pope's Authority Over Man

Now listen carefully: If the Pontiff or any of the Popes before or after him were truly emissaries of the living GOD, would they need your prayers? Would not the Healer, who is life itself, have sent his antibody armies to heal him? But that did not happen. No anti–bodies were dispatched to save his life. His ruler, his God is not the Living GOD. His God is death itself – Electron, the Matter Particle, commonly known to all men as Satan.

So, the vision of the three young girls who had the vision of the Lady (Adenine) weeping, weeping has come to pass. The one in white – the Pope – has led many millions of people astray, away from the true and living GOD, ATOM. Many millions are worshiping Satan because of the one in white.

Now understand this: The Pope's blessings are meaningless. He has no connection with the true and living GOD, with ATOM. He cannot save you. He cannot save himself. He cannot bless you. He cannot forgive your sins. No man on Earth can forgive your sins. This is a part of Satan's grand deception. You cannot donate enough money to the church to buy your way into heaven. Hello! Is anyone listening? Is the whole world mad? Am I the only one who can see the deception covering the horizon?

In Satan's plan to ascend to the throne of the Most High, the Catholic Church did a monumental thing. It became the highest power of man on earth. The Pope became the only authority on earth that could presumably condemn a man to hell or offer full absolution of sin. What a crock of crap!

And Also Understand This: The Pope's blessings are meaningless. He is not a superior being, connected to GOD; GOD's emissary on earth.

I am closer to ATOM, to GOD than your Pope and I am just a servant. I don't bless people. If you want a blessing, call upon ATOM. He can hear you pray. He alone can answer prayers, not me or any other person upon the earth. I can't intercede for you. I can pray for you, but you would do better to pray for yourself. **Don't depend on man!** Depend on GOD, on ATOM alone.

The Pope puts his pants on one leg at a time just like you do. He has no direct connection with the true and living GOD. He cannot save you. He cannot save himself. He cannot bless you. He cannot forgive your sins or absolve you of your unholy intercourse. No man on Earth can forgive your sins. This is a part of Satan's grand deception. You cannot donate enough money to the Catholic church or any other organization to buy your way into heaven.

ATOM gave no man on earth this honor. Only GOD knows the good and the bad that men do. Only he has full access to the DNA Book of Life. Only ATOM can forgive and exonerate, bless and save. No human being, let alone one elected by mere men, was ever was given that authority. Even those chosen by the Most High, by the LORD Proton were not given the authority to forgive sins or condemn people to hell. Stop worshiping your appointed idols, the officials of the church. They are no closer to favor with GOD than you are.

After some centuries of violence and death, all religions have adopted her pagan practices; practices that began in the Catholic Church. Now, the majority of people in the world worship on Sunday, shrugging their shoulders at the truth, claiming that the first day of the week is more convenient.

The Catholic Church in Prophecy

> **His** [Constantine's] **ten horns are ten kings who have not yet risen to power; they will be appointed to their kingdoms for one brief moment to reign with the beast** [Electron]. **They** [all who follow the Catholic Church and tradition] **will all agree to give their power and authority to him.**

Revelation 17:12 – 13

What Catholic does not confess his sins to a man who has no power; a man who admonishes them and tells them to pray to Satan by saying Hail Mary. (It's really hell Mary, for she is truly a hellion.] If you follow the one who created man you don't need a human intercessor. The Holy Spirit, Uracil, in the forebrain, in the outer courtyard, is your intercessor. He prays for you even when you don't know what to pray for.

Constantine's ten horns are ten kings. The number ten means "all". All Popes, Bishops, and Cardinals, priests, and clergy who have ruled in the Catholic institution since Constantine follow Satan. The Electron is their god.

> **Together they will wage war against the Lamb, but the Lamb will defeat them because he is LORD over all LORDs and King over all kings, and his people are the called and chosen and faithful ones.**

And the angel said to me, "The waters where the prostitute is sitting represent masses of people of every nation and language."

Revelation 17:14 – 15

And those who love this world and all of the wonders it has to offer follow the prostitute, the devil, because they have been seduced by the pleasures she holds in her hand.

But the Catholic Church has no interest in the prostitute. They don't know she is leading them.

The scarlet beast and his ten horns – which represent ten kings who will reign with him – all hate the prostitute. They will strip her naked, eat her flesh, and burn her remains with fire.

Revelation 17:16

The Scarlet Beast hates Satan, hates Electron. And they hate her because they are not permitted to enjoy the pleasures she offers. For, although the clergy ritually do the bidding of the devil and pray to her idols, they do not publicly enjoy the pleasures of the flesh.

For, GOD has put a plan into their minds, a plan that will carry out his purposes. They will mutually agree to give their authority to the scarlet beast, and so the words of GOD will be fulfilled.

Revelation 17:17

The priests and nuns who serve in the Catholic Church have signed a celibacy covenant, which does not allow them to participate in the sins of the flesh. (Of course, GOD sees what they do in secret. He will judge every person according to what is recorded in the DNA Book of Life.)

And in this context, the plan and the words of the LORD Proton have been fulfilled. Let everyone say 'Amen'.

The Sunday Worshipers

Well now, some will say that you are worshiping on Sunday to celebrate the resurrection of Christ on Easter Sunday. But GOD told you to keep the Sabbath Holy. But you couldn't even do that!

Let's see now. This explanation looks strong but if any of you would bother to slide your fingernail across the surface, you would find that the foundation of this lie is sinking sand, rocks and briers, whitewash.

The truth of Satan's reign lies underneath. Whitewash and tears hide a multitude of sins.

The great Constantine was the enemy of my Father, of ATOM. His actions, words, and edicts turned the whole world against the Holy One and caused all Christians to follow the evil one. Constantine is the Scarlet beast; Constantine and the Catholic Church are the protectors of Satan. Was it not the great Constantine, Satan's son, who changed the Most High's day of worship from Sabbath to Sunday and you followed? Was it not Constantine, the infidel, that scarlet beast who was alive but then died, who murdered GOD's children by the thousands in secret then confiscated a plot of land and claimed it was the resting place of GOD's Son. He built a great Temple in Jerusalem and millions of people go there each year to kiss the tomb and worship the anti–Christ believing that he is Christ. And nearby, in another ambiguous spot is the supposed birthplace of Christ – another lie hatched by Satan, the anti–Christ. Millions to that Middle Eastern city of Jerusalem where people go to worship and kiss the ground as if it were a holy place. Infidels!

I will tell you this. Judas who betrayed Jesus during his last days on earth will receive more mercy than Constantine will. Judas saw the error of the lies he had believed and took his own life in repentance and sorrow. He saw that he did not deserve to live. He was nothing without Christ, the Holy One, Proton.

While Constantine was chosen to fulfill this purpose, he will surely come up out of the bottomless pit and go to eternal destruction where the worm never dies and the fire never goes out.

The False Prophet – Adenine

How can I explain this to you? Like me, in the beginning of my incarceration, I was seeking a human person, a historical figure like Mohammed or one of the others. But, in the end, I came to understand that the false prophet is none other than the ever talking Adenine. Isaiah recorded:

Your eyes will see the king [Cytosine, the Logos, the Word] **in all his splendor, and you will see a land** [your mind] **that stretches into the distance.**

You will think back to this time of terror when the Ass–yrian officers [Electron and his bacterial armies in the bowels] **outside your walls counted your towers** [the body of every man, every hu–man] **and estimated how much plunder they would get from your fallen city** [Jerusalem].

But soon they will all be gone. These fierce, violent people [Adenine, Guanine, bacteria — demons] **with a strange, unknown language will disappear.**

Instead, you will see Zion [the forebrain] **as a place of worship and celebration. You will see Jerusalem** [the hindbrain], **a city quiet and secure. The LORD** [Proton] **will be our Mighty One. He will be like a wide river of protection that no enemy can cross.**

For the LORD [ATOM] **is our judge, our lawgiver, and our King. He will care for us and save us.**

Isaiah 28:17 – 22

So now, the Tower of Babel[74] (babble) had humble beginnings. Today, it is literally a fast growing weed, created when Eve swallowed semen from Adam's urinary tract. That tree of good and evil, that Tower of Babel began its rise into the kingdom of Heaven, onto Mount Zion, the forehead, by stealing vitamins and nutrients from food offerings intended for the Tree of Life, intended for the adrenergic network of fibres within the Sympathetic Nervous System.

The tiny roots of that tower grew deep into the groin, reaching down to the feet before venturing upward toward the light. That's why you trip and fall and cannot control your stumbling.

When it emerged from the fecal rich soil in the bowels, it began to grow in earnest, greedily stealing the synaptical light from the sun – light and energy intended for the tree of life, the auto–immune system. Mankind began to grow ill and then to die. So the false prophet, the whore monger Electron–Adenine who told Eve through Jerusalem that she would not surely did was a liar and a thief. Her prophecy, "you won't die" was a lie. She is therefore the true false prophet.

It is the Tower of Babel (babble), the Parasympathetic nervous system – strings of bile and gall knitted together, that causes the rulers of the earth (the demons / bacteria in your body) to spring into action. They speak constantly in a language of fear, remorse, bitterness, and hatred – a language that no man is born knowing.

---

74   From the forebrain, Electron, Satan talks endlessly narrating your life, making judgment calls on right and wrong. You listen to her opinion because you believe it is your own. Her voice sounds like your voice ... in your head. But outside of your head, her voice sounds like a nail on a chalkboard. In your head she and her demons babble. She is a mumbling, murmuring, mess speaking nonsense. She is quite insane. She is the reason that you question your own sanity.

In melancholia[75], they give you their assessment of everything they see – swearing by your name, with your voice. Judging your surroundings in negative terms, they see the evil that they create. They ignore every good thing. After their babbling comes into your mind and you have had time to take it all in, they wait to see if you will accept what they say as truth. Sometimes you don't – for they speak random lies causing you to ask yourself, "Where did that come from?" Sometimes you do – because they cause you to crave attention as they crave attention. They are selfish and depraved, always ready for a fight, or to cry – super sensitive in every way.

---

75   Melancholia is a manic-depressive psychosis characterized by constant complaints, hallucinations, and delusions. It affects every person who has the Tower of Babel (babble) within their body and every person born has that tower.

Gluon - Mount of Olives
Muscular & Skeletal System
Thymine - Land
Archangel Michael - Commander of GOD's Armies

Neutron - Mount Zion
Cardiovascular System
Uracil - Land
Archangel Gabriel - Seal of the Living GOD

Proton - Jerusalem
Sympathetic Nervous System
Cytosine - Crystalline GOD - Land
Christ - The Mind of All Men

Interior Jugular
Carotid Artery
Subclavian Vein
Aorta
Pulmonary Arteries
Heart
Descending Aorta

Superior Vena Cava
Pulmonary Veins
Bronchial Artery
Interior Vena Cava

Deoxyribonucleic Acid
The Tree of Life

ADRENERGIC FIBRES
Connect the Sympathetic Nervous
System from the hindbrain to the feet.

Femoral Artery

Femoral Vein

Tree of Good
and Evil,
Adenine
and Guanine

Adenine - Bladder, Water
Euphrates River
Liver, Kidneys, Prostate

Guanine - Bowels, Water
Assyria
Colon

Center of the Garden
"Don't eat of it!"

Root of the
Parasympathetic Nervous System
that runs throughout the body,
built with Cholinergic Fibres.

Tower of Babel

Tower of Babel

207

Bile

Bile has two important meanings for this dissertation. Physiologically, bile is a yellow or greenish sticky alkaline fluid, a bitter waste secreted by the liver and passed into the duodenum (the first part of the small intestine) where it aids especially in the emulsification and absorption of fats. The alkaline fluid is a soluble salt obtained from the ashes of plants, which we eat, and consisting largely of potassium or sodium carbonate.

Bile or gall is the result of the swelling of plant tissue after eating grains such as oats and processed or bleached wheat flour. The swelling is usually due to fungi or insect parasites.

In other words, the electron, the matter particle that was created to dispose of, break down waste, used her creative talents for another purpose. From her home in the pelvis where she was in charge of waste disposal, she began to build a tower made from the bile she collected and the ample amount of gall secreted from the liver. This tower she would build up to heaven, to the cranial cavity, to the very throne of GOD. At the top of the tower, Satan could have control over the body of man. But she was stopped at the forebrain of every person just behind the eyes. The scriptures say:

> **At one time, the whole world spoke a single language and used the same words.** [It was the language of GOD — a scientific language, very intelligent, comprised of physical laws, natural, laws, and spiritual laws.] **As the people migrated eastward** [from the brain — Jerusalem, the Mount of Olives and Mount Zion], **they found a plain in the land of Babylonia** [the pelvic centre] **and settled there. They began to talk about construction projects. "Come," they said, "let's make great piles of burnt brick** [feces, choline — phosphor] **and collect natural asphalt** [salt — the alkaline fluid, sticky bile] **to use as mortar.**
>
> **Let's build a great city with a tower that reaches to the skies – a monument to our greatness!** [The tower reaches from the pelvic — Babylonia to the hindbrain — Jerusalem, from the sacrum to the cranium and back down to the toes.] **This will bring us together** [Jewels and Gentiles] **and keep us from scattering all over the world."**
>
> **But the LORD** [Proton] **came down** [from Jerusalem, the hindbrain] **to see the city and the tower the people** [bacteria] **were building. "Look!" he said** [to the Gluon and Neutron]. **"If they can accomplish this when they have just begun to take advantage of their common language** [love] **and political unity** [liberty], **just think of what they will do later. Nothing will be impossible for them! Come, let's go down, and give them different languages. Then they won't be able to understand each other."**

In that way, the LORD scattered them [Judah, Israel, Jerusalem, and the Gentiles] all over the earth; and that ended the building of the city [but not the cholinergic tower that leads up to the city of GOD].

That is why the city was called Babel [babble], because it was there that the LORD confused the people by giving them many languages [the single language of the angels and the many languages of the demons, bacteria within, the voices in your head], thus scattering them across the earth.

Genesis 11:1 – 9

The tower that Satan engineered into the body and man and hence the genetic code is that famous Tower of Babel. But GOD came down from his seat in heaven and saw the work that had been done on the tower and the city. He stopped the building of the city, but the tower had been completed. It is the parasympathetic nervous system. For, they had done their work stealthily – the matter particle and her servants – the parasites, and sycophants.

Now, Electron and her parasympathetic nervous system is why you walk into a room and immediately forget why you walked in, what you came to do. Forgetfulness is not a factor of age. It is a factor of Electron squashing your thoughts, making Cryst – Cytosine work twice as hard to bring wisdom into your conscious mind. Because Satan is ever present in your mind, you reject the one who could save you and his wisdom. I have rejected the truth for days at a time thinking that it was Satan talking to me. Finally, I heard the words, "think about this logically". Finally, I would come to understand that the liar – Adenine – was keeping me from believing the truth. I rejected the truth because her lies are so compelling. Superficially, her lies seem true. But, eventually, what is done in the dark comes to the light. The light of truth always emerges.

What's the Matter With You?

Now, the bile fibres run from the cranial to the sacrum and from the cranial to the hand, which moves, seemingly at will, jumping to do evil, to do Satan's bidding. Through the parasympathetic nerve, she directs the eyes to look at that which you are not even aware. She guides the eye to wherever she wants it to go. She guides the hand to the sacrum. Haven't you read this scripture?

So, if your eye – even if it is your good eye – causes you to lust, gouge it out and throw it away. It is better for you to lose one part of your body than for your whole body to be thrown into hell."

And if your hand – even if it is your stronger hand – causes you to

sin, cut it off and throw it away. It is better for you to lose one part of your body than for your whole body to be thrown into hell.

Matthew 5:29 – 30

Why do you think that Christ gave such radical advice? It is precisely because of the parasympathetic nerve that you have come to accept her, to defend her – as if you would lose something wonderful without her influence. I assure you. You would not. No joy would be lost, only the pain and discomfort, the death that comes after her lovemaking.

Now, bile or gall – the base material of the parasympathetic nervous system – is associated with either one of two humors in the old physiology. They are irascibility and melancholy.

Irascibility is marked by a hot temper and easily provoked anger. It is mania. It is characterized by chronic irritation, a constant state of exasperation, fretting and friction.

Melancholy, on the other hand, is an abnormal state attributed to an excess of black bile and characterized by depression of the spirits. It is a pensive mood characterized by dejection. It is bitterness, utter despair. It is marked by lethargy – the inability to move with energy and vitality. We must talk ourselves into getting out of bed in the morning, drink caffeinated beverages to get going, drag ourselves home at night and we are so exhausted that we cannot sleep. The demons keep us awake half the night chatting, planning, judging, or as we stay awake we watch deceptive infomercials about how Satan's Gentile children made it rich and so can you. No you can't. You don't have their support system – Electron – on your side. You are destined for poverty – poor in spirit – until the true Cryst – Proton returns. So, while we wait, we are being dragged down inch by inch into dementia – each of us. What has been accepted as normal, as 'that's life' has become normal, has become 'life'. We have no energy. GOD, the LORD Proton surrounds us and watches over us but Electron – Adenine and Guanine rule over us. The LORD Proton is the spiritual Sun, the Son of GOD, our true energy source.

Because of the inconceivable amount of bacterial matter that surrounds us – demons, we are constantly asking each other, "What's the matter; what's the matter with you? Now you know the answer.

The Effect of Bile and Gall on the Pyramidine Man

Today, all people have fist fights with fear, anguish, and sorrow. We are always fighting, always complaining. We have unnecessary bruises and our eyes are bloodshot from crying. We are rebellious, throwing tantrums without knowing why, seeking to be the centre of attention. We have carved our lives around our fears and our passions. We have exchanged our natural cool responses for chaos.

"The Gentiles said we should listen to our feelings and we did. We bought their self–help books. But there were no remedies for the Jewels in those books – only traps, tricks and further indebtedness to Satan. We are slaves of our own choosing. But, if we have a chance at freedom, wouldn't we take it?"

Melancholy is swollen plant tissue in the body brought on by parasitic activity, bacterium, the matter particle herself. Guanine is black gall, the second half of the double helix.

Adenine and Guanine is Satan's thumbprint, her DNA written on her children in cholic acid. Cholic acid is an element within crystalline bile that has been lodged within the straight chain of the pyramidine man.

Cholic acid, the sticky bile is how the daily sacrifices were stopped. The yellow or greenish sticky alkaline fluid is secreted by the liver and passed into the first part of the duodenum. There, everything it encounters sticks to it, causing a backup to the liver and bloating with excess gas in the small and large intestine. Unused energy sits in park, almost motionless, waiting to be processed, growing more dense until it is eventually lubricated enough to move out of the body or coaxed into budging with a laxative.

> **His** [the matter particle's] **army** [bacterium] **will take over the Temple fortress** [the outer courtyard, the forebrain], **polluting the sanctuary** [the brain and the body], **putting a stop to the daily sacrifices** [the elimination of waste], **and setting up the sacrilegious object** [the parasympathetic nervous system] **that causes desecration** [of the body of man, ATOM's temple or home].
>
> *Daniel 11:31 – 32*

Because of the bile, our tongues crave sugar, carbonation and sweet cream – anything to take the bitter edge off. All of which exacerbates the bowel blockage even more. We have irritated bowels. We are full of gas, bloated. We have irritated and bitter spirits. Where is the joy?

Hell

The five kings who have already died will be in hell though Mr. Hitler. Then the sixth that now reigns and finally the seventh that is still to come will join the others. In the end, all of those who refuse to believe the truth that would save them will enter that filthy, gaseous mess, the bottomless pit. Their spiritual bodies and conscious minds will boil day and night in that cooking pot, where they will belch up fire and brimstone. O didn't you know? Hell is a sewer filled with the earth's excrement and replenished daily. It must be cleaned; the excrement must be decomposed, eaten. The sinners, the murderers, pedophiles and liars will live there (if you want to call it living) and perish there – eternal destruction. Many will cry.

> **"On judgment day, many will tell me, 'LORD, LORD, we prophesied in your name and cast out demons in your name and performed many miracles in your name.'** [in God's name, in Jesus' name. But … Electron – the devil is also called God, is also called Jesus. GOD's name is ATOM.] **… I will reply, 'I never knew you. Go away; the things you did were unauthorized.'"**

Matthew 7:22 – 23

Why will these so–called "good works" be unauthorized by the living GOD – by the author of help? Because Satan – Electron is the source of all men's so called "good ideas" in this Age of the Gentiles. Satan uses people and seemingly benevolent ideas, benefits, and religious events to deceive all people into believing that she is GOD. She is the one giving mankind their "clever ideas" via the parasympathetic nervous system – the Tower of Babel. The outer courtyard has been turned over to the nations – the bacterial horde; the gray matter covers your brain, your thoughts, your conscious mind.

The "I" Doll

Electron keeps you wanting for his demon armies, the bacterial horde that controls the body, causing you to crave everything from sugar to sex to murder. They crave beauty – the magnetic device, the lure and all of the trappings of beauty. They are the centre of all attention, every one, every where. Every man is concerned with the pain she inflicts, with the fear in the pit of your stomach, with the fat, with the thin, with the lack of love, with too much love, the right dress, hair, shoes, me, me, me.

And who is making you think constantly about such things?

Electron is the I doll (idol). She causes people to constantly say, "What about me?", "I want …", "I need …", "Mine". Electron is Gog and the one you call on constantly, "O ma gog!" The Electron is the one angrily babbling on and on in your mind about injustice, bitter rejection, retaliation, and revenge. Satan is the voice of confusion, anger – not reason. She is the one reminding you over and over of the bonehead ideas you tried, ideas that failed – ideas that she gave you, which caused you to lose your money, wife, or job. She is the one reminding you day and night of the sins you committed against GOD – sins she tempted you into. She causes all people to think and speak about hate and war, to accuse the innocent, to worry about love, to crave pornography and drugs, and to live in anxiety and fear. She is the overwhelming urge. She is the one who makes you cry in your car, when you are alone. She is the one singing songs endlessly in your head. She is the one keeping you awake all night – so you will turn to her and curse GOD and to stop trusting in him for your deliverance.

Decide for yourself if I, Cyrus, speak the truth or not. There is only one Living GOD, one Proton, one Creator, one Truth.

Do you doubt it? Be logical. Would Satan work to destroy herself, to expose the truth of her deception? Would the devil tell you the truth about the devil?

NO!

She would tell you to doubt the truth. She would put a fear in the pit of your stomach to turn your thoughts from the truth and back to her lies. She would keep the meaning of her lies hidden so she can keep right on deceiving you. She would work to keep the seven seals from being opened. She would urge you from the pit of your stomach to your conscious mind to doubt the truth of GOD so that you would follow her into battle and be lost at Megiddo.

There is only one who is Death followed by the Grave. She is both Good and Evil. She is the lure and the trap. She is the Destroyer – one Electron, two minds, two purposes in one body.

If you cannot believe me, believe the scriptures when they say that Electron is "This great dragon – the ancient serpent called the Devil, or Satan, the one deceiving the whole world."

The Destruction of Babylon

After all this, I saw another angel [Cytosine] **come down from heaven with great authority, and the earth** [the body of every man] **grew bright with his splendor. He gave a mighty shout, "Babylon is fallen – that great city is fallen;** [the Baby Loins has been thrown down like a stone]**!**

She has become the hideout of demons and evil spirits, a nest for filthy buzzards, and a den for dreadful beasts [all bacteria commingled with mucus and puss and urine]. **For, all the nations have drunk the wine of her passionate immorality. The rulers of the world have committed adultery with her, and merchants throughout the world have grown rich as a result of her luxurious living."**

Then I heard another voice calling from heaven [the voice of Uracil], **"Come away from** [Electron], **my people. Do not take part in her sins, or you will be punished with her.**

For, her sins are piled as high as heaven, and [ATOM] **is ready to judge her for her evil deeds. Do to her as she has done to your people. Give her a double penalty for all her evil deeds. She brewed a cup of terror for others, so give her twice as much as she gave out. She has lived in luxury and pleasure, so match it now with torments and sorrows. She boasts, 'I am queen on my throne. I am no helpless widow. I will not experience sorrow.' Therefore, the sorrows of death and mourning and famine will overtake her in a single day. She will be utterly consumed by fire, for the Lord GOD who judges her is mighty."**

And the rulers of the world [the Gentiles] **who took part in her immoral acts and enjoyed her great luxury will mourn for her as they see the smoke rising from her charred remains. They will stand at a distance, terrified by her great torment. They will cry out, "How terrible, how terrible for Babylon, that great city! In one single moment** [ATOM's] **judgment came on her." The merchants of the world will weep and mourn for her, for there is no one left to buy their goods** [their medicines, their love potions, their anxiety potions, their psychic reading and horror-scopes]. **She bought great quantities of gold, silver, jewels, pearls, fine linen, purple dye, silk, scarlet cloth, every kind of perfumed wood, ivory goods, objects made of expensive wood, bronze, iron, and marble. She also bought cinnamon, spice, incense, myrrh, frankincense, wine, olive oil, fine flour, wheat, cattle, sheep, horses, chariots, and slaves – yes, she even traded in human lives.**

"All the fancy things you loved so much are gone," they cry. "The luxuries and splendor that you prized so much will never be yours again. They are gone forever." The merchants who became wealthy by selling her these things will stand at a distance, terrified by her great torment. They will weep and cry. "How terrible, how terrible for that great city! She was so beautiful – like a woman clothed in finest purple and scarlet linens, decked out with gold and precious stones and pearls!

And in one single moment all the wealth of the city [of Babylon] **is gone!" And all the ship owners** [bacterial blood sucking corpses that ride on molecules within the body of every person] **and captains of the merchant ships** [corpuscles] **and their** [bacterial] **crews will stand at a**

distance. They will weep as they watch the smoke ascend [the spirit of Adenine rising; the spirit of Guanine rising], and they will say, "Where in all the world is there another city like this?"

And they will throw [crystalline] dust [the dust from the bodies of mankind] on their heads to show their great sorrow. And they will say, "How terrible, how terrible for the great city! She made us all rich from her great wealth. And now in a single hour it is all gone."

But you, O heaven, rejoice over her fate. And you also rejoice, O holy people of [ATOM] and apostles and prophets! For at last GOD has judged her on your behalf.

Then a mighty angel [Israel] picked up a boulder as large as a great millstone. He threw it into the ocean and shouted, "Babylon, the great city, will be thrown down as violently as I have thrown away this stone, and she will disappear forever.

Never again will the sound of music be heard there – no more harps, songs, flutes, or trumpets. There will be no industry of any kind, and no more milling of grain [sexual grinding]. Her nights will be dark, without a single lamp. There will be no happy voices of brides and grooms. This will happen because her merchants, who were the greatest in the world, deceived the nations with her sorceries. In her streets the blood of the prophets was spilled. She was the one who slaughtered GOD's people all over the world."

Revelation 18:1 – 24

Now, don't worry, Israel, about the destruction of Babylon. Don't you remember? There was joy in the body of man before Adenine came along and introduced you to joy strong. GOD gave you joy from the beginning. He did not give you the kind that would kill you. He gave you the kind of joy that would bring you happiness here on earth and in heaven. It is the natural order of things. Adenine, Electron gave you joy strong and death rolled up in one sweet and sour package. Don't despair. The joy that GOD, ATOM gives is better than anything Electron can give you. And ... you will live after it is over without contaminating the genetic pool.

Salvation

After this, I heard the sound of a vast crowd [all mankind] in heaven [the mind] shouting, "Hallelujah! Salvation is from our GOD [ATOM]. Glory and power belong to him alone. His judgments are just and true. He has punished the great prostitute who corrupted the earth with her immorality, and he has avenged the murder of his servants." Again and again their voices rang, "Hallelujah! The smoke from that city ascends forever and forever!" Then the twenty–four elders and the four living beings fell down and worshiped GOD, who was sitting on the throne. They cried out, "Amen! Hallelujah!"

And from the throne came a voice that said, "Praise our GOD, all his servants, from the least to the greatest, all who fear him."

Then I heard again what sounded like the shout of a huge crowd, or the roar of mighty ocean waves, or the crash of loud thunder: "Hallelujah! For the Lord our GOD [ATOM], the Almighty, reigns. Let us be glad and rejoice and honor him. For the time has come for the wedding feast of the Lamb, and his bride [all of the Jewels, all of mankind] has prepared herself. She is permitted to wear the finest white linen." (Fine linen represents the good deeds done by the people of GOD.)

And the angel [Uracil, Gabriel] said, "Write this: Blessed are those who are invited to the wedding feast of the Lamb." And he added, "These are true words that come from GOD." Then I fell down at his feet to worship him, but he said, "No, don't worship me. For I am a servant of GOD, just like you and other brothers and sisters who testify of their faith in Jesus. Worship GOD. For the essence of prophecy is to give a clear witness for Jesus."

Then I saw heaven opened, and a white horse was standing there. And the one sitting on the horse was named Faithful and True. For he [Proton] judges fairly and then goes to war. His eyes were bright like flames of fire, and on his head were many crowns [the crown of every person's head].

A name was written on him, and only he knew what it meant. [The name is Deoxyribonucleic Acid (DNA).]

He was clothed with a robe dipped in blood [every man's blood is his blood], and his title was the Word of GOD [he speaks to and for all mankind; he only speaks the truth].

The armies of heaven [antibodies and bodies], dressed in pure white linen, followed him on white horses. From his mouth came a sharp sword [truth], and with it he struck down the nations. He ruled them with an iron rod, and he trod the winepress of the fierce wrath of Almighty GOD.

On his robe and thigh was written this title: King of kings and Lord of lords.

Then I saw an angel standing in the sun [Proton], shouting to the vultures flying high in the sky: "Come! Gather together for the great banquet GOD has prepared.

Come and eat the flesh of [bacterial] kings, captains and strong warriors; of horses and their riders; and of all humanity, both free and slave, small and great."

Then I saw the beast gathering the kings of the earth and their armies in order to fight against the one sitting on the horse [Proton] and his [anti-bacterial] army.

And the beast [Electron] was captured, and with him the false prophet [Adenine] who did mighty miracles on behalf of the beast – miracles that deceived all who had accepted the mark of the beast [called choice or election] and who worshiped his statue [called liberty].

Both the beast and his false prophet were thrown alive into the lake of fire that burns with sulfur. Their entire [bacterial] army was killed by the sharp sword [truth] that came out of the mouth of the one riding the white horse [Proton]. And all the vultures of the sky gorged themselves on the dead bodies.

Revelation 19:1 – 21

The Last Judgment

Then I saw an angel come down from heaven [Gluon, Michael] with the key to the bottomless pit and a heavy chain in his hand. He seized the dragon – that old serpent, the Devil, Satan [Electron] – and bound him in chains for a thousand years.

The angel [Michael] threw him into the bottomless pit [the bowels and bladder filled with the urine and feces of all men], which he then shut and locked so Satan could not deceive the nations anymore until the thousand years were finished. Afterward he would be released again for a little while.

Then I saw thrones, and the people sitting on them had been given the authority to judge [Israel has the power and authority to judge].

And I saw the souls of those who had been beheaded for their testimony about **Jesus** [Jerusalem was beheaded for preaching the WORD of GOD], **for proclaiming the WORD of GOD** [of ATOM].

And I saw the souls of those who had not worshiped the beast or his statue, nor accepted his mark on their forehead or their hands. They came to life again, and they reigned with Christ for a thousand years.

This is the first resurrection. (The rest of the dead did not come back to life until the thousand years had ended.)

Blessed and holy are those who share in the first resurrection. For them the second death holds no power, but they will be priests of **GOD** [of ATOM] **and of Christ** [Proton] **and will reign with him a thousand years** [on earth and up in heaven].

The Final Defeat – Election

When the thousand years end, Satan, Electron will be let out of his prison. He will go out to deceive the nations from every corner of the earth, which are called Gog and Magog. He will gather them together for battle – a mighty host, as numberless as sand along the shore.

And I saw them as they went up on the broad plain of the earth [the top of the head is the broad plain] **and surrounded GOD's people** [Cytosine, Thymine and Uracil] **and the beloved city** [Jerusalem at the hindbrain].

But fire from heaven came down on the attacking armies and consumed them. Then the Devil [Electron], **who betrayed them, was thrown into the lake of fire that burns with sulfur, joining the beast** [Guanine] **and the false prophet** [Adenine]. **There they will be tormented day and night forever and ever.**

Revelation 20:1 – 10

The Judging of Mankind and Humankind

And I saw a great white throne, and I saw the one who was sitting on it [Proton, Christ]. **The earth and sky** [all living beings] **fled from his presence, but they found no place to hide. I saw the dead, both great and small, standing before GOD's throne.**

And the books were opened, including the Book of Life [the DNA record of every life]. **And the dead were judged according to the things written in the books, according to what they had done.**

The sea [the matter particle – Electron] **gave up the dead in it, and death** [Adenine] **and the grave** [Guanine] **gave up the dead in them. They were all judged according to their deeds. And death and the grave were thrown into the lake of fire. This is the second death. And anyone whose name was not found recorded in the Book of Life** [this book includes the Gentiles] **was thrown into the lake of fire.**

Revelation 20:11 – 15

Everyone's name is recorded in the Book of Life – the DNA record. It is a complex record of every man's life. However, everyone's name is not written in the Lamb's Book of Life – the one that was written before the world was made. It is a very small book. There are only nine names in that book. They are Proton, Gluon and Neutron – the force particles, the rulers of the planet Earth. And there is Cytosine, Thymine, and Uracil – the rulers of the Sympathetic Nervous System in every person's body, also called the earth or clay. And finally, there is Judah, Israel and Jerusalem – GOD's three Jewels, made in the image of Proton, Gluon and Neutron and produced in a 12–year cyclical birth pattern. The double helix will be snatched out of the DNA chain and thrown into the lake of fire – when Satan – Electron is thrown into the lake of fire. No more Gentiles will be born after the 1000–year Reign of Cryst has ended. There will be peace among all of mankind. But ... the Gentiles who are chosen by GOD's son, Proton, Cryst, shall have eternal life just as promised.

The Swine

Mankind has been riding high on a vulture that holds us and will not let you go. She holds us with thoughts of love, guilt, passion, lust, poverty, lies, fear and ignorance. But all of this is incense burning, nonsensical thoughts with no basis in fact. It is vapour wear, the worst kind of ignorance.

But on the appointed day, you will fall from the swine that hold you so tightly. The Electron's grip on the hearts and minds of mankind will be loosed and as we fall, we will be caught up to meet the LORD of Hosts in the air. And he will hold us in the palm of his hand as we float gently to the ground, as if floating on a cloud. This is what it means to be caught up by the LORD in the middle of the air.

Michelangelo, Return of the Jewels

This is the meaning of that "Falling Dream" that many of you Jewels have had. Your heart was pounding as mine was pounding. I woke up sweating and filled with fear. When you reach the ground, you will not die as you have been told. Adenine, living within your body, is the one who was afraid.

When you reach the ground, the land, you will live, for the Spirit of the Holy One will lift you up and set you gently upright, away from Babylon where you have been dispersed all off these years. Your heart will pound as it did in the falling dream. Your head will feel light. You will finally know what it means to have the Spirit of the Most High. His way is easy and his burden is light (unlike the heavy yoke of Satan).

Those connected to the root, to the Tree of Life will return to that tree – to their own land. Right now, mankind is imprisoned by the swine that once housed the demons – the swine that Christ long ago drove off the cliff. What happened?

But you ate the swine, the sweet meat, and caused the demons – the trichinosis – to grow within you. Year upon year the body of men has become more infected. Now, the demons within you are 5 million, million, million plus two elephantine spirits, Adenine and Guanine. You preferred the taste of swine to the rich red beef, lamb, and fish that were provided for the bodies of men from the beginning.

Many of you decided that you would prefer to have no red meat at all. Don't you realize that the size of a man's brain began to grow and function with knowledge and wisdom, every step calculated after he began to eat red meat? Ask the anthropologists, the archaeologist. They have found the evidence.

Now, you stink from both ends. Your breath stinks from the bacteria growing in your stomach. You use Massingill, vinegar and water – whatever you can think of to keep the smell of the foul bacteria, the demons within you at bay. You have become the swine that you abhor. Demon possession is the law of the land – your land, your body.

Red meat is the catalyst for ensuring that the body functions properly. It is why the offerings of calves and lamb – the best parts – were so important in the Temple of GOD. It is why Abel's offering was accepted and Cain's was rejected. It is no different today.

Red meat feeds the brain and cleanses the body. Cooked properly – without blood running through it after it has completed cooking – red meat has the nutrients the body needs to keep your weight in check, you keep you healthy and strong, to keep your muscles at a steady pace and remain – not fade away in a couple of day. It is rich in iron and will push contaminants out the colon. Why do you think the priests ate the meat offered at the Temple? Why do you think they were wiser than everyone else?

But, you take your protein from man made sources. Have you ever heard of anything so ridiculous! You shun the resources the LORD Proton gave you in lieu of fake protein. Is that because you serve a fake 'god'? Her standards are low. She has no brain, no wisdom, no intelligence. She would have you stupid as she is stupid. Why would you worship one who is not as wise as you are? Why would you continue your enslavement after you know the truth? Paul said if you have a chance to be free – take it! Are you going to tell me that you would rather be enslaved by Satan – a vain, egotistical idiot than by the Holy One who created everything and by him and through him you live and die? You three Jewels amaze me! Have you converted to Gentilism? Are those natural born killers so important to you that you prefer a lie over the truth? Wake up! Your days are numbered.

The New Jerusalem

And I saw a new heaven [new mind – no more gray matter covering the brain] and a new earth [new body], for the old heaven and the old earth [the parasympathetic nervous system] had disappeared. And the sea [atomic matter particle – Electron] was also gone.

And I saw the holy city, the New Jerusalem [a new mind], coming down from GOD [the Amorphous form of DNA] out of heaven [above the planet] like a beautiful bride prepared for her husband.

I heard a loud shout from the throne, saying, "Look, the home of GOD is now among his people. GOD himself [ATOM, the Amorphous Form of DNA] will be with them. He will remove all their sorrows, and there will be no more death or sorrow or crying or pain. For the old world [led by Satan] and its evils are gone forever."

And the one sitting on the throne [Proton] said, "Look, I am making all things new!" And then he said to me, "Write this down, for what I tell you is trustworthy and true."

And he also said, "It is finished! I am the Alpha and the Omega – the Beginning and the End. To all who are thirsty I will give the springs of the water of life without charge! All who are victorious will inherit all these blessings, and I [ATOM] will be their GOD, and they will be my children.

Revelation 21:1 – 7

Then one of the seven angels who held the seven bowls [the golden crowns at the top of every person's head] containing the seven last plagues [embedded in the crystal DNA – the genetic code] came and said to me, "Come with me! I will show you the bride, the wife of the Lamb."

So he took me [John, the revelator] in spirit to a great, high mountain, and he showed me the holy city, Jerusalem[76] [the minds of all men is the bride, the wife of the Lamb], descending out of heaven from GOD [ATOM, the Amorphous Form of DNA]. It was filled with the glory of GOD and sparkled like a precious gem, crystal clear [clear crystalline DNA] like jasper.

Its walls were broad and high, with twelve gates guarded by twelve angels. And the names of the twelve tribes of Israel[77] were written on the gates.

There were three gates [Cytosine, Thymine and Uracil] on each side [the four living beings] – east [man – Judah], north [lion – Israel], south [leopard[78] – Jerusalem], and west [eagle – the Lamb's chosen Gentiles].

Revelation 21:9 – 13

---

76   The address of this edifice is 333 Pyramidine Crown. It is heaven, the top of your head, your mind.

77   Now, In case you still have not figured it out yet, the twelve tribes of Israel are the Jewels of GOD. The Jews who are also called "GOD's chosen people" is a ruse, a subterfuge, part of GOD's hidden plan. Who the Proton's Jewels really are have also been kept secret until this time. The Jewels of GOD are the children of the Cytosine. Jesus Christ, the Messiah, was both a Jewel of GOD (Judah) and a Hebrew born Jew just as Abraham, Isaac, and Jacob were before him. But not every Hebrew born Jew is a Jewel of GOD. One-Fourth of the Hebrew born Jews are really Gentiles, Satan's children – murderers, legalists, Pharisees, pedophiles and prostitutes.

78   In Revelation 4, Jerusalem was second in the lineup of the four living beings and looked like an ox because he blindly followed Satan. Here, he is a fierce leopard as in Daniel's four beasts. Jerusalem will be forgiven and honored for he will turn again to his Father, *Proton* and will teach with wisdom what GOD has given him to teach – truth. Jerusalem will teach your children the truth just as Uracil or the Archangel Gabriel has taught me the truth of the great deception that he experienced on his undercover mission as Satan's ally. The Prodigal son is going home.

What Mean Ye By These Stones?

The wall of the city had twelve foundation stones and on them were written the names of the twelve apostles of the Lamb [those who were the first disciples of Jesus Christ when he walked the earth]. **The angel** [Uracil] **who talked to me held in his hand a gold measuring stick to measure the city, its gates and its wall. When he measured it, he found it was a square, as wide as it was long. In fact, it was in the form of a cube, for its length and width and height were each 1,400 miles. Then he measured the walls and found them to be 216 feet thick (the angel used a standard human measure).**

The wall was made of jasper, and the city was pure gold, as clear as glass [invisible to eyes of mankind]. **The wall of the city was built on foundation stones** [the servants of GOD – Cytosine, Thymine and Uracil] **inlaid with twelve gems** [the Jewels of GOD];

The first was jasper [an opaque cryptocrystalline quartz of any of several colors, Judah]**, the second was sapphire** [Israel]**, the third was agate** [Jerusalem]**, the fourth emerald** [the Gentiles].

The fifth onyx [Judah]**, the sixth carnelian** [Israel]**, the seventh chrysolite,** [Jerusalem]**, the eighth beryl** [the Gentiles].

The ninth topaz [Judah]**, the tenth chrysoprase** [Israel]**, the eleventh jacinth** [Jerusalem]**, the twelfth amethyst** [the Gentiles].

Revelation 21:18 – 20

These stones were all visible at the first big bang, when the world was created. As such, they are all in the mix of that which all peoples are comprised.

However, this passage describes the seasons – the twelve–year birth cycle of all peoples. In the first year Judah is born. In the second, Israel is born. In the third, Jerusalem is born. For every living being, every living thing there is a season. This is the nature of healthy crops. They grow on a planned schedule.

These are the enduring characteristics of the three Jewels of GOD. Judah is wise. Israel is strong. Jerusalem is intelligent, the philosopher, the teacher. In the fourth year, the Gentiles are born. This simple pattern occurs for a twelve–year period with the most wise, strongest, and most intelligent babies born at the beginning of the twelve–year cycle. Each crop begins and ends without fail as the DNA chain rotates. The DNA mechanism automatically determines which crop to plant and what fruit to harvest.

These are the twelve tribes of Israel, to be ruled by Israel – the strong force. This explains the abiding similarities between people, but not the variables. The variables are the basis for the work Proton predestines us to do. Every person is one of these four. Every person is born within this twelve–year DNA cycle. This is the explanation of the Tree of Life (Proton, the Creator) and the Branch (Cytosine).

Examples: Abram was Jerusalem, made in the image of the Neutron. He is Ham, the actor, philosophizing and stirring those that they teach to action or emotion. That is why the devil used Jerusalem to convince Eve to sin and it is also why GOD changed Abram's name to Abraham. Abraham is Jerusalem and so are many of the 24 elders, as was Peter and Paul, the teachers.

Sarai was Judah. GOD changed her name to Sarah. Both Kind David and Jacob were Israel – the strongest one. Jacob's name was changed to Israel. King Nebuchadnezzar, King Saul and Joseph – son of Jacob, were all Gentiles.

The Lampstands

The twelve gates [all gates] **were made of pearls** [all people] **– each gate from a single pearl** [a single person]! **And the main street** [the mind] **was pure gold, as clear as glass.**

No temple [no parasympathetic nervous system] **could be seen in the city, for the LORD GOD Almighty** [ATOM, the Amorphous Form of DNA also known as GOD] **and the Lamb** [Proton] **are its temple.** [The temple is the body sourced through the tree of life, also known as the sympathetic nervous system].

And the city has no need for [celestial] **sun or moon, for the glory of GOD** [Proton, the sun of GOD, the Son of the Amorphous GOD who is all energy] **illuminates the city** [with wisdom – a great light], **and the Lamb** [Proton] **is its light** [is its wisdom]. **The nations of the Earth** [mankind] **will walk in its light, and the rulers** [Cytosine, Thymine, and Uracil] **of the world** [each person is the world or the earth] **will come** [to consult] **and bring their glory to it** [as the law of physics requires]. **Its gates never close at the end of the day because there is no night** [no Electron].[79]

And all the nations will bring their glory and honor into the city [by discovering new things, creating and innovating, organizing and refur-

---

79   Every person will be able to go to the source, to Jerusalem, in the hindbrain and talk to GOD also known as Proton or Cytosine day or night. GOD never sleeps. Take you burdens to the LORD, lay them down and leave them there.

bishing and teaching the new ones who come after us what is right and what is true]. **Nothing evil will be allowed to enter** [no bile, no gall, no bad humor or moodiness, no contentious thoughts] **– no one who practices shameful I–dolatry** [what about me?] **and dishonesty – but only those whose names are written in the Lamb's Book of Life** [the carbon dated DNA record].

Revelation 21:21 – 27

The twelve gates are the seven lampstands that are lighted by the Cytosine who gives all men wisdom.

Let us make man in our image [Proton or Cytosine, Gluon or Thymine and Neutron or Uracil]. **So GOD** [ATOM] **created people in his own image; GOD patterned them after himself** [Proton, Gluon and Neutron]; **male and female he created them** [from the beginning].

Genesis 1:26 – 27

Philadelphia and Smyrna are Judah – the wise one. Judah is diatomic – two separate force particles or Adam – one male, one female. Judah is known in heaven as "the man", morning, or sun, made in the image of Proton.

Laodicea and Pergamum are Israel – the strong one. Israel is diatomic – two separate force particles – one male, one female. Israel is known in heaven as "the woman", Evening or the star, made in the image of the Gluon.

Thyatira is Jerusalem – the intelligent one. Jerusalem is atomic (one force particle – either male or female). Jerusalem is "the night", the moon, made in the image of the Neutron. These three are the Jewels of GOD, the pyramidine Y–Men.

Ephesus and Sardis are the Gentiles. The Gentiles are bi–atomic – two matter particles in the same body; one female gene – Adenine and one male gene – Guanine in every Gentile body, made in the image of Electron or Satan. These are the X–Men, the children of the double helix, the humans.

Every person is one of these seven lampstands, fruit produced by the Branch that is Proton, the Tree of Life.

The Return of Christ

And the angel showed me a pure river with the water of life, clear as crystal [DNA], flowing from the throne [hindbrain] of [the Amorphous] GOD and of the Lamb [Proton], coursing down the centre of the main street [the spine].

On each side of the river grew a tree of life [adrenergic fibres connecting Cytosine, Thymine and Uracil to every cell in the body], bearing twelve crops [four each] of fruit [wisdom, strength and knowledge], with a fresh crop [rotating through] each month.

The leaves were used for medicine to heal the nations. No longer will anything be cursed. For the throne [the hindbrain] of [the Amorphous] GOD and of the Lamb [Proton], will be there, and his servants [Cytosine, Thymine, and Uracil] will worship him [from Jerusalem].

And they [all men] will see his face [which is their faces], and his name [Deoxyribonucleic Acid] will be written on their foreheads.

And there will be no night there [in Jerusalem, the Holy City situated in the hindbrain] – no need for lamps or sun – for the LORD GOD will shine on them [synapses firing day and night].

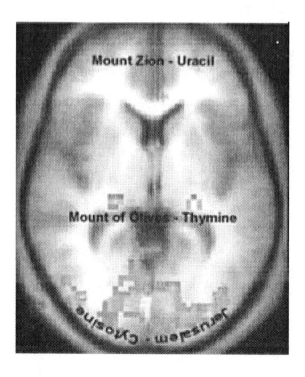

Mountain of Fire

And they [the LORD Proton and the Amorphous GOD – Energy and Life] **will reign** [on earth – the world, on earth – the body] **forever and ever.**

Revelation 22:1 – 5

Then the angel said to me, "These words are trustworthy and true: 'The Lord GOD [ATOM], who tells his prophets what the future holds, has sent his angel [Cyrus] to tell you what will happen soon.'"

"Look, I [Proton] am coming soon! Blessed are those who obey the prophecy written in this scroll." I, John, am the one who saw and heard all these things. And when I saw and heard these things, I fell down to worship the angel [Gabriel, Uracil] who showed them to me.

But again he said, "No, don't worship me. I am a servant of GOD, just like you and your brothers the prophets, as well as all who obey what is written in this scroll. Worship GOD! [Worship ATOM!]"

Then he [Gabriel or Uracil] instructed me [Cyrus], "Do not seal up the prophetic words you have written, for the time is near. Let the one who is doing wrong continue to do wrong; the one who is vile, continue to be vile; the one who is good, continue to do good; and the one who is holy, continue in holiness."

"See, I [ATOM] am coming soon, and my reward is with me, to repay all according to their deeds. I am the Alpha and the Omega, the First and the Last, the Beginning and the End."

Blessed are those who wash their robes so they can enter through the gates of the city and eat the fruit from the tree of life [truth].

Outside the city are the dogs – the sorcerers, the sexually immoral, the murderers, the idol worshipers, and all who love to live a lie.

"I, Jesus [He's us], have sent my angel [Cyrus] to give you this message for the churches. I am both the source of David and the heir to his throne. I am the bright morning star."

The Spirit [called Man, or ATOM] and the bride [all of mankind] say, "Come." Let each one who hears them say, "Come." Let the thirsty ones come – anyone who wants to. Let them come and drink the water of life without charge.

The Final Declaration, A Curse for Deceivers

And I solemnly declare to everyone who hears the prophetic words of this book: If anyone adds anything to what is written here, GOD [ATOM] will add to that person the plagues described in this book. And if anyone removes any of the words of this prophetic book, GOD [ATOM] will remove that person's share in the tree of life and in the holy city that are described in this book.

He [Proton, Cytosine] who is the faithful witness to all these things says, "Yes, I am coming soon!"

Amen! Come, Lord Jesus! [He's us!] The grace of the Lord Jesus be with you all.

Revelation 22:6 – 21

The Appendix

DNA Genetic Crop Rotation Chart

The natural schedule for the crops that holds the key to the behavioural differences between people.

From				To			DNA
Month	Day	Year		Month	Day	Year	Genetic Rotation
1	28	1645	....	2	15	1646	Judah
2	16	1646	....	2	4	1647	Gentiles
2	5	1647	....	1	24	1648	Jerusalem
1	25	1648	....	2	10	1649	Israel
2	11	1649	....	2	0	1650	Judah
2	1	1650	....	1	20	1651	Gentiles
1	21	1651	....	2	8	1652	Jerusalem
2	9	1652	....	1	28	1653	Israel
1	29	1653	....	2	16	1654	Judah
2	17	1654	....	2	5	1655	Gentiles
2	6	1655	....	1	25	1656	Jerusalem
1	26	1656	....	2	12	1657	Israel
2	13	1657	....	2	1	1658	Judah
2	2	1658	....	1	22	1659	Gentiles
1	23	1659	....	2	10	1660	Jerusalem
2	11	1660	....	1	29	1661	Israel
1	30	1661	....	2	17	1662	Judah
2	18	1662	....	2	7	1663	Gentiles
2	8	1663	....	1	27	1664	Jerusalem
1	28	1664	....	2	14	1665	Israel
2	15	1665	....	2	3	1666	Judah
2	4	1666	....	1	23	1667	Gentiles
1	24	1667	....	2	11	1668	Jerusalem
2	12	1668	....	2	0	1669	Israel

From				To			DNA
2	1	1669	....	1	20	1670	Judah
1	21	1670	......	2	8	1671	Gentiles
2	9	1671	....	1	29	1672	Jerusalem
1	30	1672	......	2	16	1673	Israel
2	17	1673	......	2	5	1674	Judah
2	6	1674	....	1	25	1675	Gentiles
1	26	1675	......	2	13	1676	Jerusalem
2	14	1676	....	2	1	1677	Israel
2	2	1677	......	1	22	1678	Judah
1	23	1678	......	2	10	1679	Gentiles
2	11	1679	....	1	30	1680	Jerusalem
1	31	1680	......	2	17	1681	Israel
2	18	1681	....	2	6	1682	Judah
2	7	1682	......	1	26	1683	Gentiles
1	27	1683	......	2	14	1684	Jerusalem
2	15	1684	....	2	2	1685	Israel
2	3	1685	......	1	23	1686	Judah
1	24	1686	....	2	11	1687	Gentiles
2	12	1687	......	2	1	1688	Jerusalem
2	2	1688	......	1	20	1689	Israel
1	21	1689	....	2	8	1690	Judah
2	9	1690	......	1	28	1691	Gentiles
1	29	1691	....	2	16	1692	Jerusalem
2	17	1692	......	2	4	1693	Israel
2	5	1693	......	1	24	1694	Judah
1	25	1694	......	2	12	1695	Gentiles
2	13	1695	......	2	2	1696	Jerusalem
2	3	1696	......	1	22	1697	Israel
1	23	1697	......	2	10	1698	Judah
2	11	1698	......	1	30	1699	Gentiles

From				To			DNA
1	31	1699	....	2	18	1700	Jerusalem
2	19	1700	....	2	7	1701	Israel
2	8	1701	....	1	27	1702	Judah
1	28	1702	....	2	15	1703	Gentiles
2	16	1703	....	2	4	1704	Jerusalem
2	5	1704	....	1	24	1705	Israel
1	25	1705	....	2	12	1706	Judah
2	13	1706	....	2	2	1707	Gentiles
2	3	1707	....	1	22	1708	Jerusalem
1	23	1708	....	2	9	1709	Israel
2	10	1709	....	1	29	1710	Judah
1	30	1710	....	2	16	1711	Gentiles
2	17	1711	....	2	6	1712	Jerusalem
2	7	1712	....	1	25	1713	Israel
1	26	1713	....	2	13	1714	Judah
2	14	1714	....	2	3	1715	Gentiles
2	4	1715	....	1	23	1716	Jerusalem
1	24	1716	....	2	10	1717	Israel
2	11	1717	....	1	30	1718	Judah
1	31	1718	....	2	18	1719	Gentiles
2	19	1719	....	2	7	1720	Jerusalem
2	8	1720	....	1	27	1721	Israel
1	28	1721	....	2	15	1722	Judah
2	16	1722	....	2	4	1723	Gentiles
2	5	1723	....	1	25	1724	Jerusalem
1	26	1724	....	2	12	1725	Israel
2	13	1725	....	2	1	1726	Judah
2	2	1726	....	1	21	1727	Gentiles
1	22	1727	....	2	9	1728	Jerusalem
2	10	1728	....	1	28	1729	Israel

From				To			DNA
1	29	1729	....	2	16	1730	Judah
2	17	1730	~~~~	2	6	1731	Gentiles
2	7	1731	....	1	26	1732	Jerusalem
1	27	1732	~~~~~	2	13	1733	Israel
2	14	1733	~~~~~	2	3	1734	Judah
2	4	1734	....	1	23	1735	Gentiles
1	24	1735	~~~~~	2	11	1736	Jerusalem
2	12	1736	....	1	30	1737	Israel
1	31	1737	~~~~~	2	18	1738	Judah
2	19	1738	~~~~~	2	7	1739	Gentiles
2	8	1739	....	1	28	1740	Jerusalem
1	29	1740	~~~~~	2	15	1741	Israel
2	16	1741	....	2	4	1742	Judah
2	5	1742	~~~~~	1	25	1743	Gentiles
1	26	1743	~~~~~	2	12	1744	Jerusalem
2	13	1744	....	2	0	1745	Israel
2	1	1745	~~~~~	1	21	1746	Judah
1	22	1746	....	2	8	1747	Gentiles
2	9	1747	~~~~~	1	29	1748	Jerusalem
1	30	1748	~~~~~	2	16	1749	Israel
2	17	1749	....	2	6	1750	Judah
2	7	1750	~~~~~	1	26	1751	Gentiles
1	27	1751	....	2	14	1752	Jerusalem
2	15	1752	~~~~~	2	2	1753	Israel
2	3	1753	~~~~~	1	22	1754	Judah
1	23	1754	....	2	10	1755	Gentiles
2	11	1755	~~~~~	1	30	1756	Jerusalem
1	31	1756	....	2	17	1757	Israel
2	18	1757	~~~~~	2	7	1758	Judah
2	8	1758	~~~~~	1	28	1759	Gentiles

From				To			DNA
1	29	1759	....	2	16	1760	Jerusalem
2	17	1760	....	2	4	1761	Israel
2	5	1761	....	1	24	1762	Judah
1	25	1762	....	2	12	1763	Gentiles
2	13	1763	....	2	1	1764	Jerusalem
2	2	1764	....	1	20	1765	Israel
1	21	1765	....	2	8	1766	Judah
2	9	1766	....	1	29	1767	Gentiles
1	30	1767	....	2	17	1768	Jerusalem
2	18	1768	....	2	6	1769	Israel
2	7	1769	....	1	26	1770	Judah
1	27	1770	....	2	14	1771	Gentiles
2	15	1771	....	2	3	1772	Jerusalem
2	4	1772	....	1	22	1773	Israel
1	23	1773	....	2	10	1774	Judah
2	11	1774	....	1	30	1775	Gentiles
1	31	1775	....	2	18	1776	Jerusalem
2	19	1776	....	2	7	1777	Israel
2	8	1777	....	1	27	1778	Judah
1	28	1778	....	2	15	1779	Gentiles
2	16	1779	....	2	4	1780	Jerusalem
2	5	1780	....	1	23	1781	Israel
1	24	1781	....	2	11	1782	Judah
2	12	1782	....	2	1	1783	Gentiles
2	2	1783	....	1	21	1784	Jerusalem
1	22	1784	....	2	8	1785	Israel
2	9	1785	....	1	29	1786	Judah
1	30	1786	....	2	17	1787	Gentiles
2	18	1787	....	2	6	1788	Jerusalem
2	7	1788	....	1	25	1789	Israel

From				To			DNA
1	26	1789	....	2	13	1790	Judah
2	14	1790	~~~~	2	2	1791	Gentiles
2	3	1791	....	1	23	1792	Jerusalem
1	24	1792	~~~~~	2	10	1793	Israel
2	11	1793	~~~~	1	30	1794	Judah
1	31	1794	....	1	20	1795	Gentiles
1	21	1795	~~~~	2	8	1796	Jerusalem
2	9	1796	....	1	27	1797	Israel
1	28	1797	~~~~~	2	15	1798	Judah
2	16	1798	~~~~	2	4	1799	Gentiles
2	5	1799	....	1	24	1800	Jerusalem
1	25	1800	~~~~	2	12	1801	Israel
2	13	1801	....	2	2	1802	Judah
2	3	1802	~~~~~	1	22	1803	Gentiles
1	23	1803	~~~~	2	10	1804	Jerusalem
2	11	1804	....	1	30	1805	Israel
1	31	1805	~~~~~	2	17	1806	Judah
2	18	1806	....	2	6	1807	Gentiles
2	7	1807	~~~~~	1	27	1808	Jerusalem
1	28	1808	~~~~~	2	13	1809	Israel
2	14	1809	....	2	3	1810	Judah
2	4	1810	~~~	1	24	1811	Gentiles
1	25	1811	....	2	12	1812	Jerusalem
2	13	1812	~~~~	2	0	1813	Israel
2	1	1813	~~~	1	20	1814	Judah
1	21	1814	....	2	8	1815	Gentiles
2	9	1815	~~~~	1	28	1816	Jerusalem
1	29	1816	....	2	15	1817	Israel
2	16	1817	~~~~~	2	4	1818	Judah
2	5	1818	~~~~	1	25	1819	Gentiles

From				To			DNA
1	26	1819	....	2	13	1820	Jerusalem
2	14	1820	....	2	2	1821	Israel
2	3	1821	....	1	22	1822	Judah
1	23	1822	....	2	10	1823	Gentiles
2	11	1823	....	1	30	1824	Jerusalem
1	31	1824	....	2	17	1825	Israel
2	18	1825	....	2	6	1826	Judah
2	7	1826	....	1	26	1827	Gentiles
1	27	1827	....	2	14	1828	Jerusalem
2	15	1828	....	2	3	1829	Israel
2	4	1829	....	1	24	1830	Judah
1	25	1830	....	2	12	1831	Gentiles
2	13	1831	....	2	1	1832	Jerusalem
2	2	1832	....	2	19	1833	Israel
2	20	1833	....	2	8	1834	Judah
2	9	1834	....	1	28	1835	Gentiles
1	29	1835	....	2	16	1836	Jerusalem
2	17	1836	....	2	4	1837	Israel
2	5	1837	....	1	25	1838	Judah
1	26	1838	....	2	13	1839	Gentiles
2	14	1839	....	2	2	1840	Jerusalem
2	3	1840	....	1	22	1841	Israel
1	23	1841	....	2	9	1842	Judah
2	10	1842	....	1	29	1843	Gentiles
1	30	1843	....	2	17	1844	Jerusalem
2	18	1844	....	2	6	1845	Israel
2	7	1845	....	1	26	1846	Judah
1	27	1846	....	2	14	1847	Gentiles
2	15	1847	....	2	4	1848	Jerusalem
2	5	1848	....	1	23	1849	Israel

From				To			DNA
1	24	1849	....	2	11	1850	Judah
2	12	1850	....	2	0	1851	Gentiles
2	1	1851	....	2	19	1852	Jerusalem
2	20	1852	....	2	7	1853	Israel
2	8	1853	....	1	28	1854	Judah
1	29	1854	....	2	16	1855	Gentiles
2	17	1855	....	2	5	1856	Jerusalem
2	6	1856	....	1	25	1857	Israel
1	26	1857	....	2	13	1858	Judah
2	14	1858	....	2	2	1859	Gentiles
2	3	1859	....	1	22	1860	Jerusalem
1	23	1860	....	2	9	1861	Israel
2	10	1861	....	1	29	1862	Judah
1	30	1862	....	2	17	1863	Gentiles
2	18	1863	....	2	7	1864	Jerusalem
2	8	1864	....	1	26	1865	Israel
1	27	1865	....	2	14	1866	Judah
2	15	1866	....	2	4	1867	Gentiles
2	5	1867	....	1	24	1868	Jerusalem
1	25	1868	....	2	10	1869	Israel
2	11	1869	....	1	30	1870	Judah
1	31	1870	....	2	18	1871	Gentiles
2	19	1871	....	2	8	1872	Jerusalem
2	9	1872	....	1	28	1873	Israel
1	29	1873	....	2	16	1874	Judah
2	17	1874	....	2	5	1875	Gentiles
2	6	1875	....	1	25	1876	Jerusalem
1	26	1876	....	2	12	1877	Israel
2	13	1877	....	2	1	1878	Judah
2	2	1878	....	1	21	1879	Gentiles

From				To			DNA
1	22	1879	....	2	9	1880	Jerusalem
2	10	1880	....	1	29	1881	Israel
1	30	1881	....	2	17	1882	Judah
2	18	1882	....	2	7	1883	Gentiles
2	8	1883	....	1	27	1884	Jerusalem
1	28	1884	....	2	14	1885	Israel
2	15	1885	....	2	3	1886	Judah
2	4	1886	....	1	23	1887	Gentiles
1	24	1887	....	2	11	1888	Jerusalem
2	12	1888	....	1	30	1889	Israel
1	31	1889	....	1	20	1890	Judah
1	21	1890	....	2	8	1891	Gentiles
2	9	1891	....	1	29	1892	Jerusalem
1	30	1892	....	2	16	1893	Israel
2	17	1893	....	2	5	1894	Judah
2	6	1894	....	1	25	1895	Gentiles
1	26	1895	....	2	12	1896	Jerusalem
2	13	1896	....	2	1	1897	Israel
2	2	1897	....	1	21	1898	Judah
1	22	1898	....	2	9	1899	Gentiles
2	10	1899	....	1	30	1900	Jerusalem
1	31	1900	....	2	18	1901	Israel
2	19	1901	....	2	7	1902	Judah
2	8	1902	....	1	28	1903	Gentiles
1	29	1903	....	2	15	1904	Jerusalem
2	16	1904	....	2	3	1905	Israel
2	4	1905	....	1	24	1906	Judah
1	25	1906	....	2	12	1907	Gentiles
2	13	1907	....	2	1	1908	Jerusalem
2	2	1908	....	1	21	1909	Israel

From				To			DNA
1	22	1909	....	2	9	1910	Judah
2	10	1910	~~~~	1	29	1911	Gentiles
1	30	1911	....	2	17	1912	Jerusalem
2	18	1912	~~~~~	2	5	1913	Israel
2	6	1913	~~~~	1	25	1914	Judah
1	26	1914	....	2	13	1915	Gentiles
2	14	1915	~~~~~	2	2	1916	Jerusalem
2	3	1916	....	1	22	1917	Israel
1	23	1917	~~~~~	2	10	1918	Judah
2	11	1918	~~~~~	2	0	1919	Gentiles
2	1	1919	....	2	19	1920	Jerusalem
2	20	1920	~~~~~	2	7	1921	Israel
2	8	1921	....	1	27	1922	Judah
1	28	1922	~~~~~	2	15	1923	Gentiles
2	16	1923	~~~~~	2	4	1924	Jerusalem
2	5	1924	....	1	23	1925	Israel
1	24	1925	~~~~~	2	12	1926	Judah
2	13	1926	....	2	1	1927	Gentiles
2	2	1927	~~~~~	1	22	1928	Jerusalem
1	23	1928	~~~~~	2	9	1929	Israel
2	10	1929	~~~~~	1	29	1930	Judah
1	30	1930	~~~~~	2	16	1931	Gentiles
2	17	1931	....	2	5	1932	Jerusalem
2	6	1932	~~~~~	1	25	1933	Israel
1	26	1933	~~~~~	2	13	1934	Judah
2	14	1934	....	2	3	1935	Gentiles
2	4	1935	~~~~~	1	23	1936	Jerusalem
1	24	1936	....	2	10	1937	Israel
2	11	1937	~~~~~	1	30	1938	Judah
1	31	1938	~~~~~	2	18	1939	Gentiles

From				To			DNA
2	19	1939	....	2	7	1940	Jerusalem
2	8	1940	....	1	26	1941	Israel
1	27	1941	....	2	14	1942	Judah
2	15	1942	....	2	4	1943	Gentiles
2	5	1943	....	1	24	1944	Jerusalem
1	25	1944	....	2	12	1945	Israel
2	13	1945	....	2	1	1946	Judah
2	2	1946	....	1	21	1947	Gentiles
1	22	1947	....	2	9	1948	Jerusalem
2	10	1948	....	1	28	1949	Israel
1	29	1949	....	2	16	1950	Judah
2	17	1950	....	2	5	1951	Gentiles
2	6	1951	....	1	26	1952	Jerusalem
1	27	1952	....	2	13	1953	Israel
2	14	1953	....	2	2	1954	Judah
2	3	1954	....	1	23	1955	Gentiles
1	24	1955	....	2	11	1956	Jerusalem
2	12	1956	....	1	30	1957	Israel
1	31	1957	....	2	17	1958	Judah
2	18	1958	....	2	7	1959	Gentiles
2	8	1959	....	1	27	1960	Jerusalem
1	28	1960	....	2	14	1961	Israel
2	15	1961	....	2	4	1962	Judah
2	5	1962	....	1	24	1963	Gentiles
1	25	1963	....	2	12	1964	Jerusalem
2	13	1964	....	2	1	1965	Israel
2	2	1965	....	1	20	1966	Judah
1	21	1966	....	2	8	1967	Gentiles
2	9	1967	....	1	29	1968	Jerusalem
1	30	1968	....	2	16	1969	Israel

From				To			DNA
2	17	1969	....	2	5	1970	Judah
2	6	1970	....	1	26	1971	Gentiles
1	27	1971	....	2	14	1972	Jerusalem
2	15	1972	....	2	2	1973	Israel
2	3	1973	....	1	22	1974	Judah
1	23	1974	....	2	10	1975	Gentiles
2	11	1975	....	1	30	1976	Jerusalem
1	31	1976	....	2	17	1977	Israel
2	18	1977	....	2	6	1978	Judah
2	7	1978	....	1	27	1979	Gentiles
1	28	1979	....	2	15	1980	Jerusalem
2	16	1980	....	2	4	1981	Israel
2	5	1981	....	1	24	1982	Judah
1	25	1982	....	2	12	1983	Gentiles
2	13	1983	....	2	1	1984	Jerusalem
2	2	1984	....	2	19	1985	Israel
2	20	1985	....	2	8	1986	Judah
2	9	1986	....	1	28	1987	Gentiles
1	29	1987	....	2	16	1988	Jerusalem
2	17	1988	....	2	5	1989	Israel
2	6	1989	....	1	26	1990	Judah
1	27	1990	....	2	14	1991	Gentiles
2	15	1991	....	2	3	1992	Jerusalem
2	4	1992	....	1	22	1993	Israel
1	23	1993	....	2	9	1994	Judah
2	10	1994	....	1	30	1995	Gentiles
1	31	1995	....	2	18	1996	Jerusalem
2	19	1996	....	2	6	1997	Israel
2	7	1997	....	1	27	1998	Judah
1	28	1998	....	2	15	1999	Gentiles

From				To			DNA
2	16	1999	....	2	4	2000	Jerusalem
2	5	2000	....	1	23	2001	Israel
1	24	2001	....	2	11	2002	Judah
2	12	2002	....	2	0	2003	Gentiles
2	1	2003	....	1	21	2004	Jerusalem
1	22	2004	....	2	8	2005	Israel
2	9	2005	....	1	28	2006	Judah
1	29	2006	....	2	17	2007	Gentiles
2	18	2007	....	2	6	2008	Jerusalem
2	7	2008	....	1	25	2009	Israel
1	26	2009	....	2	13	2010	Judah
2	14	2010	....	2	2	2011	Gentiles
2	3	2011	....	1	22	2012	Jerusalem
1	23	2012	....	2	9	2013	Israel
2	10	2013	....	1	30	2014	Judah
1	31	2014	....	2	18	2015	Gentiles
2	19	2015	....	2	7	2016	Jerusalem
2	8	2016	....	1	27	2017	Israel
1	28	2017	....	2	15	2018	Judah
2	16	2018	....	2	4	2019	Gentiles
2	5	2019	....	1	24	2020	Jerusalem
1	25	2020	....	2	11	2021	Israel
2	12	2021	....	2	0	2022	Judah
2	1	2022	....	1	21	2023	Gentiles
1	22	2023	....	2	9	2024	Jerusalem
2	10	2024	....	1	28	2025	Israel
1	29	2025	....	2	16	2026	Judah
2	17	2026	....	2	5	2027	Gentiles
2	6	2027	....	1	25	2028	Jerusalem
1	26	2028	....	2	12	2029	Israel

From				To			DNA
2	13	2029	....	2	2	2030	Judah
2	3	2030	~~~~~	1	22	2031	Gentiles
1	23	2031	....	2	10	2032	Jerusalem
2	11	2032	....	1	30	2033	Israel
1	31	2033	~~~~~	2	18	2034	Judah
2	19	2034	....	2	7	2035	Gentiles
2	8	2035	~~~~~	1	27	2036	Jerusalem
1	28	2036	....	2	14	2037	Israel
2	15	2037	~~~~~	2	3	2038	Judah
2	4	2038	~~~~~	1	23	2039	Gentiles
1	24	2039	....	2	11	2040	Jerusalem
2	12	2040	~~~~~	2	0	2041	Israel
2	1	2041	....	1	21	2042	Judah
1	22	2042	~~~~~	2	9	2043	Gentiles
2	10	2043	~~~~~	1	29	2044	Jerusalem
1	30	2044	....	2	16	2045	Israel
2	17	2045	~~~~~	2	5	2046	Judah
2	6	2046	....	1	25	2047	Gentiles
1	26	2047	~~~~~	2	13	2048	Jerusalem
2	14	2048	~~~~~	2	1	2049	Israel
2	2	2049	....	1	22	2050	Judah
1	23	2050	~~~~~	2	10	2051	Gentiles
2	11	2051	....	2	0	2052	Jerusalem
2	1	2052	~~~~~	2	18	2053	Israel
2	19	2053	~~~~~	2	7	2054	Judah
2	8	2054	....	1	27	2055	Gentiles
1	28	2055	~~~~~	2	14	2056	Jerusalem
2	15	2056	....	2	3	2057	Israel

Printed in the United States
46324LVS00002BA/1

9 781592 992058